UNLEARNING THE COLONIAL CULTURES OF PLANNING

For Mum and Dad

Unlearning the Colonial Cultures of Planning

LIBBY PORTER
University of Glasgow, UK

Routledge
Taylor & Francis Group
LONDON AND NEW YORK

First published 2010 by Ashgate Publishing

Published 2016 by Routledge
2 Park Square, Milton Park, Abingdon, Oxon OX14 4RN
711 Third Avenue, New York, NY 10017, USA

Routledge is an imprint of the Taylor & Francis Group, an informa business

Copyright © Libby Porter 2010

Libby Porter has asserted her right under the Copyright, Designs and Patents Act, 1988, to be identified as the author of this work.

All rights reserved. No part of this book may be reprinted or reproduced or utilised in any form or by any electronic, mechanical, or other means, now known or hereafter invented, including photocopying and recording, or in any information storage or retrieval system, without permission in writing from the publishers.

Notice:
Product or corporate names may be trademarks or registered trademarks, and are used only for identification and explanation without intent to infringe.

British Library Cataloguing in Publication Data
Porter, Libby, 1973-
   Unlearning the colonial cultures of planning.
   1. Indigenous peoples--Great Britain--Colonies.
   2. Regional planning--Great Britain--Colonies. 3. Great
Britain--Colonies--Ethnic relations.
   I. Title
   323.1'1'09171241-dc22

Library of Congress Cataloging-in-Publication Data
Porter, Libby, 1973-
   Unlearning the colonial cultures of planning / by Libby Porter.
       p. cm.
   Includes bibliographical references and index.
   ISBN 978-0-7546-4988-5 (hardback) -- ISBN 978-0-7546-9260-7
(ebook) 1. Indigenous peoples--Great Britain--Colonies. 2. Regional planning--Great Britain--Colonies. 3. Great Britain--Colonies--Ethnic relations. I. Title.

JV1035.P67 2010
323.1109171'241--dc22
                                                                                  2009045783

ISBN 13: 978-0-7546-4988-5 (hbk)

Contents

List of Figures and Tables vii
Acknowledgements ix
List of Abbreviations xi

1   Introduction: Culture, Colonialism and Planning   1

2   Indigenous People and their Challenge to Planning   21

3   A Colonial Genealogy of Planning   43

4   Systematizing Space: 'Natures', 'Cultures' and Protected Areas   77

5   Managing the Sacred   107

6   Modes of Governance: The Difference Indigeneity Makes to Progressive Planning   125

7   Unlearning Privilege: Towards the Decolonization of Planning   151

Bibliography   *159*
Index   *177*

List of Figures and Tables

Figures

1.1	Nyah Forest, Victoria	8
1.2	Brambuk building in Gariwerd, Victoria	10
4.1	Gariwerd rock art	86
5.1	Nyah's cultural heritage 'sites'	116
6.1	Committee structure of planned integration of Brambuk and National Park Visitor Centre, Gariwerd	130
6.2	New signs of welcome in Tjapwurrung at the National Park Visitor Centre, Gariwerd	131
6.3	Scarred tree at Brambuk and Visitors Centre, Gariwerd	135

Tables

4.1	Western scientific knowledge base in Gariwerd	84
4.2	Naming in Gariwerd: A case of split identity?	92
4.3	Western scientific knowledge base in Nyah	99
6.1	Interpretive themes planned for Gariwerd	138

Acknowledgements

I respectfully acknowledge the Wadi Wadi, Wemba Wemba, Wotjobaluk, Gunditjmara, Jardwadjali, Tjapwurrung and Kirrae Wurrung peoples of southeastern Australia, whose country was the focus of much of the research presented here. This book would not have been possible without the generosity and energetic commitment of many people in those and other Indigenous communities, for which I am very grateful. Special thanks to Doug Nicholls, Marilyne Nicholls, Uncle Sam Morgan, Uncle Brien Nelson, Jenni Beer, the Wotjobaluk Traditional Land Council, Levi Lovett, Tim Chatfield and others at Brambuk Living Cultural Centre who generously gave me so much of their time and energy. The original primary research would also not have been possible without the commitment of many non–Indigenous people in Victoria, particularly staff at the (former) Department of Natural Resources and Environment, Forestry Victoria, Parks Victoria and Aboriginal Affairs Victoria. I am particularly grateful to Grahame Parkes, Patrick Fricker and the team at the Grampians National Park office. Also to Peter Kelly and his team at the DNRE Mildura office. The time and assistance of Jacqui Kelly and the Friends of the Nyah–Vinifera Forest group, and also Natalie Moxham was also extremely helpful. I was supported in doing the original fieldwork by a grant from the Australian Institute of Aboriginal and Torres Strait Islander Studies. The Department of Town and Regional Planning at the University of Sheffield provided a small resource to allow me to undertake a portion of the archival work, and the British Library and University of Glasgow library were invaluable resources. There are many other people to thank who acted as mentors and guides through my doctoral work (and beyond): Leonie Sandercock, Ruth Fincher, Lisa Palmer, Marcus Lane, Marcia Langton, and Jane Jacobs. Thanks also to those who have provided more recent support, including challenging and constructive discussions on early drafts or emerging ideas: Margo Huxley, Gesa Helms, Sophie Bond and Leonie Sandercock. Chapter 3 in particular benefited from a lively and challenging discussion with colleagues at the University of Sheffield, and I am grateful to them all for their engagement and input. I am very grateful to Ashgate Publishing, and particularly Val Rose, for waiting so patiently for the manuscript, and for continuing to encourage. A huge thanks to my Dad, who edited, refined, polished and proofread a near–final draft (the mistakes are all mine). And to Mum, many thanks for doing the tedious work of the bibliography with such enthusiasm and care. Finally, thanks to Ewan and my girls, Jessie and Catriona, who have put up with this book for far too long and have provided love, support and a renewal of energy when most needed.

With acknowledgement to Gayatri Chakravorty Spivak (1994) for the term 'unlearning'.

List of Abbreviations

AAV	Aboriginal Affairs Victoria
BC	British Columbia
DNRE	Department of Natural Resources and Environment
DSE	Department of Sustainability and Environment
FMA	Forest Management Area
FONVF	Friends of the Nyah–Vinifera Forest
IUCN	International Union for the Conservation of Nature
LCC	Land Conservation Council
NFPS	National Forest Policy Statement
NPVC	National Park Visitor Centre
NZHPT	New Zealand Historic Places Trust
UN	United Nations
UNESCO	United Nations Educational, Scientific and Cultural Organization
USA or US	United States of America
WCPA	World Commission on Protected Areas

Chapter 1
Introduction:
Culture, Colonialism and Planning

Let it be known as of April 21, 1984, we the Clayoquot Band, do declare Meares Island a Tribal Park...[for] Total preservation of Meares Island based on title and survival of our Native way of life...The Native people are prepared to share Meares Island with non–Natives, providing that you adhere to the Laws of our Forefathers; which were always there.

(Excerpts from Tribal Park Declaration signed by George Frank, Alex Frank Sr and the Clayoquot Band Council 1984)

Nearly suffocated with imposed labels and structures, Aboriginal peoples have had no other choice than to insist on our right to speak back, to do as the old man said: to build and represent our own world of meaning and significance.

(Dodson 1994b, 4)

Indigenous struggle against colonisers has always been present. These two quotes offer insights into the diverse ways that struggle continues to be waged, and across how many fronts (discursive, political, institutional) Indigenous people must work for justice. The first quote is an extract from the Tribal Park Declaration made by the hereditary chiefs of the Clayoquot people, and the Clayoquot Band Council, over Meares Island in Canada's Pacific northwest region. They sought to re–assert their law, sovereignty and rights in the face of major development pressure (in the form of logging) on the Island. Their declaration brought the environmental planning processes and institutions in the region to a standstill, and was a formative moment in shaping alternative approaches to land use and management.

That declaration, as a politically enacted form of Dodson's urge for Indigenous people to 'speak back', mounted a quite specific challenge in a specific field: land use planning. The declaration not only invoked a continuing domain of Indigenous sovereignty and law, but prioritized that domain in a subversion (a very direct 'speaking back') of colonial power relations. It challenged the authority of modern institutions and laws, and in particular the practice of modern planning, in a particular place.

Indigenous claims for land justice, self–determination and sovereignty, like this one at Meares Island, are unsettling the certainties and central tenets of modern land use planning across the world. All sorts of shifts (multiple, fragmented, hardly coherent) in various aspects of planning are occurring in response. How should we understand these shifts, and the nature and importance of the claims Indigenous people make upon Western state–based planning? To ask a practitioner–oriented question: how should planning respond? This book addresses these kinds of questions, but not in the sense of producing a handbook on planning practice with Indigenous peoples, nor to offer a series of 'best practice' case studies. Instead, I ask two critical questions raised by the Indigenous challenge to planning and explore the different directions these questions lead our practice and analysis. The first question concerns the work planning itself has done in locally specific colonizing processes: its complicity in colonialism. The second asks how the assumptions of that colonial work, the ontologies and epistemologies that gave it shape and agency, persist.

The consequences of the answers to these questions are very challenging. For Indigenous peoples to 'speak back' suggests at least the possibility of a relational quality: of 'listening to'. This book is about how planning theory and practice might conduct that listening, as an urgent political project for our times. In investigating these two questions, my purpose is to show how planning is a cultural practice, in the sense of being embedded within as well as creating its own meanings. Seeing planning as a cultural practice makes it become specific to particular peoples, life views, times and spaces, even as planning theory tends to mythologize its universal features and norms. I am embarking on this work because I am weary of hearing the universalist voice in planning (both its theory and practice), and I am particularly disillusioned with left critiques that give alternative or radical practices of planning a newly rendered universality.

Let me briefly set out the project and argument of the book, before turning to some important methodological and theoretical points. My definition of planning here is broadly conceived as the social practice of spatial ordering, and more specifically, the modern form of that practice in the West: state–based land use or spatial planning. The aim is to address how this practice is not just complicit in, but actively produces, social injustice for Indigenous peoples. It pursues a line of thinking recently developed by Ananya Roy in the relations between empire and planning:

> ...empire is not simply an unfortunate backdrop to planning, one that can be simply denied allegiance. Rather, empire is planning's 'present history'. It is an inaugural moment. It is a trace. It is a haunting. It is a seduction. (Roy 2006, 8)

The book stems from a deep concern with how planning – my own chosen profession – dominates discursive practices in and about place, and in doing so has marginalizing and oppressing effects upon the rights and lives of Indigenous peoples. The political orientation of the book is about how to unsettle this dominance, and so find ways to undo it. I ask how this is possible, and where we should look: what theoretical notions might help; which institutional contexts and mechanisms offer possibility; what forms of struggle, resistance and critical politics might give hope some shape?

My argument is that an approach to answering these questions must do some 'archaeological' work on planning itself. We need to make available for analysis the ontological philosophies and discursive rationalities that make possible this social practice of spatial ordering in the first place. This is why I seek to make planning a culturally positioned subject, even as I explore and sometimes write against, the variety of essentializing tendencies that operate within such a project. It seems not only possible but *necessary* to the political project for Indigenous land justice to contextualize and historicize planning as a practice and theory: to show planning as only one (of many) cultural responses to questions of human–environment relations. What that analysis reveals, as the rest of the book will show, is the extent to which modern planning is constituted within colonialism itself, and the possibility that modern planning, far from being merely an 'export' of Britain, is the product of colonial relations.

I have written the book within and against a range of literatures, an activity I find both challenging and humbling. These different fields of thought and action seem to have something to say about my core concern: the colonial constitution of planning and its oppressive implications for Indigenous peoples. I am inspired and challenged by the unfaltering activism and insightful reconstitution of colonial questions by Indigenous thinkers and activists. I am intellectually engaged by critical authors whose work helps expose relations between practice, knowledge and the will to power. I am troubled by emerging dominances of theorizing planning that simply fail to notice (because they don't historicize and contextualize) that planning has its own culturally specific positionality. This chapter sets out those various debates and influences, and where the book makes its contribution. Before I turn to that, however, it is important to clarify the boundaries of the project, and the context from which the original research material in the book is drawn, and make some opening comments about the two places encountered most frequently in the chapters that follow.

Defining Settler States

Colonialism has historically been enacted in many ways, by many different states. Forms of land annexation and occupation differ widely over time and between places, depending on historical circumstance and local conditions as well as prevailing views and ideologies. In this book, I look at one variant of colonialism: the British settler colony, and more specifically, the settler colonies of what is often described as the 'New World', while recognizing all of the discursive erasures that such a name enacts. These are the states of Australia, Aoteoroa–New Zealand, the USA and Canada.

The British were relative latecomers to imperial expansion. In 1584, Richard Hakluyt presented Queen Elizabeth I with a programme for English expansion derived out of a study of both Portugese and Spanish approaches. His *Principall Navigations* (1599) set out a mode of imperial expansion that would simultaneously 'satisfy all England's imported wants, at once relieving the mother country of surplus population and rendering it independent of foreign suppliers' (Zahedieh 2002, 51). It was to the Atlantic world that Hakluyt looked to achieve this purpose, but Columbus had already sailed for the Atlantic 'New World' in 1492, and so the English were forced to operate within the terms of competition set by other imperial powers.

Industrialization in northwest Europe began to assert a new kind of superiority in the eighteenth century. Britain displaced Dutch supremacy in many regions and London had become a centre of world trade. The Spanish monopoly of trade in the Americas had been eroded by vigorous British expansion, and Spain and Portugal began to 'lose' much of their South American dominance as revolutions brought independence to key states such as Argentina and Mexico (Blue 2002, 6). By the late eighteenth and early nineteenth centuries a second wave of colonialism was emerging with Britain the dominant force (Blue 2002). By this time, the British East India Co. controlled Bengal and most of the Indian subcontinent, and Britain had also established new colonies in Australia and Aoteoroa–New Zealand. The result was a different colonial order, one that

> constituted a diversified system involving many different types of state in a complex hierarchy of domination that spanned the globe...At the heart of the system was the finely honed, bifurcated framework of direct and indirect rule, in both parts of which the cultivation and manipulation of local allies and collaborators were essential tools of control. (Blue 2002, 8)

The relative autonomy of individual colonies from the British Crown meant that many colonial processes in the New World centred around localized state building. British colonialism contributed to the proliferation of modern states, and it is on a selection of British settler colony states that I will focus in this book. While there are always differences, these countries offer a broadly coherent framework in which to work. It is at that broad, schematic level that the framework is useful and used, because there are at least four basic historical conditions operating in Aoteoroa–New Zealand, Canada, the US and Australia.

First, prior to British colonisers arriving, the 'New World' was an occupied world owned by multiple nations of Indigenous peoples, each with distinct cultures and languages, who were responsible to territorial districts, both land and waters. Second, colonies within these contemporary nation–states were annexed to Britain at some point during their history via broadly similar processes of occupation of territory, and administration of colonial affairs by Westminster. Third, the reality of encounters between colonisers and Indigenous peoples in these contemporary nation–states bear broadly similar characteristics. Declaration of sovereignty by Britain over the territories brought colonial administration and effort to bear on the people and places within them. Dispossession of Indigenous people involved a suite of mechanisms. Lands were sometimes bought or bartered, but rarely fairly. Forced removal to obtain land was widespread, enacted through violent battles with Indigenous groups, destruction or disruption of economic and subsistence sites, murder, poisoning, starvation, and exploitation. Introduced diseases took their toll. Systems of government and religious reserves were established to begin a civilizing and assimilatory process. Fourth, Indigenous peoples across these nation–states, in their struggle against marginalization and racial oppression, have continually agitated for justice and seek to regain their land and secure recognition of their rights and self–determining status.

Such points of similarity are meaningful at a very general level, and perform the useful function of containing what would otherwise be an unwieldy project. At another level, however, there are so many specificities of colonial encounter and process that such statements deserve scrutiny. It is not my intention to claim that these 'New World' states are the same as each other, nor significantly different from other places who also have colonial histories. The aim is not to look for differences or similarities as this is not offered as a comparative framework, but instead to explore the specific moments of encounter and re–encounter and ask how they shape our understanding of contemporary land justice questions and dilemmas.

Research Trajectory

The origins of my research journey are in Australia, more particularly the southeastern state of Victoria. Much of the empirical material in the book was produced during original research conducted in two places: Nyah Forest and Gariwerd National Park, both located in western Victoria. I extend the frame of reference to the three other settler states (and other places within Australia), where this proves illuminating. It will strike the critical reader that there is a distinct imbalance between the rich detail of the material from Nyah and Gariwerd and the other places I discuss in the book. This is indeed the case, and the outcome of the constraints of publishing a work that has its roots in small places, far away from the corridors of publishing power and consumer markets for academic books. I have no claim to a coherent comparative framework across settler states, but suggest that the insights offered through the two specific cases of Nyah and Gariwerd might have resonance in other contexts. A comparative case analysis might be a fruitful avenue for further work.

The research work I undertook in Nyah and Gariwerd adopted an interpretive ethnographic approach (following Agar 1996). I was interested in how planning produced space and place, by what mechanisms and spatial practices, and through what discursive tones. It was a study of the 'practices of everyday life' (Agar 1996, 10) of those people performing that spatial cultural production. In particular, the research was focused on that production in places where there was contest between Indigenous people and state–based planning. The research work, then, was oriented to understanding how and through what mechanisms that contest occurred, not as a search for universal laws about such contests but to explore the meanings of places and events within social contexts: the 'webs of significance' (Geertz 1973, 5) spun by social actors.

In both settings the study adopted a range of methods including interviews, document analysis, and participant observation with Indigenous and non-Indigenous peoples. I spent time visiting country with Indigenous participants, worked with both Indigenous and non–Indigenous works crews and rangers, volunteered in local organizations, attended meetings, accessed a wide range of documentary sources in government offices and people's homes, and conducted around 40 interviews. I used field notes to record observations and events, taped and transcribed interviews, and analysed, using a proforma framework, about 180 documents. You will hear the voices of many of the participants in the research at different points.

Fieldwork of this nature inevitably involves the negotiation of complex insider/outsider positions. As a white Australian, I was conscious of all the privileges and histories that dispossession has offered, thereby enabling me to be in the position of researcher (see Porter 2009). My participant observation of planners particularly revealed my position as both an insider and an outsider to the field. As a person with a planning qualification, I was able to access the vernacular of planning and was accepted by some of the participants as 'a planner'. Yet I was also an outsider by virtue of my peculiar position as (at that time) a student, without any formal training in environmental planning and ultimately, as time progressed, by the extent to which I became involved with particular Indigenous people. Navigating a constantly shifting insider–outsider status is never easy and there are always defining moments when certain affiliations and local politics radically delimits the possibilities for the research (see Agar 1996; Denzin 1997). These certainly occurred in my fieldwork, particularly around the politics of logging in Nyah Forest as I will go on to explore in later chapters.

Taking a critical stance in research of this nature, as I do in this book, adds further complexity to this 'insider–outsider' question. The question of values and politics within research projects continues to be a subject of debate within the social sciences. There will no doubt be those who do not see my approach here as rigorous or scientific because I indicate a viewpoint, an 'interest' instead of dispassionate disinterest. It is in such moments when qualitative research methods, critical ethnography perhaps particularly, comes under attack from the canon of western science (see for example Flyvbjerg 2001). In this sense, my ideal of 'objectivity' in research has not been to be dispassionately disinterested but to be passionately interested and methodologically rigorous. There was never the possibility that I could 'uncover' truths in the research, or access and verify unmediated 'facts'. Instead, I have attempted to take an openly self–reflexive approach, in the view that such reflexivity is neither a luxury nor self–absorbed angst, but instead a core component of critical ethnographic work (Clifford and Marcus 1986; Clifford 1998).

At this point, I need to make some disclaimers. The purpose of the research was not to document the lifeways, beliefs, and culture of Indigenous people in

Victoria, or anywhere else. This book does not constitute an anthropological study of Indigenous polities and practices in Nyah, Gariwerd, or any other place, and I have no claim to the validity or otherwise of land title claims, or of the veracity of expressed knowledge about place presented in the book. I appreciate the sensitivity of these questions, as Indigenous people now work, under very limiting rules of proof, to establish their connection to land through the systems and structures established by dominant non–Indigenous cultures. The ethical dilemmas inhering within this kind of project are also always present. In undertaking the fieldwork, I negotiated an ethical code of conduct that governed my relationship with Indigenous participants in the research. This used a proforma document covering aspects such as intellectual property, confidentiality, sensitive data, publishing, and reciprocity which was then negotiated (and amended where necessary) with each individual participant. In some cases, that negotiation was with a larger body, such as a native title claimant group or organization.

The definition of Indigenous polities and groupings is varied, complex and sometimes the site of contentious politics within and between Indigenous groups. Indigenous people in many parts of urban and rural Australia, for example, have come to define their identity by language group rather than the (usually smaller) clan groupings that have been the focus of anthropological literature (see Sutton 1998). Identity formation around the contemporary complexities of Indigenous life experience is of critical importance in the anthropological literature, and to the cut and thrust of specific land claims. While I have nothing empirical to add to these kinds of questions, I am aware that the material reported here is inevitably bound up in those questions. Throughout the book, you will hear the voices of Indigenous people who are currently claiming some form of land title, as well as those who are considered to have an historical connection (rather than a traditional one) to the places discussed. Where appropriate, I will identify those voices as much as possible, as either 'native title claimants' or 'traditional owners', to respect this differentiation within the polity.

At certain points, I will move beyond Nyah and Gariwerd and draw together material from other places across the four settler states on which I have chosen to focus. I have done no original research work in Aoteoroa–New Zealand, Canada or the United States, and all of what I report here is based on a reading of multiple types of secondary sources: existing academic literature and research findings, government reports, guidelines and policy. The historical material presented in Chapter 3 was developed through archival work undertaken in the British Library and the library of the University of Glasgow. This research was a document analysis of a selection of historical records from across the four settler states that are my focus, including: journals, despatches and other correspondence between colonial governors and the Colonial Office in London, House of Commons committee reports, and legislation. In some cases, I was able to access a copy of the full and original source; other times, I used secondary texts.

Such a wide range of sources, time periods and regional contexts does not lend itself to comparison, and so I have not set out to achieve this. The interpretive analysis I offer of the many cases that appear throughout the book is intended to explore the complexity within the particular case, rather than the commonalities across all cases. This is particularly so for the two primary fieldwork areas of Nyah and Gariwerd, where I have tried to give a deep narrative of their particulars, rather than a cruder observation of their similarities. Having said this, my point is, of course, to also show the connections, the interlocking nature of colonial spatial cultures, as I will call them, that give rise to these particular circumstances. The structure of the book is not, then, symmetrical in its treatment of particular cases, but instead interweaves the stories together in a variety of different depths and ways. In order to understand the material from Nyah and Gariwerd found throughout the book, some background and context is necessary.

About Nyah

Nyah is a place of the Wadi Wadi people, an interconnected landscape of living, sentient beings, significant due to it being the home of ancestral spirits, important places of significance (see Figure 1.1), and social and economic sustenance.[1] Nyah is a Wadi Wadi word meaning 'big river bend' and now designates an area of forest in Wadi Wadi country, situated on a bend in the river now known as the Murray River, in the northwest of the state of Victoria, Australia.

Figure 1.1   Nyah Forest, Victoria

---

1   I respectfully acknowledge the Wadi Wadi people here, and their permission to speak about Nyah Forest and its importance in these terms.

Nyah State Forest, as a specifically bounded place, is a small area of just under 1,000 hectares of public land, about 30 kilometres northwest of the regional town of Swan Hill. A small township called Nyah is located at the southern edge of the forest. I use the term 'Nyah' in this book to designate the forest area, rather than the township. Swan Hill and surrounding district has a significant Indigenous population (3.65 per cent compared with 0.5 per cent in Victoria in total), made up of Wadi Wadi people, those from the neighbouring Wemba Wemba group, and other Indigenous people with historical associations to the region. The Wadi Wadi people are involved in two native title[2] claims in the region. The first is a claim covering only the lands within both Nyah and neighbouring Vinifera forests, and the second is a wider regional claim, in connection with the North West Nations Clans. This is an umbrella body set up by different native title claimant groups in the region to better represent wider native title issues.

Contemporary associations with Nyah Forest for Wadi Wadi people in particular are focused on Tyntynder homestead, situated on the edge of the forest, to the south of Nyah township. Tyntynder, a Wadi Wadi word meaning 'song of birds' (Baxter et al. 1990) was established as a pastoral run in 1846 by the first British squatters to the area – Andrew and Peter Beveridge. Relatively amicable relations between the squatters and Wadi Wadi people were enjoyed at first (Cerutty 1977) but this soon soured and resulted in the death by spear of Andrew Beveridge and the subsequent hanging of two Wadi Wadi people by Melbourne police. Peter Beveridge continued to operate the run at Tyntynder, Indigenous people constituting around half the staff at the homestead at any one time (Penney 1979) such that Wadi Wadi people have continued to live in the region. In 1996, the Indigenous Land Corporation purchased Tyntynder homestead, on behalf of Wadi Wadi people. The land is considered a Dreaming area (Baxter et al. 1990), and an important part of the social and cultural history of Wadi Wadi people. It is now operated as a tourist venture and orchard farm by Wadi Wadi people.

The forest itself is predominantly river redgum trees and is a floodplain of the Murray River. Being state forest, it is managed as public land by the Department of Sustainability and Environment (DSE). When the research was undertaken, however, that Department operated as the Department of Natural Resources and Environment (DNRE) with its forest resource extraction arm managed by Forestry Victoria. Throughout discussions of Nyah Forest, I will refer to these organizations by the name relevant to the time under discussion, or to the organization that authored the documents under discussion. Nyah Forest is also the site of contest between Wadi Wadi people and the public authorities over logging. Due to its stands of river redgum trees, Nyah is a prized hardwood forest. Yet it is also a sacred area to the Wadi Wadi people, who have joined forces with other local Indigenous and non–Indigenous people to resist plans to log in Nyah Forest.

---

2   These are claims for recognition of continued title in land that survived British annexation, under the *Native Title Act 1993 (Cth)*, which forms the legislative response to the Australian High Court's decision in Mabo.

About Gariwerd

Gariwerd is a place significant to the Wotjobaluk, Tjapwurrung, Jardwadjali, Gunditjmara and Kirrae Wurrung peoples. The word Gariwerd means nose–like or pointed mountains in both Tjapwurrung and Jardwadjali languages. This significant set of mountain ranges and valleys is located in what is now the western part of Victoria, Australia and is known to non–Indigenous people as the Grampians National Park. As a national park, it is Victoria's fourth largest and is often referred to as 'the Kakadu of the south', denoting its importance as a tourist destination and area of natural beauty. Gariwerd is managed as a national park by Parks Victoria, an agency appointed by the Victorian Government's Department of Sustainability and Environment to manage all national parks in the State. I use the term 'Gariwerd' to name this place, as it is the accepted name for the mountain ranges amongst Indigenous communities. Naming in Gariwerd has a history of controversy, when attempts were made to restore Indigenous names to both the park and some of its features (see Birch 1997 and Chapter 4). Indigenous participants in this research used the name Gariwerd and expressed aspirations to widen its usage. I also use the term Gariwerd because it reminds us that the place itself – its stories, associations and knowledge – leak outside the boundaries of what might otherwise be known as 'the park'. This naming points to and plays on important differences in naming and knowing places, such that Indigenous communities know the place as Gariwerd, and park managers know the place as the Grampians. As an Indigenous place for the

Figure 1.2   **Brambuk building in Gariwerd, Victoria**

Wotjobaluk, Gunditjmara, Tjapwurrung, Jardwadjali and Kirrae Wurrung peoples and Indigenous peoples with strong historical links to the region, Gariwerd is the source of economic and social practices, cultural responsibility, and the presence of significant cultural places.

During the 1980s, five Indigenous communities in Victoria's southwest region including Framlingham, Goolum Goolum, Gunditjmara, Kerrup Jmara, and Kirrae Wurrung, began discussing how to develop new initiatives to meet their aspirations. Those ideas came to fruition in the Brambuk Living Cultural Centre, opened in late 1989 and located within the park on the edge of the small township of Halls Gap. Brambuk was established to provide employment and training for local Indigenous people, and education and awareness about Indigenous culture and values to the wider community. As a building, Brambuk Living Cultural Centre has become an iconic feature of the Gariwerd landscape. 'Brambuk' means white cockatoo, an important Indigenous totem for Gariwerd, and the Brambuk building is shaped to represent the white cockatoo in flight (see Figure 1.2).

The issue of native title is a difficult and contested one for Indigenous communities in the region, due to its particular colonial history (Clark 1998b, 1995; Critchett 1990) and consequently Gariwerd is not wholly covered by native title claims despite its importance to a number of Indigenous nations in the region.

Theoretical Starting Points

Students of planning today can read many excellent texts that set out the multitude of ways in which planning is implicated in, and has a responsibility toward, communities of difference. The project of interculturalism is one that has found a clear voice in planning theory, with calls to attend to a politics of difference hitherto swept under planning's 'universal public good' carpet (see Sandercock 2003 and 1998a; Forester 1999; Healey 1997; Burayidi 2003; Beebeejaun 2004; Thomas 2000). Sandercock's call for a new multicultural praxis in the face of such challenges entails, in part, the recognition of multiple publics and the development of multicultural literacies (1998b, 30). Other texts point out practical ways by which planning can do this work, by thinking through the implications of equal opportunity legislation (Reeves 2005), including voices from culturally diverse communities, and more transparently mediating land use conflicts that are enframed by a politics of difference (Sandercock and Kliger 1997; Harwood 2005).

Recognizing, celebrating, understanding and developing good transactive and collaborative dialogues with sociocultural groups that are 'other' to planning is an essential and laudable aim. Yet those approaches consistently miss what I believe is the first and most important theoretical and practical work to be done: to turn our analysis toward the culture of the practice of planning. Even when power relations are well theorized, and local histories and cultural nuances sensitively understood, to pretend that planning is the position from which the clamour of 'difference' in (post)colonial settings can be heard, translated and mediated is to forget that planning's own genealogy is colonial and its work a fundamental activity to the ongoing colonial settlement of territory. Forgetting to theorize planning's own cultural position can render the 'inclusion' of Indigenous people in land management decisions a new form of colonial oppression.

There is some attention in the planning field of differently identified 'cultural' ways of doing planning. A collection of essays brought together by Sanyal (2005) explores planning cultures as different 'styles' of planning, of varying responses to challenges, change, and context. That collection demonstrates the local nuances of a wide range of planning 'cultures' that emerge and change in relation to their historically, geographically and culturally specific settings and recognizes that planning as an activity of spatial ordering 'cannot possibly be divorced – as a rational, technical exercise – from the general traditions that inform it' (Booth 2005, 260). Planning actions and behaviours are mapped onto a wider set of social, cultural and political variations and shifts. My interest here is different because I see continuities, a continuing performance, of colonial sensibilities in contemporary planning practices that need exposure and analysis. This entails an approach to the (post)colonial not as a beyond, but as a reconstitution of structures of feeling and meaning born of the historically specific emergence of colonial cultures. Unsettling the myth of progress beyond the 'colonial' moment, troubling the sense of sustained contemporary reflection at multiple removes from the historical quirks under investigation, must be a core strategy for anticolonial analysis and resistance (Thomas 1994).

Understanding the 'culture' of planning is not a question of analysing the cultural or ethnic makeup of the planning profession, although the white domination of the profession in many otherwise culturally diverse places is widely regarded a problem of structural inequality, and should be addressed. The only conclusion possible from that kind of analysis is that 'more Indigenous people should be employed as planners': positive in terms of equal opportunities, but it basically misses the point and detracts our analytical attention. For an Indigenous person to be employed to implement a new land use plan somewhere is a victory for equality of opportunity, and for a greater recognition of ever present cross–cultural issues. It does not, however, help us understand how planning discursively constructs itself, and the position of 'othered' Indigenous people in relation to itself, and how the very practice of 'implementing a land use plan' has colonial roots that powerfully shape conceptions of and actions in place, whether performed by an Indigenous person or not. My definition of culture is not, then, about styles or traditions but about 'structures of feeling'. I draw from the work of Raymond Williams to develop an approach of cultural materialism to the questions I pose to see that

> Culture never stands alone but always participates in a conflictual economy acting out the tensions between sameness and difference, comparison and differentiation, unity and diversity, cohesion and dispersion, containment and subversion. (Young, R.C. 1995, 53)

In working against the tendencies of relativism, I try to explore the questions I am raising through an historicized investigation of detailed events and moments, with planning's historically and culturally determined 'self' at its centre. I am looking to see if we can produce a 'critical ontology of ourselves' (in Rabinow 1984, 40). 'Ourselves' includes those of us involved in planning, conceived of here in its broadest sense as the social practice of spatial ordering.

I write here as a non–Indigenous person and a planner, and I will use throughout the book terms like 'us' and 'them': terms I am uncomfortable with but for which I have failed to find suitable alternatives. In the sense, however, that I write as an 'insider' to planning, educated in its discipline and professional orientations, the 'us' has a certain appropriateness. I want to speak *to* that discipline and profession and of course I speak *from* it. My analysis, then, is fully located in a variety of 'centres': the centre of a dominant culture, an authoritative system of government (planning), a prestigious University, within the colonial metropole (see also Porter 2009 for further reflection on these questions). But I read the critiques of this very positioning (Spivak 1994; Prakash 1996; Chakrabarty 2000; hooks 1992; Smith 1999) also as a rejection of disavowal. As Prakash observes 'we do not have the option of saying no to the determinate conditions of history' (1996, 201) and so the work here must be situated as an analysis of the 'contingent, contentious, and heterogenous subaltern positions' (ibid) arising out of those conditions. Being the subject of those critiques, because of my positionality, does not absolve me of the responsibility of writing. In that sense, I am conscious of the privilege and politics of my location and the extent to which that privilege is built upon the historical fact of Indigenous disposesssion (see Porter 2009). There is a requirement to write responsibly (Noxolo 2009).

This book provides, then, a genealogy of *planning*, not an anthropology of Indigenous people in settler states trying to influence planning decisions. It is an exploration of planning's 'spatial cultures' as I will call them, of the 'us' that is a wider civic body of people grappling with the ongoing contemporary endurances of colonialism's culture. If colonial culture is indeed 'expressive and constitutive of colonial relationships in themselves' (Thomas 1994, 2) then the focus of inquiry should be the everyday relationships between Indigenous and non–Indigenous people, played out in countless mundane settings across the world.

Why is this a critical part of the work? In explicating how we have never, in fact, been modern, Latour names what he sees as a second 'Great Divide' in the world (the first is between nature and culture), that between 'Westerners' and all others:

> Whatever they do, Westerners bring history along with them in the hulls of their caravels and their gunboats, in the cylinders of their telescopes and the pistons of their immunizing syringes. They bear this white man's burden sometimes as an exalting challenge, sometimes as a tragedy, but always as a destiny. They do not claim merely that they differ from others as the Sioux differ from the Algonquins, or the Baoules from the Lapps, but that they differ radically, absolutely, to the extent that Westerners can be lined up on one side and all the cultures on the

other, since the latter all have in common the fact that they are precisely cultures among others. In Westerners' eyes the West, and the West alone, is not a culture, not merely a culture. (Latour 1991, 97)

It is the Western, modern distinction between moderns and the rest that enables only moderns to establish a total separation of Nature from Culture, as I will explore in later chapters, and in so doing situate themselves as 'meta–cultural'.

Latour suggests that the notion of culture could simply be dissolved altogether in order to remove the difference that the West sets up for itself from its Others (Latour 1991, 106). If we see how all 'collectivities', as he calls them, 'sort out what will bear signs and what will not' (ibid, 106) we equalize the terrain of conversation. If we accept that what Latour offers here is a way of reformulating modern existence to render difference less absolute yet simultaneously hardly relativist, it seems we need to first expose the work done in constructing the very edifices Latour describes. In other words, to see the West as hardly different (except by virtue of organization) from any other collective requires a thorough exposition of Western ways of being in order to demote them from their pedestal of 'meta–cultural'. For my project here, it means making western planning cultural and thereby unsettle the hegemony it produces for itself in marking off nature from culture, things from being.

Critical to my approach to this project is Lefebvre's notion that '(social) space is a (social) product' (1991, 26). In a sense I am responding, in a small way, to his call for a 'science of space' applied to all 'modes of production' of space (ibid) by bringing the particular mode of settler colonialism under analysis. Lefebvre's conceptualization of the production of space (as opposed to its creation, or to 'works') orients that analysis toward producers and process: the labour (conceived broadly) of production predominates and highlights the reproducibility of space (ibid, 71). This is important, because it *enables* an investigation of those productive processes and efforts, and the kinds of producers involved. In other words, it renders space visible and real by making visible and real the practices which bring space into being.

Lefebvre's approach is also illuminating because it makes puncture and rupture, the dialectic, an inevitable part of those productive practices. The 'differential space' Lefebvre observes (1991, 52) affirms the inability of those productive practices to entirely contain, or master, space. Space is its own source of contradictions, of rupture, of immanent difference (a theme I will explore time and again throughout the book), and so an orientation to the production of space also proffers the possibility of transformation.

In conceptualizing the production of space, Lefebvre offers an analytical triad for investigating productions of spaces as follows:

1. Spatial practice, or 'perceived' space,
2. Representations of space, or 'conceived' space,
3. Representational space, or 'lived' space.

Perceived space, or 'firstspace' in Soja's interpretation (2000) is the material engagement with the space of the city, the daily interactions and routes of the social in the city, the 'concrete forms and specific patternings of urban as a way of life' (Soja 2000, 10). Conceived space for Lefebvre is the space of the 'scientists, planners, urbanists, technocratic subdividers and social engineers' (Lefebvre 1991, 38) which is 'in thrall to both knowledge and power' (ibid, 50). It is the 'mental or ideational field' of spatial imagination that is the work of dominant systems of thinking for the purposes of administering and remaking space. Lived space is the 'life story of space' (Soja 2000, 11) that encapsulates the everyday lived experience and expression of the social in space. A key concern is the extent to which conceived space has come to 'penetrate and dominate the way we live today' (Healey 2007, 204) and in doing so reduce space as an analytical category to be explained rather than a lived phenomenon (Soja 2000).

Much of the work of colonialism, it could be interpreted, is to impose (often violently) a conceived space upon the lived spaces of Indigenous peoples. My argument in this book will focus in this direction, but not in the sense of determining an Indigenous 'lived space'. My focus will be on conceived space as the dominant space of a society tied to its relations of production and its production of knowledge. In particular, I will be looking at conceived space as it is coded within planning. Yet I aim to do this by seeing the dialectical relationship between the elements that Lefebvre insists on, and in particular the relations and interwoven–ness of spatial practice and conceived space. I read this as the practice of giving space shape and form, the crystallization of the relationship between society and its spaces, 'revealed through the deciphering of its space' (Lefebvre 1991, 38). In short, then, I will look at the variety of modes of producing colonial space, what is given meaning through that production, or rather how we can see what is given meaning through analysing what gets produced. I bring conceived space under critical analysis in terms of its role in producing abstract colonial space as a form of dominance, sometimes a violation, of the already existing lived spaces of the 'New World'. This is a contemporary reading, also: the purpose of the book is to show the dialectical relationship that manifests as a struggle – between Indigenous people and planning – over the production of space: between conceived and lived space.

If we agree that space is produced then that leads to the requirement, argues Lefebvre, for a history of space, historicized according to modes of its production. Historicized, contextualized: these are the theoretical and methodological commitments necessary to the work of making spatial practices available for analysis. In the context of colonialism, it is neither theoretically, nor logically, possible to talk about colonialism across places as diverse as India, Burma, Taiwan, Palestine, Aoteoroa–New Zealand and Iraq (as a random selection of examples) in any coherent way. There can be no unifying theory of colonialism and its effects, as 'only localized theories and historically specific accounts can provide much insight into the varied articulations of colonizing and countercolonial representations and practices' (Thomas 1994, ix).

Furthermore, that we might now speak of a state of (post)colonialism should not be taken as a triumphant liberation from past colonial violence, now clearly seen from the vantage point of twenty–first century values. (Post)colonial societies remain deeply implicated in past events, but more importantly the *cultural* traits of colonialism endure, as 'a variety of colonial representations and encounters both precede and succeed periods of actual possession and rule' (Thomas 1994, 16). To be 'post' colonial is to be always and forever implicated, though in constantly shifting ways, in colonialism's enduring philosophies, hence my use of parentheses. (Post)colonial is a way of writing 'against the grain' (Gregory 2001, 612), but always with an attention to its project as more than writing, as a responsible contribution to the work of anticolonial resistance.

This deeply fractured, pluralized theorization of colonialism, as one 'mode of production' of space, renders void any attempt to undertake a universalizing analysis of planning's colonial culture. How, then, can I write of this 'colonial culture' of planning? We can do this in the same way as we can speak of planning in its 'modernist paradigm', or planning as a 'technocratic activity': by making available for analysis the everyday specific spatial practices that are of interest. Investing planning objects with meaning, history and identity can only be approached through a detailed analysis of selected specific planning 'moments', both contemporarily and in historical times. That analysis, as I will suggest in the book, exposes not a universal and coherent 'Culture' of planning, but instead a porous and by no means coherent, *structure of meaning* (Williams 1965) enframing planning activities. It makes visible a colonial logic embedded within planning's philosophy and action–in–the–world, its practice. What I argue is that what shapes planning practice in settler societies – the structures of meaning and authorities of truth that give planning agency in the world – are drenched in colonial historiographies, and so the colonial relations of domination and oppression are ever present.

Planning, then, becomes the subject, it becomes a 'cultural artifact' (Sharma and Gupta 2006, 5) of colonialism. Different kinds of questions then become possible: what are the cultural conditions under which planning came to be able to operate in settler colonies, and how do those shape what planning becomes, how it is practiced, and the material realities it produces? If planning is a producer of place, what does it claim is worth producing and how is this particular view of the world continually mediated and reconstituted? In particular, I wish to expose the fact that such modes of seeing are not only able to be discerned, but further constitute a potential field of action for a more progressive planning theory and practice. If planning started out by convincing itself it was rational, that myth has been deeply unsettled by the continuing work of those exposing how planning is political and social. This book will show how planning is also culturally enframed – a structure of feeling that continually reproduces its sensibilities and rationalities through its daily practice. This focus on the intricate network of feelings, rationalities and practices helps unsettle the 'conceit of reason and the celebration of rationality on which imperial authority has been seen to rest' (Stoler 2004, 4).

In treating planning here as a 'discourse' I am drawing on Foucault's work to see that discourse as *whatever* constrains – but also enables – writing, speaking and thinking within such specific historical limits' (McHoul and Grace 1993, 31 original italics). The elision of colonial sites from Foucault's work, and the extent to which colonies were the places where subjectivities and governmentalities were produced and recast, is well established (Spivak 1994; Legg 2007b; Stoler 1989 and 1995; Thomas 1994). Ways of seeing the intersection of power and knowledge that Foucault's work illuminates is nonetheless useful. By considering the mechanics of rule and workings of power in an anthropological sense (in the everyday, mundane practices) enables us to see power, especially state power, in disaggregate form (Sharma and Gupta 2006).

This is aided by a deconstructive stance, one that I borrow, after a fashion, from Spivak (1988). Deconstruction is an effort to historicize our own practice, analyses and intellectual efforts, as a stance it seeks to investigate hidden ethical and political agendas and to see the 'situational product of those concepts [we use for analysis] and our complicity in such a production' (Spivak 1988, 84). A work, then, can acknowledge that it is produced within and through the very structures it sets out to critique (Spivak 1993, 281), and the 'master narratives' already existing that give critical analysis its voice (Mouffe 1999). Yet Spivak tries to reclaim that dilemma by denoting deconstruction as a kind of transformative analytical 'gift' (Spivak 1988, 201). The work of investigating the ideological formations, spatial rationalities, and colonial complicities of planning will require working within a framework that sees these constructs as patterns already available for analysis. To speak of an 'Indigenous polity', or to speak of 'settler states', as if these were coherent and accessible 'natural' (or first order) categories, is always potentially essentializing. The very subject positions 'Indigenous' and 'planning' (not to mention 'colonial') are possible only because of the conditions of our existence. In subjecting them to further analysis (even while we might position that analysis as 'more progressive'), we are always nearing complicity with the form of domination of 'knowledge as power', and tendencies toward reification.

The message of this book is bounded within this very same complex identity politics conundrum. My central argument is that western settler states, and their planning systems especially, produce space in ways broadly coherent with their modes of production. More importantly, that this formation of space production is quite distinct from Indigenous productions of space. My argument rests, then, on the establishment of difference, on a sometimes reified binary of (post)colonial relations. The potential for my argument to turn on a stylized and reified identification of difference is very present. In Chapter 3, for example, I attempt to convey a sense of a colonial spatial culture that was not only constituted within the various specificities of (historical) colonial experiences, but continues to shape our (post)colonial presents. Following from this, the rest of the book discusses contests between that colonial spatial culture and differently constructed Indigenous ontological and epistemological philosophies of place over the power and authority to practice those spatial cultures. A binaric difference is very visible.

Necessarily, then, I argue that difference exists and is materially relevant to our social practices and relations, especially the practices of (post)colonial planning as other scholars have shown (see Lane and Williams 2008; Tipa and Nelson 2008; Watson and Huntington 2008).

But the problem of difference is not difference itself. Our concern should not be with why difference exists and what our political position on difference might be, but instead how a politics of difference is made manifest within those social practices and relations. My concern is that this difference, or more accurately the invisibility of planning's own spatial ontology, will always act as a a basis of pervasive forms of colonial dominance and continue to oppress and marginalize Indigenous peoples. Always: unless we turn some attention to undoing that ontology. That is why the analytical orientation of the book is firmly on identifying where, and by what mechanisms, that politics of difference reconstitutes colonial power relations and how injustice results. To have any chance of finding more progressive (post)colonial politics, especially in planning, this is where we must begin.

Outline of the Book

In Chapter 2, I look at the ways in which Indigenous people have actively resisted and shaped colonialism and what kinds of questions, dilemmas and challenges this raises for planning in contemporary settler states. Indigenous struggles to reclaim dispossessed lands raises a series of complex dilemmas for planning: particularly, what dispossession is and planning's role inside of the processes of dispossession; and the identity questions concerning sovereignty and difference that such claims are based upon. The chapter explores the workings of Indigenous resistance and struggle in settler states, questions about dispossession and cultural difference that both identify a sovereign Indigenous domain and structure the reception of Indigenous land claims by the state.

In Chapter 3, I focus on how colonial space actually came to be produced, through what technologies and practices. I do this through an analysis of archival material from a range of different settler states. The chapter argues that those technologies and practices constitute the early forms of planning in settler states. While the designation of a profession of planning was some way off in time, the spatial desires, rationalities and technologies – what I will term, 'spatial cultures' – practiced in the production of colonial space are the very same that today underpin modern planning systems. This chapter is about exposing both how planning was a fundamental practice of colonialism, and how planning remains bound within its colonial spatial culture.

Chapter 4 then takes that historical investigation and attempts to historicize the emergence of a distinct hierarchisation of place within the particular canon of environmental management and protected area planning. I begin at the global level, looking at the inscription of a hierarchy of spaces within global environmental planning frameworks. The chapter then looks in some detail at a range of cases (Nyah, Gariwerd, Clayoquot Sound and Aoraki/Mt Cook) and asks what particular spatial cultures have been brought to bear on these places and with what outcomes for Indigenous claims.

One manifestation of those relations in contemporary planning is cultural heritage management, which is theorized in Chapter 5 as a particular governmentality of modern settler states. This chapter draws specifically on material from Nyah Forest and looks at how the production of Nyah as a 'forest' both limits Indigenous claims at the same time as it is the site of transformative possibilities. I then widen the analysis to other cases to explore the renegotiation of power and agency in space occurring through cultural heritage management in different settler states.

In Chapter 6 I turn to the question of new and shifting forms of planning and management for protected areas and in the environment more widely. While there is a significant literature looking at the emergence of 'community–based' forms of protected area management, this chapter will take a close look at what difference Indigeneity makes to the assumptions of processes steeped in the principles of deliberative democracy. It explores whether the collaborative forms of planning being tried in different places might, where they don't attend to planning's own cultural specificity and its own spatial culture, be a new form of colonial domination.

The final chapter explores the kinds of work (theoretical, empirical–analytical, practical and political) that needs to be done within the planning field to enable more transformative (post)colonial politics. In short, what would a project of decolonizing planning look like? And what ethical orientations do we need to locate the possible moments for that project? I suggest that the critical and practical work ahead needs to encompass (at least) three such orientations: recognizing the rights of Indigenous peoples; continuing the analytical work required to expose planning as cultural; and locating our radical politics in an ethic of love.

Chapter 2
Indigenous People and their Challenge to Planning

> I am earthspeaking, talking about this place, my home, and it is, first, a very small story. Tell it softly so that someone might by chance hear you. One valley. A tree with a crooked branch where children swung with children's hands, a soft look of the pasture in the buttery afternoon light. The cold scent of dew on purple–tipped flatgrass, grass that can be stripped and played like a gumleaf if you know how. It is land with a small *l*. The people? They are off to the side somewhere. They are important, yes, but they aren't the whole story. Nothing is the whole story, by itself. Not the people and not the land either. They need each other. So gather round. This earthspeaking is a small, quiet story in a human mouth, or no story at all.
>
> (Lucashenko 2006, 23)

Just as colonialism is not a monolithic process, neither does it simply 'get done' to passive native peoples. Indigenous resistance, in multiple and changing forms, physically and performatively shaped, and continues to shape, the production of colonial space in settler states. This chapter sets out some key ideas to shape our understanding of the importance of land justice for Indigenous peoples to the planning field. What kind of challenges do Indigenous people make to planning, and how should we conceptualize those challenges in their historical context? What is the nexus between Indigenous rights in land and the practice of state–based planning? This chapter is about the challenge that the difference of Indigeneity makes to planning. Important to this understanding is to appreciate the link between Indigenous claims over, and struggles for, land; questions of sovereignty and citizenship, and the contemporary recognition, in its varied forms, of Indigenous rights in settler states. Underpinning all these is the fact of dispossession of Indigenous peoples, and the effects of its discourses. First, though, some context on the scale and nature of Indigenous resistance and struggle is necessary.

The Lived Space of Indigenous Struggle

The histories of Indigenous struggle and resistance around the world are many and varied. Settler colonialism encountered resistance and the active agency of Indigenous peoples everywhere it went. Violent conflicts between colonists and native groups were common, as were more conciliatory relationships built through trade, exchange and intermarriage (see Dyck 1985 on indirect and direct forms of confrontation). The fur trade in the Canadian northwest, for example, integrally involved Indigenous communities, and Native American groups often allied themselves with different colonial governments (sometimes British, sometimes French) during war (see Fleras and Elliott 1992).

Indigenous peoples also successfully negotiated treaties with colonial powers. Two of particular significance are the Treaty of Waitangi in Aoteoroa–New Zealand agreed in 1840, and the James Bay Cree Treaty in Ontario, Canada of 1905. However, despite the presence of treaties and agreements, Indigenous peoples have consistently been betrayed by settler states as treaty clauses have been ignored, redefined or interpreted away over time. For example, it is only since 1975 with the establishment of the Treaty of Waitangi Tribunal, that Maori have been able to bring claims of grievance against the state for breaches of that treaty. In the US, despite the presence of local treaties and agreements regarding land reservations, the US government continues to occupy land illegally (see Churchill 1998).

More contemporarily, Indigenous peoples have advocated for their rights, and fought (not always successfully) threats from governments, developers and multinational corporations through protest, lobbying, occupation of territory, and legal proceedings. The Gurindji people's stand at Wave Hill in Australia's Northern Territory in 1966, ostensibly about wages and conditions, led to the first land rights legislation in Australia. The Six Nations protests and resistance against infrastructure projects in New York State in the 1950s, and the occupation of Alcatraz by Indian people fighting for better conditions and rights from 1969 to 1971 brought better conditions and rights recognition for American Indian Nations. First Nations protests throughout Canada in the 1980s, best exemplified in Clayoquot Sound, blockading logging and other natural resource extraction activities had a global impact and raised the difficult (post)colonial dilemmas inherent between conservation and land justice. In Aoteoroa–New Zealand, campaigns by Maori and non–Maori throughout the 1970s and 80s to have the Treaty of Waitangi recognized and enforced successfully culminated in the establishment of the Treaty of Waitangi Tribunal, finally affording Maori the ability to seek restitution and compensation for loss of land and resources (for excellent accounts of these and other aspects of Indigenous activism and struggle, see Vine Deloria and Lytle 1984; Johnson, Nagel and Champagne 1997; Fleras and Elliot 1992; Evison 1997; Jentoft, Minde and Nilsen 2003; Wilson and Yeatman 1995; Tennant 1990; Willems–Braun 1997; Bandler 1989; Toyne and Vachon 1983; Peterson and Langton 1983; Gelder and Jacobs 1998).

Litigation and negotiation have become particularly important strategies of Indigenous politics in recent years, and considerable advances in rights recognition has occurred through these means. Cases such as *Delgamuukw v the Queen* in Canada, and *Mabo v Queensland [No. 2] (1992) 175 CLR 1* in Australia (hereafter the 'Mabo' case) have redefined the nature of Indigenous rights in those two countries, even as their original spirit remains largely unfulfilled. As Bunton argues in relation to British imperialism in Palestine in the 1920s:

legal proceedings became an important arena for opposing imperial measures, an area where the colonial state, less monolithic and omnipotent than is often presumed, was forced to confront unwelcome opposition to its self–perception as an objective authority neutrally exercising the rule of law over indigenous parties. (2002, 148)

This common law doctrine concerning Indigenous title is now well established enough to be globally influential (see Gilbert 2007, 585; and also Daes 2001, 10–11). Indigenous people from different nation–states have recognized commonalities in their colonial experiences and developed new alliances in the geopolitical order, now reflected in the United Nations Draft Declaration on the Rights of Indigenous Peoples which declares the fundamental right of all people to self–determination and the pursuit of economic, social and cultural development (Gibson 1999). The intensity of struggle and global alliances achieved by Indigenous peoples in recent years constitutes a 'distinctive force in world politics with a capacity to embarrass and exert leverage on national governments' (Fleras and Elliott 1992, 3).

This global alliance has successfully reformed some aspects of land and environmental planning to recognize Indigenous rights and interests more fully at the global level. Prior to the Declaration of the Rights of Indigenous Peoples in 2007, the United Nations (UN) had begun to codify Indigenous interests in a variety of treaty areas. In 1997, the World Heritage Convention was amended to include a third category of heritage site called 'cultural landscapes'. These offered Indigenous peoples a new forum to mobilize international support for the recognition and protection of sacred lands threatened by development. The first cultural landscape to be designated under the new category was Uluru in central Australia (Barsh 1998, 229). Changes have been made to the classification category of protected areas, where the International Union for the Conservation of Nature (IUCN), in 1972, recognized the right of Indigenous peoples to live in protected areas and use the economic resources of their homelands (Stevens 1997). Building on this, the IUCN developed a set of guidelines for developing joint management partnerships between nation–states and Indigenous peoples to manage protected areas (Beltran 2000). Similarly, the Convention on Biological Diversity adopted at the Rio Earth Summit in 1992 specifically identified Indigenous peoples as 'actors in the conservation of resources and ecosystems' (Barsh 1998, 230). Following considerable efforts raising the profile of and documenting Indigenous knowledge systems, Indigenous peoples successfully fought for changes to UNESCO's Man and the Biosphere Programme to adopt a new goal of understanding 'human ecology' by recognizing that the 'system of knowledge most useful for the understanding of an inhabited ecosystem…is the science of the people who originally inhabited it' (Barsh 1998, 229). These moves signify a shift in the way that Indigenous issues are appreciated within international, particularly environmental, treaties.

The record of national and provincial governments, however, is more fragmented, and as Barsh cautions 'international conventions and declarations are only useful to the extent that they can be translated into national policy' (1998, 223). The next section and following chapters will look at some of these specific responses. For now it is important to be aware that major inequities between Indigenous and non–Indigenous peoples. Indigenous peoples represent approximately 5 per cent of the world's population, but comprise around 15 per cent of the world's poor, and suffer grossly disproportionate rates of poor health, poverty, violence, early death, incarceration and poor quality housing and infrastructure than non–Indigenous peoples (see International Fund for Agricultural Development, no date).

In contemporary times, then, there is an essential tension around which settler states manage their territory – that between Indigenous people advocating their right to survive as Indigenous peoples, and that of nation–states seeking to 'reconcile demands for special aboriginal status and rights with the existing institutional arrangements and ideological foundations of Western nation–states' (Dyck 1985, 2). The nature of this dilemma as it arises for planning constitutes one of the important foci of this book, and I will return repeatedly to this question of the difference that Indigeneity makes.

Rights Claims, Sovereignty and Citizenship

In the US, Canada, Aoteoroa–New Zealand and Australia, conflicts concerning land use and natural resource management continue to define the political landscape. These questions of land and waters have been the site of greatest effort and confrontation for Indigenous peoples over the last thirty years, because access, control and responsibility for custodial land and waters is central to Indigenous culture, economy, religion and philosophy.

These same contests between Indigenous peoples and nation–states also give rise to the related issue of the location from where such rights spring. Settler states tend to see such rights as being conferred upon, or granted to, Indigenous peoples by the state either through a treaty arrangement (which entails greater parity between the parties) or as a form of 'delegated' right from the state (Fleras and Elliott 1992, 29). In the latter view, the state acts benevolently to bestow additional rights upon one group of citizens that are not available to others. Indigenous people contend, and this has long been recognized in international law, that their rights pre–exist modern settler states and are inherent to their status as original inhabitants of contested territory (see Fleras and Elliott 1992; Dyck 1985; Scholtz 2006).

It is not only cultural conceptualizations of space and place that constitute potentially gulf–like differences between Indigenous and non–Indigenous parties in territorial disputes. How the parties conceptualize the nature and purpose of the struggle is also different:

> land claims...tend to be viewed by corporations and governments as issues involving control of access to valuable commodities, whereas for indigenous peoples these claims stand not only for a different set of economic interests but also for the protection of their culture and community. (Dyck 2985, 7–8)

Further, they stand for the need to control local economies and achieve self-determination. This difference profoundly unsettles the notion of citizenship that underpins modern liberal democracies. The assertion of one single category of citizenship, and the universality that underpins the legal regimes of modern liberal states (see Tully 1995) tend to foreclose on the possibility of separate citizenship claims and stakes to territory (see Dyck 1985) in the way that Indigenous peoples seek to do.

Indigenous sovereignty, and consequently rights to self–determination, is at the heart of these arguments. Sovereign rights have been seen as fundamental to not only addressing poverty and socioeconomic marginalization, but also to securing land rights and respect for Indigenous systems of land tenure (see Senese 1991). As Churchill (2002) observes in relation to North America:

> This, then, is the context in which the native liberation struggle in North America should be viewed. The agendas of the American Indian Movement (AIM) and the more organic warrior societies which have lately (re)emerged in several indigenous nations – as well as armed confrontations at places like Wounded Knee, Oka and Gunnison Lake – have nothing to do with attaining civil rights and other forms of 'equality' for native people within the U.S. and Canadian systems. Nor are they meant to foster some 'revolutionary' reorganization either. Rather, the purpose is, quite specifically, to reassert the genuinely sovereign and self–determining status to which our nations are and have always been entitled. (26)

What is sovereignty and what does it mean in these contexts? While sovereignty clearly infers 'supreme power', sovereignty is a concept that unlike power is not a 'fact' until a network of other circumstances and practices give it effect (Kuehls 2003, 181). One part of this network of circumstances and practices is land, or more particularly the production of property in land. Property creates sovereignty, because sovereignty is spatial in its manifestation and jurisdiction. Sovereignty over and in territory is a concept in both Indigenous and non–Indigenous philosophies of place governance, and of territorial control. Indigenous struggle, as I have shown in this section, is really about sovereignty and self–determination, expressed through recognition of rights to land. These rights link sovereignty and territory: the right to use and enjoy land, to control access, to determine its management, and so on.

Sovereignty in and over territory is also the aspiration of colonialism. The act and process of colonizing territory is to enable sovereignty over that land, and its peoples. Central to Western notions of the link between sovereignty and territory has been, and remains, John Locke's concept of property. I will discuss Lockean theories of property in detail in Chapter 3. For now, it is important to say that Locke created a definition of property (sovereignty over territory) that was rendered legible through the addition of labour to land, its use and improvement.

> In order for sovereignty over land to exist...there must first be property in the land. And in order for property to exist, the land has to be used in specific ways...that meant enclosing ground, maintaining said ground with domesticated cattle, and establishing permanent dwellings. (Kuehls 2003, 182)

Such a theorization of property had very specific implications for colonialism. Sovereignty, in western terms, exists over land, it becomes recognizable, through specific land use, the improvement of land. Chapter 3 will look in more detail at how important this notion of improvement is in the continual process of creating and asserting sovereignty through colonialism, and how it underpins modern land use planning. It has also been important to the justification of colonialism in settler states, where land has been stolen from Indigenous peoples. Locke's property discourse – of sovereignty existing only where use and improvement can be measurable and recognized – linked to the intrinsic racism and violence of colonialism, was one of the mechanisms of securing imperial power over territory. Indigenous peoples were not recognizably 'improving' their territory and therefore could not be recognized as sovereign rulers of that territory (or indeed as owners of property). Indigenous land politics is all about exposing the racialized hierarchies embedded within this notion of property and its application in colonialism, and asserting the recognition of their sovereignty expressed differently over territory. Indigenous land claims, then, are fundamentally contests about identity, sovereignty and the recognition that Western/colonial approaches to property are one cultural expression of the sovereignty–territory relationship.

By consistently *unsettling* settler activity, Indigenous resistance is constantly renegotiating the meanings of place as well as the physical structuring of space in colonial society. Just as early periods were characterized by warfare, violence, trade and struggle, so the contemporary period is marked by continued resistance especially through lobbying, protest and legal challenge. These struggles, and the shifting sociopolitical contexts in which they unfold, are renegotiating the multiple fields of recognition and governance between Indigenous peoples and settler states. It is important now to look more closely at exactly what kinds of forms this recognition has taken in the four settler states that are the focus in this book, as these become pertinent to the discussions in later chapters.

USA

Recognition of the sovereignty and territorial rights of Indigenous nations in the United States, while obviously highly differentiated, was both generally understood, and specifically perceived in legal terms. Thomas Jefferson, the author of the American Declaration of Independence recognized Indian sovereignty in 1793 and in doing so implicitly recognized that the new America did not have title rights but rather could simply replace England to the 'right of pre–emption' (Jefferson quoted in Churchill 2002, 44). Chief Justice Marshall of the US Supreme Court, who as I will detail in a moment declared some of the most significant legal rulings on Indigenous sovereignty and territory rights, also recognized this (Churchill 2002, 40). Between 1778 and 1871, the US Senate ratified around 400 treaties with Indigenous nations, treaties being recognized in the US Constitution (Churchill 2002, 41). The existence of such treaties has meant that Indigenous nations in the US and Canada have a recognizable sovereignty, jurisdiction and territory.

However, as Churchill shows, other rulings of the Supreme Court in the US failed to understand the actual intent and meaning of the Doctrine of Discovery and Marshall himself ultimately managed to subvert it too in his famous trilogy of rulings (Churchill 2002, 61). The Marshall trilogy constitutes three separate landmark decisions by the then Chief Justice of the American Supreme Court, John Marshall. Essentially, through these three rulings, Marshall

> argued that while discovery divested Indians of ultimate fee simple ownership of the United States, the tribes did maintain rights of use and occupancy. The United States could acquire these remaining rights through agreement and consent of the tribe. (Scholtz 2006, 161)

In 1871, American Congress declared that Indians were henceforth wards of the state, representing a fundamental shift in power relations (Fleras and Elliott 1992, 144), as the US state would no longer be required to treat with them as they were not considered nations. This closed the treaty making period, after which the US government adopted a litigation approach to land claims particularly through the Court of Claims. It was between this 1871 Act, the *General Allotment Act of 1887* (known as the *Dawes Act*) and the establishment of the Bureau if Indian Affairs (BIA) to implement and enforce the Congressional legislation, that the modes of dispossession of Indigenous peoples in America were regulated. The 1887 *General Allotment Act* was particularly important. Based on paternalistic notions of acculturation and assimilation (Fleras and Elliott 1992, 144) this Act allocated Indian 'heads of households' that met certain criteria with a 160–acre parcel of land. It thereby undermined communal governance and ownership of land, and then made the balance of land unallotted available to non–Indigenous settlers (Churchill 2002, 47). This has resulted in the situation whereby there are non–Indigenous landholders within Indian reservations today who do not recognize the jurisdiction of tribal government (Scholtz 2006, 165).

The *Indian Reorganization Act 1934* marked another turning point. While it rested on the principle of self–government, after a damning report of 1928 concerning Indian reservations, the basis of self–government was dictated by the state and the reserve system itself, and failed to recognize Indigenous systems of law (Fleras and Elliott 1992, 149). Over 90 tribal governments were established between 1935 and 1945 under this legislation, which reshaped the nature of Indigenous governance and tribal structure. The next stage of the allotment policy was known as 'termination' which 'identified tribes as ready for liberation from federal supervision and control' …and 'called for Congress to disperse tribal assets (read reservation land and claim settlement awards) among tribal members, dissolve the tribal trust status, and send Indians into the mainstream' (Scholtz 2006, 183). This drew a mixed reaction from Indian nations, but was considerably opposed such that by the mid 1960s a significant Indian protest movement emerged. In 1978, the Bureau of Indian Affairs created a system for formally recognizing tribal status. This is set out in the US Code of Federal Regulations (25 CFR 83.7), with seven mandatory criteria that tribes must meet including such aspects as being a 'distinct community' on a 'substantially continuous basis since 1900' (Bureau of Indian Affairs 2003). These criteria are especially difficult to meet given the history as described above of forced dispossession and relocation onto reserve systems, the working of the *Allotment Act* to undermine traditional affiliations with land and long–standing policies of assimilation. While these policies and regulations have also fundamentally served as a means of dispossession and assimilation, they are also the primary means for contemporary Indigenous communities in the US to control their own land and resources (see Hibberd 2006).

Canada

In Canada, Britain had explicitly recognized Indigenous rights through the Royal Proclamation of 1763, which had also recognized continuity of Indigenous land title (Tennant 1990, 12). The proclamation established 'the principle of exclusive Crown acquisition of aboriginal lands' (Fleras and Elliott 1992, 31) thus recognizing that Indigenous rights and tenure existed. Indigenous Canadians see the 1736 Royal Proclamation as proof that the British sovereign 'acknowledged aboriginal rights' and explicitly recognized 'continuity of land title...while continuity of self–government was implicitly sanctioned' (Tennant 1990, 12). Thus, treaties made in accord with the proclamation also recognize those continuing rights. Such treaties are looked upon with great seriousness and care by Indigenous peoples, who see them as 'semi–sacred, binding documents according to which land and resources were transferred to central authorities in exchange for guarantees of protection, control over aboriginal land and resources, and various goods and services' (Fleras and Elliott 1992, 31).

Treaties in Canada are very numerous and varied in their content and intent, and indeed First Nations peoples made treaties with both British and French imperial powers. First Nations Canadians made treaties to secure trade and prove territorial possession against other rival colonising powers, others were peace treaties, and others actually involved land cession in exchange for money or other benefits for Indigenous peoples (McKee 2000, 8). British treaty policy was explicitly set out between 1871 and 1921, which gave rise to the agreements known as the 'numbered treaties' across the Prairie provinces and northestern British Columbia (McKee 2000, 8). Thirteen 'numbered' treaties were signed between 1871 and 1929 encompassing much of the territory west of the Quebec/Ontario border. Most treaty terms involved land and the 'terms stipulated that, in return for vast tracts of land, the government would set aside reserve land for the local aboriginal population on a per capita basis...and grant special privileges' (Fleras and Elliott 1992, 31–32).

Yet, treaties have been the source of considerable contestation in Canadian history. The Canadian state has often been the centre of attention concerning whether it has complied with treaty obligations and the treaty making process has been described as a process that is riddled with deceit (Fleras and Elliott 1992, 32). Policies of assimilation and protectionism became much more prominent in the latter half of the 1800s, as Indigenous resistance waned and as colonists sought to expand territorial conquest. Treaties were still in force yet the focus had become the reservations. The elimination of the 'Indigenous problem' was a keen policy concern but was coupled with emerging liberal concerns about Indigenous welfare and protection. Reserves were widely seen as the solution to both containment and welfare, serving as 'holding pens' (Fleras and Elliott 1992, 41) for cultural assimilation purposes, and clearing the land of Indigenous presence (see also Harris 2002).

In the postwar period, policy focus shifted to the re–integration of Indigenous peoples into 'mainstream' society and away from reserves. This was overtly justified through the burdensome cost reservations policy had become on governments. It was recommended in the late 1940s to abolish 'separate' status of Indigenous Canadians and bring them under the same citizenship rights and requirements as all other Canadians. In 1969, a white paper attempted to do away with the constitutional recognition of Indigenous status and end 'Aboriginal privileges' and thereby accelerate absorption into the mainstream (Fleras and Elliott 1992, 43). This policy agenda sparked outcry particularly from Indigenous peoples. Far from seeking equality, Indigenous peoples wanted to be treated as special, with unique status, and treated with formally as sovereign nations (Fleras and Elliott 1992, 44). The Canadian government retracted its proposals in 1971 and formally moved to a position of negotiation of land claims in 1973. This approach attempted to take land claims out of the court system and establish separate treaty process, though these are undertaken at provincial level (Scholtz 2000; Tennant 1990; McKee 2000).

In 1986, the government established the Comprehensive Land Claims Policy which reaffirmed this principle of negotiation for claims resolution. The aim of the policy is to clarify and thereby provide certainty about Indigenous rights to land. Indigenous peoples have to fulfil certain criteria before the state will negotiate: first, the claimant group must establish it is an 'organized society with exclusive occupancy of a specific territory prior to European contact' (Fleras and Elliott 1992, 34); second that it has continued this occupation and use of land to the present; and third that Indigenous title and rights remain intact and have not been traded through treaty or other legal means.

There are two types of land claim made in Canada, today – specific and comprehensive claims. Specific claims are based on 'perceived violations by federal authorities of their lawful treaty obligations' (Fleras and Elliott 1992, 34). Comprehensive claims are more like modern–day treaty claims and based on traditional occupancy and ongoing Indigenous use of lands and waters. These modern agreements involve:

large land masses as well as complex governmental, social, and economic institutions and guarantees. They also confer on the Aboriginal peoples modern–day equivalents of the benefits contained in the numbered treaties. (McKee 2000, 9)

Alongside and within the treaty process is the complex of governance arrangements and agreement–making models that are prolifterating in Canada, along the lines of 'nation to nation relationships' (Palmer 2006). Many such agreements are being made within the realm of natural resource management and planning, such as the control of industrial resource development, mining and other natural resource development and are substantially challenging the 'separation, allocation and distribution of space' (Borrows 2002, 443) that underpins western natural resource management and planning approaches.

Aoteoroa–New Zealand

The Treaty of Waitangi is the foundational document of Aoteoroa–New Zealand. It was signed in 1840 by Maori chiefs and representatives of the British Crown, under instruction from the Colonial Office in London (Cant 1998, 323). In 1852, British authority was devolved from London to Aoteoroa–New Zealand and what had been a relatively successful implementation of treaty rights up until then started to be disregarded. The goodwill that existed during negotiation of the Treaty 'disappeared in the face of settler greed for land and control' (Fleras and Elliott 1992, 181). What became known as the Maori wars of the 1860s identify the significant Maori resistance that settler greed met with, but many lands were settled and consolidated at Maori expense. Cant (1998) argues that the Treaty was 'lost from *pakeha*[1] memory from the 1850s to the 1930s' (323). Indeed during an 1877 legal challenge, the judge declared the Treaty to be 'a legal nullity with no standing in domestic law' (ibid). A strongly assimilationist policy was introduced between 1865 and 1945, particularly through the wholesale dismissal of Maori language (Fleras and Elliott 1992, 181) and then similarly to Canada, integration became the policy objective in the postwar era.

Maori resurgence, as Indigenous politics elsewhere, was well underway through the 1960s. In 1975, the Labour Government moved to honour promises made in the 1930s and legislation was passed to set up the Treaty of Waitangi Tribunal in 1975, which was given powers to investigate Maori grievances and hear claims against the Crown for actions arising after 1975. Ten years later that was extended to hear grievances dating back to the 1840 signing date (Cant 1998, 323). This was followed by the Tu Tangata policy in 1978, enshrining the development of the Maori people and their resources (Fleras and Elliott 1992, 183). Yet these were only advisory moves. It wasn't until 1984 that there was a reinvigoration of the Treaty. At this point, Aoteoroa–New Zealand's government

---

1 Pakeha refers to non–Maori New Zealanders.

adopted a policy of negotiating land claims with Maori in 1989, prior to this there had not been a functioning and effective claim remedy system (Scholtz 2006, 4). Since then, Maori people have successfully sought their land claim redress through the Tribunal system, and there has been a very significant resurgence of Maori culture and language. Fleras and Elliott (1992) consider this

> nothing short of astonishing. In less than a decade, the Maori have moved from the margins of society into the mainstream – in large part because of activist and organizational pressure for redefining Maori status and relations with the state. (218)

Australia

Australia has no such history of treaties or agreement making with Indigenous peoples. British colonization of Australian territories in 1788 was based on the legal myth of *terra nullius* (empty land), despite Cook being despatched from England with specific instructions to treat with native peoples. The Doctrine of Discovery set out the conditions in international law under which territory could be colonised by European powers. This was in itself a fundamentally racist suite of laws which assumed an inferior status of Indigenous peoples: the language of 'discovery' shows the dominance of the West and the disregard for Indigenous histories, politics and law. Yet that Doctrine set out that territory could only be colonised in certain kinds of ways, and one of these was if colonisers came upon land that was in fact empty of people.

The fundamentally racist and violent application of *terra nullius*, wrongly and illegally, in Australia served as the basis of Australian law for 200 years (for an excellent analysis see Reynolds 1992). Colonists in Australia clearly saw that the land was occupied by Indigenous peoples, but considered these people to be so 'low' on a racialized hierarchy of 'civilization' that they failed to countenance or recognize the existence of Indigenous sovereignty, territory, jurisdiction and law. This justified colonial activities, practices and laws that forcefully, regularly violently, removed Indigenous peoples from lands. Like in Canada, reserves and missions became central aspects of colonial land policy, and a strong assimilation ethic was at work.

It was not until the High Court's famous decision in the Mabo case in 1992 that Indigenous laws (by virtue of the continued operation of Indigenous property rights) survived British colonization. The court agreed that

> the common law recognizes a form of native title which, in cases where it has not been extinguished, reflects the entitlement of the Indigenous inhabitants in accordance with their laws or customs to their traditional lands. (French 1994, 74)

Such an approach accords with the Indigenous view of rights as pre–existing colonization and being consequently recognized by settler states, rather than a set of new rights invented by the modern state and bestowed upon Indigenous peoples. In legal terms, native title was found by the High Court to be a continuing burden on the Crown's radical title of Australian territory by recognizing that Indigenous property rights and law survived British colonization. In this way, the recognition of native title confers a unique status upon native title registered claimants and landowners. It begins to recognize that Indigenous people 'are born with an inchoate, inherited and transmissible right in a "country"' (Langton 1997, 1).

Ultimately, then, what the Mabo decision did was to recognize Indigenous people as landowners with unique property tenure rights, not only as citizens of the Australian nation–state, and thereby require Australian governments to deal with Indigenous rights in unique ways. (For more detail on native title and the Mabo decision see Pearson 1993; Butt and Eagleson 1996; Stephenson and Ratnapala 1993.)

The common law of native title was developed into Australian statute through the passing of the *Native Title Act 1993 (Cth)*, and each State and Territory in Australia have since passed legislation to be consistent with this national statute. The 1993 Act protects future extinguishment of native title and sets up procedures, primarily through the National Native Title Tribunal, to determine applications for the recognition of native title. However, many crucial protections and rights enshrined within the 1993 Act were subsequently whittled away by the conservative Howard Government when it was elected in 1996, in a series of amendments.

The actual process of recognizing specific cases of native title (and its content) has proved a difficult process, unsurprisingly fraught with (post)colonial dilemmas. Both the tribunal and the courts have tended to take a particularly limited 'traditionality–based' approach to assessing the existence, form and content of native title in particular applications. In this view, native title claimants must assert that their native title continues to exist by proving an unbroken and ongoing physical connection to their country, similar to the Comprehensive Land Claims policy in Canada.

The decision by Olney J in the Yorta Yorta native title claim in southeastern Australia, and the upholding of that decision on appeal to the High Court (*Members of the Yorta Yorta Aboriginal Community v Victoria [2002] HCA 58 (12 December 2002)*) is a particular testament to the devastation that can be revisited upon Indigenous people by Western conceptualizations of authentic Indigenous cultural practices, and the linking of those practices to territorial rights (see Atkinson 2002; Weiner 2002; Strelein 2003). The Yorta Yorta claim was for recognition of their native title over lands and waters in the Murray Valley district in the two Australian states of Victoria and New South Wales. The claim was overturned and the Yorta Yorta denied recognition because of the application of a narrow conceptualization of tradition and culture. Strelein, in her examination of the findings, determined that:

contemporary practices that the Yorta Yorta saw as cultural traditions, such as the protection of sites of cultural significance and involvement in the management of land and waters in their traditional areas, were rejected because they were not of a kind that were exercised by, or of significance to, the pre–contact society. (Strelein 2003, 2)

Requiring Indigenous people to prove their continuing cultural practices and connection to country is fundamentally an issue of power, because the burden of proof lies with the claimants, who come to the table with no recognized rights. Power relations inhere in all native title mediation and litigation experiences, indeed, in the very structures and processes of the native title regime as it is structured in Australian law (see Dodson 1996; Choo and O'Connell 1999; Atkinson 2002; Muir 1998).

Even in areas where native title claims have been successful, some claimant groups have found it to be a profoundly disappointing experience. The Nharnuwangga, Wajarri and Ngarla people are three language groups, whose country is situated in the Upper Gascoyne region of Western Australia, who came together to jointly assert native title over that country. In August 2000, their native title rights were recognized, and as with most successful native title claims that emerge now in Australia, the groups enjoyed significant media attention about their 'historic victory' (Riley 2002). One traditional owner, however, speaks of her people's 'win' as one of 'pain, disappointment and sorrow' because of the consequences of that recognition in administrative, legal and bureaucratic terms. Riley reflects that her people now have 'drastically fewer rights', an 'unbearable burden of administration', and a range of 'complex and conflicting obligations' imposed by non–Indigenous laws (ibid). However, despite these wider disappointments and difficulties, native title remains one of the most significant ways by which Indigenous people in Australia can gain a seat at the decision–making table on issues that affect their country.

The Difference Indigeneity and Dispossession Makes

The practice of identity politics for Indigenous peoples, then, is both necessary and fraught. Indigenous claims to unique status as original inhabitants who are the custodians of particular cultural, economic and religious traditions provide a necessary potency required for success, constituting a form of 'strategic essentialism' (Spivak 1994). Yet, the difference and traditionality invoked in such claims are also tools of manipulation in working against Indigenous claims.

Settler societies are actually deeply 'unsettled'. Indigenous people continue to assert their rights, and point to the illegality and injustice of the founding moments of settler colonies, and in doing so are daily requiring the renegotiation of the politics of recognition and difference which positions them in a relationship with western states and modes of government. I have been discussing so far in this chapter some of the ways we might conceptualize the location and expression of Indigenous claims and the ways that expression has taken place in four states. Those claims are clearly a challenge to assumptions of universal human experience and liberal rights. The irruptions caused by those claims have led governments, courts, policy-makers and theorists to reconceptualize citizenship, participation and democracy amongst culturally diverse and even incommensurable polities (see Tully 2004). When we come to look more closely at where the specific state activity of spatial ordering and management comes into this debate, we need to look at the concrete territorial manifestations of these issues. One of the significant bases of relations between Indigenous and non-Indigenous peoples and states is both the fact and discursive operation of territorial dispossession. Dispossession is a fact that state-based planning is not only confronted by, but complicit with.

Dispossession is also woven into the politics of difference that is operating when Indigenous peoples make particular kinds of territorial claims on settler states. Dispossession and difference, and the interwoven-ness of their characteristics and manifestations, are of critical importance to reconceptualizing planning in settler contexts. Difference, of varying categories and types, is a fundamental concern of any social science research endeavour in the twenty-first century. Our contemporary society is marked by struggles that concern the recognition of difference amongst, between and within social groups. Decades of both empirical and theoretical endeavour have entirely recast both philosophical and popular conceptualizations of difference and what it means for our relations as human beings. Difference, then, underpins our social relations in every facet of those relations, spaces and times. In colonial encounters, and therefore in (post)colonial contexts, that difference is particularly manifest.

To explore the salience of the difference of Indigeneity for planning in settler states, we need to explore three particular facets of difference. First, is the existence of difference as what I will call a 'social fact' in the world. Difference exists in real, material terms and thus is a fact. Yet it is a construct of our social relations, it is constituted in our social relations (rather than prior to them as a 'natural law'). Second, is the discursive construction of difference as a tool of domination and oppression – the fifth face of oppression that Young (1990) identifies as 'cultural imperialism'. Third, is the discursive mobilization of difference as a politics of liberation (see Young 1990, Tully 2004). The discussion that follows, then, weaves together an understanding of these three particular facets of the politics of difference that underpin Indigenous struggles over and for recognition, and how these relate to the critical territorial issue of dispossession.

Indigenous Difference and the Politics of Identity

Identifying Indigeneity is automatically a relational act within a politics of difference. To be Indigenous is to be marked in a relational sense with something else, it is to be an Other to the norm 'non-Indigenous'. I have already written explicitly (see Chapter 1) about the various literatures that inform our understanding of the particular operations of power, domination and racism that have come to shape those identity positions – and then the attempts to reclaim those for emancipatory ends. Yet it is worth repeating here, to again engage with these difficult (post)colonial dilemmas of working *in* 'difference' as a socially constructed but nevertheless material reality.

Our histories and conditions of existence in (post)colonial settler states is what gives rise to our ability to speak with coherence of such groupings as 'Indigenous polity' or 'settler states', as if they were first order categories. To leave them with the status of first order categories is an act of essentializing those subject positions, and not making them available, as theorists such as Spivak (1998) and Mouffe (1999) suggest, for critical and deconstructive analysis. In every way, this book is bound up in (and perhaps reproduces) these tensions and conundrums. I am exploring, in this book, the relational nature of Indigenous difference with western state–based planning, and by definition require an assumption that we can 'know' these two subject positions, even if we acknowledge them as highly fragmented. A potentially essentializing, reifing and therefore destructive binary of difference underpins the argument and narrative of this book. It is an issue about which I am persistently vexed. Yet, difference exists and is materially relevant to our social practices and relations, even as it is constituted within those very social and historical relations: it is a 'social fact', in that sense. To suggest, for instance, that difference doesn't exist (or shouldn't) between Indigenous and non–Indigenous groups would be not only nonsensical but certainly offensive to Indigenous peoples.

The problem of difference is not difference itself. Our concern should not be with why difference exists and what our political position on difference might be. Such questions lead to some blind alleys both conceptually and in terms of realizing more socially just outcomes, as Young (2000, 83–87) points out in her own critique of the 'critics of difference'. Difference is problematic when it is reified in ways that produce domination and oppression, and the peculiar forms of colonial domination and oppression in particular. My concern, following authors such as Young (1990 and 2000), Tully (1995), Sandercock (2003) and Spivak (1998), is to turn our political, analytical and theoretical attention to elucidating and analysing that reification of difference in colonial social relations.

The construction of difference, of an Other to Europe, is a central feature of the processes of colonialism. That construction is, coupled with the physical violence of colonial encounters, the most pervasive operation of colonial power and domination. Said's (1978) analysis of how Europe established, categorized and produced its Others illuminates the power of the discursive form when linked to the production of knowledge about Othered peoples. Indigenous peoples in northern America, Aoteoroa–New Zealand and Australia came to be constructed as 'Indigenous' (or native, Aboriginal, Indian) *through* colonial encounter. The relational nature of that construction as I outlined earlier (Indigenous is not non–Indigenous) is an ever–present limitation on Indigenous freedom (Dodson 1994b) because it cannot escape its constitution within the language of colonialism.

In colonialist discourse, the difference between European/Indigenous is made explicitly and racially hierarchical. The binary is constructed around, becomes a shorthand for, good and evil, culture and nature, civilized and primitive. These meanings are then normalized, becoming the (natural) compartmentalization of the colonial world along racial lines based on white superiority and black inferiority, the violent hierarchy of imperial power (Fanon 1963 and 1967; Said 1978; JanMohamed 1985).

That colonial hierarchy, like other hierarchies of social order, is at least in part produced through scientific discourses of, and knowledge production about, the body. And in particular, different 'kinds' of bodies. The normalizing gaze that Foucault expounded in *Discipline and Punish* (1977), and indeed his identification of the 'sciences of man' as a particular epistemological formation and expression of power (Foucault 1970), is analytically helpful in working out precisely how the colonial hierarchy is produced and functions. In extending (and critiquing) Foucault's analysis Stoler (1995) shows how the colonial was a reference point of difference, and also desire. The 'savage' was a counterpoint of the West in a way that shaped the very discourses of sexuality that Foucault studied (Stoler 1995, 7). Put differently, Stoler wants (post)colonial critical analyses to demote its attention to the self–referential construction of colonial bourgeois identity construction and the concomitant relational production of Others, but instead to see how colonial bourgeois identity was itself *relational*. In this sense, Young's (1990) reading of the scientific scaling of bodies is helpful:

> In the nineteenth century in Europe and the United States the normalizing gaze of science endowed the aesthetic scaling of bodies with the authoritativeness of objective truth. All bodies can be located on a single scale whose apex is the strong and beautiful youth and whose nadir is the degenerate. The scale measured at least three crucial attributes: physical health, moral soundness, and mental balance. The degenerate is physically weak, frailo, diseased. Or the degenerate is mentally imbalanced: raving, irrational or childlike in mental simplicity. But most important, moral impropriety is a sign of degeneracy, and a cause of physical or mental disease. (Young 1990, 128)

Such a scaling of bodies allows the construction of powerful 'formal theories of race, sex, age and national superiority' (Young 1990, 125). And there is a concomitant spatialization, or spatial practice, of that scaling of bodies, as I will investigate in Chapter 3.

A strange ambivalence works within and through this violent hierarchy of imperial power. A desire to position the non–Indigenous, modern self in the landscape is confounded by an identity crisis, a sense of the 'unhomely' (Gelder and Jacobs 1998; Kristeva 1991). To be not quite at home (for non–Indigenous people) is to have a condition marked by both familiarity and strangeness, comfort and unease, desire and fear. It is that which we desire (to be at home, to be 'indigenous'), but on desiring it and making it emerge, are fearful of it (Kristeva

1991, 182–5; see also Young 1990). These are pervasive themes in nation–building efforts in the US, Canada, Aoteoroa–New Zealand and Australia. Consequently, relations with Indigenous people are at once strange and familiar, settling and yet unsettling, desirous but engendering of fear (Torgovnick 1997; Goldie 1989). An ambivalence operates toward the 'Indigenous question' in settler states, where the dominant culture is equally and simultaneously enthralled and revulsed by Indigenous people (Gelder and Jacobs 1998). That ambivalence is exposed in the simultaneous 'cherishing' and 'denigration' of Indigenous people and culture (Thomas 1994): the cherishing of a 'more natural, more spiritual' (Indigenous) mode of being is at the same time a denigration, because of its patronizing desire to nurture something for its exotic, fading value. It is also a stereotype, an 'anxious repetition' of what is already 'known' about the other (Bhabha 1994, 66). Stereotype, for Bhabha is simultaneously a play for fantasy and defence, it turns on the notion of fetishism, the desire for originality that is then threatened by the difference that erupts.

A popular stereotype (there are many) that circulate in the settler states of Australia, Aoteoroa–New Zealand, Canada and the United States is that of primitivism. Torgovnick argues that Western conceptualizations of Indigeneity are structured by a 'passion for primitivism': the 'utopian desire to go back and recover irreducible features of the psyche, body, land, and community – to reinhabit core experiences' (Torgovnick 1997, 5). This is an important (post)colonial trope here, because it draws on certain renderings of the discourses of identity, difference and dispossession in ways that shore up difference on the side of the dominant culture. Primitivism renders Indigenous people the absolute Other of the modern, rational world. It constructs Indigenous people as (having) lived an ahistorical existence, without capacity for change and without capacity to survive modernity in any authentic way. Indigenous peoples are therefore profoundly threatened by modernity. According to this logic, there is no room for hybridity, change, flux, appropriation (Thomas 1994). The discursive construction of difference, and the scaling of bodies (Young 1990) in a hierarchy of colonial power is a primary means of colonial domination and oppression.

Yet the discursive construction of difference is also the fundamental premise around which an Indigenous politics of difference has been able to interrupt the certainty of settler states in recent years. This is the third facet of difference I described earlier – difference as a tool for liberation. Indigenous claim to territory and self–determination rest on the assertion of an entirely different status within, and indeed relationship with, the nation–state than all other peoples. Assertions of Indigeneity (as opposed to membership of an 'ethnic group'),

> permits the formulation of arguments based on the legal consequences of prior occupancy of territory. This is not so much an appeal to the laws of aboriginal peoples in opposition to those of liberal democracies, as an appeal based upon major inconsistencies in the historical treatment accorded by imperial, colonial

> and national legal systems to indigenous peoples, especially with respect to their
> lands and the taking of these for settlement. (Dyck 1985, 13)

Indeed, as one Indigenous observer wryly observed 'we are not ethnic groups. Ethnic groups run restaurants serving "exotic" foods. We are *nations*' (Brooklyn Rivera quoted in Churchill 2002, 19). Not only do Indigenous people perceive their claims in different ways from the modern state as I explored earlier in this chapter, but the very moral authority of those claims are predicated on difference. Such difference is constituted in the Indigenous status of 'original inhabitants' of territory, but also more fundamentally in terms of the ontological and epistemological philosophies underpinning culture, law, society and economy.

There is an important literature on the concept of sovereign and continuing Indigenous 'domains' or polities distinct from the settler nation–state. Such domains constitute, 'the very distinct networks of interaction, with spatial correlates, which divide Aborigines and non–Aborigines' (Keen 1988, 10). Identifying this domain constitutes Indigenous peoples as distinct peoples. As Dodson describes in relation to Australia, Indigenous people are:

> united by common territories, cultures, traditions, histories, languages,
> institutions and beliefs. We share a sense of kinship and identity, a consciousness
> as distinct peoples and a political will to exist as distinct peoples. (1994a, 69)

Indigenous people continually point out the (co)existence of 'two systems of law' operating within settler states: Indigenous laws and non–Indigenous laws (Tipa and Nelson 2008; Langton 1997). The very basis of Indigenous struggles for recognition and restitution of lands is the assertion of specific and different socioeconomic structures, cultural practices, and forms of knowledge production that pre–exist colonial settlement. Appreciating the particular claims of this facet of difference for Indigenous peoples requires a more thorough–going discussion of dispossession. This is because dispossession is one of the primary material realities against which Indigenous people orient their struggles.

Dispossession

Dispossession: the very word suggests an ultimate colonial power erasing all traces of Indigenous presence and knowledge in place. Indigenous people have indeed been dispossessed, in some cases profoundly so. Yet as the earlier part of this chapter has shown, dispossession is never complete. Not only is colonial space continually unsettled (repossessed) by Indigenous claims, but also the work of colonial dispossession persists. The sociopolitical reality of settler states, then, is the continuing presence of dispossession as a manifestation of injustice, the site of struggle, the foundation of Indigenous political strategy, and a continuing colonial project.

The discourses of dispossession and primitivism activates an unjust burden of proof–of–authenticity for Indigenous people and very easily renders those who are 'just not Indigenous enough' out of any of the mechanisms currently available to amend conditions of gross socioeconomic disadvantage. The romanticisation of the 'closeness' of Indigenous people to land and nature, and a continued focus on 'traditions' as some kind of immutable, fixed body of culture is a radical Othering (Langton 1996) and a strategic limitation on Indigenous claims. To be modern, in (post)colonial states, and to be Indigenous is a difficult role to play. 'Real' Indigenous people should exhibit, in the popular non–Indigenous imagination, those essential characteristics determined by traditional anthropological studies of 'real' Aborigines or 'real' Indians. It means not displaying the trappings of modernity. Where cultural and social practices, including languages, are seen to have been radically disrupted, such thinking generates an enormous question mark in the popular imagination about the authenticity of Indigenous claims to self–determination, sovereignty, and land. The cases of the Yorta Yorta people in southeastern Australia outlined earlier in this chapter, exemplifies this problem. To fight for land rights through the institutionalized (white) court system is not so much a 'difficult paradox' for Indigenous people navigating between the imagined 'poles' of tradition and modernity, but instead a (re)negotiation of the power relations inherent in everyday life that either restrict or allow agency in particular places.

To be 'dispossessed' places Indigenous people strangely. It has a material reality of injustice in the everyday lives of Indigenous people, and yet because it establishes the legitimacy and urgency of Indigenous claims *upon* and through the nation–state (as the dispossessor) for land reparations, dispossession is central to Indigenous political strategy. At the same time it can confound the identity politics simultaneously crucial to the project of recovering rights, as I detailed earlier in the case of the Yorta Yorta people. Dispossession activates loss, it flirts with the idea that Indigenous people have 'lost' culture. Loss is a discursive strategy employed in different ways, at different moments, and with different effects, in (post)colonial relations in settler states. One powerful discursive effect of 'loss' is the diagnosis of fatal impact, where non–Indigenous people can be left nostalgic and regretful for the destruction that their colonial forebears wrought on precolonial societies, without having to attend to the (post)colonial difficulties which they now face (Thomas 1994).

This is particularly important for the role of planning in (post)colonial contexts, as the rest of the book investigates. Planning, if we see it as the Western practices of spatial ordering, has played a starring role in dispossessory strategies and activities, a history that I will explore in depth in Chapter 3. It is impossible, then, for planning to claim to be the forum in which, suddenly, Indigenous rights can easily be translated into the existing institutions of land use decision–making. A strategic politics of dispossession for Indigenous people, both within planning and in wider arenas, concerns the survival of Indigenous *possession*: of connection, knowledge and relations with land.

The 'fatal impact' assessment, or the assumed finality of dispossession amongst non–Indigenous conceptualizations of the 'place' of Indigenous people in settler states, returns us to the notion of difference. A great deal of anthropological work has attempted to show the relationship between Indigenous people and place, and of course anthropology itself is another site of Indigenous struggle to maintain control over the production of knowledge, and in particular the production of what comes to be seen as 'Indigenous' as a direct result of that knowledge production. These studies suggest that Indigenous relations to place cannot be described outside social relations, stories, language events and activities that come to constitute that place (see for example Myers 1989; Povinelli 1993; Merlan 1998). Questions of what rightfully constitutes an 'Indigenous world view' or 'appropriate Indigenous aspirations' also powerfully shape the politics of place. Such a connection fails to comprehend the reality of everyday life for Indigenous people today, which is a constant negotiation absorbed into changing cultural practices and social relations (see for example Povinelli 1993; Swain 1993; Merlan 1998).

While I recognize the importance of that debate and contest over the production of anthropological knowledge, that debate is not where my attention is focused. I want to look more closely at a different question, one that is not about whether and how Indigenous people and place are connected, but how that connection might become a powerful notion circulating in discourses about Indigeneity and rights, particularly in relation to land. My questions then are not about the 'truth' or otherwise of Indigenous relations to place, but how different kinds of truth production about that question operate, particularly in the field of planning. In other words, it is in the discursive mobilization of difference, Indigeneity and dispossession, especially within non–Indigenous polities, that is the focus in order to see what kinds of effects they have.

My argument in this book, to reiterate, is that western settler states, and their planning systems especially, have a particular way of seeing space, and that this is quite distinct from Indigenous ways of seeing space. Moreover, this produces manifestly unjust outcomes, oppression and marginalization. Once again, while the argument rests on the establishment of difference, the 'problem' of difference is not in difference itself. It is in acknowledging that difference is materially relevant to our social practices and relations, because it constitutes and reconstitutes colonial power relations and injustices. These must occupy our critical attention.

(Post)colonial Dilemmas and the Challenge for Planning

The predicament of (post)coloniality in settler states is to simultaneously occupy positions that are both *within* the enduring structures of colonialism and 'located beyond or "after" them' (Gelder and Jacobs 1998, 24). My usage of parentheses in the term (post)colonial seeks to highlight this predicament. There are some peculiar features of this predicament for contemporary planning in settler states. Planning systems are premised on a decision–making system that values scientific knowledge, and seeks to utilize 'knowledge' as an instrumental feature of that decision–making: the evidence–based policy approach. Planning systems assume a relationship between humans and land that is constructed entirely around property relations (ownership and exchange). Planning systems institutionalize processes that seek to incorporate stakeholder interests in order to make decisions for a generalized 'public good'. When Indigenous people contest western assumptions (and intentions) of land use and management, they unsettle these features of planning in settler states.

The presumption of scientific knowledge and human relations with place in planning is unsettled when Indigenous people present different ontological and epistemological understandings of place. Often, that knowledge is orally constituted, refers to inter–generational sources, and is evidenced not in relation to empirical inquiry but in reference to custodial responsibilities, narrative, or spiritual awareness. When, for example, Indigenous sacred sites 'appear', usually because they are threatened by modern uses, differently constructed Indigenous knowledges about place (their sacred construction in a secular, modern space) threaten that modernity (Gelder and Jacobs 1998).

The appearance of the Waugul spirit at a site (known as the Swan Brewery site) marked for redevelopment in the Western Australian city of Perth challenged planning's way of knowing that same site. A plot of property, with a certain proximity to a river and Perth's city centre, with a certain land value (making it especially ripe for redevelopment) all of a sudden became something unfamiliar – the resting place of a spirit, knowledge about which was conveyed through inter–generational narrative (see Jacobs 1996). Plans for a new waste water treatment plant to discharge into the Kaituna River in Aoteoroa–New Zealand, a response to concerns about sewage pollution of Lake Rotorua, were unsettled when Ngati Pikiao women took action against the plan through the Treaty of Waitangi Tribunal. They described the importance of the River to their economic and cultural practices of weaving:

> The only area to take women for fieldwork is the area alongside the Kaituna River...kiekie [a forest plant used for weaving] is there...it needs a natural environment...to get the whiteness it has to be soaked in clear running water... the only stream we have is the Kaituna... (evidence from Schuster provided to the Waitangi Tribunal, quoted in Cant 1998, 329)

Such disruptions of planning's certainty of knowledge and value in place give rise to the peculiar dilemma increasingly present for planners in (post)colonial settler states: how to 'treat' (and I mean in the sense of 'treat with') Indigenous people as different kinds of 'stakeholders'. The difference that Indigeneity expresses, as demonstrated in these vignettes, raises the question of the location of those interests in modern liberal democracies. As expressions of sovereignty in place, they challenge at least the ability of planning processes to deal with Indigenous interests as one of many interest groups. At most, they challenge the very authority of modern planning systems to make those decisions.

One response to this particular dilemma is for planning systems to establish additional forums in which Indigenous interests can be addressed, to the exclusion of other interests. A good example of this is an informal meeting space for native title claimants set up in the western district of Victoria, Australia to more directly address Indigenous native title interests in planning decisions (I have written about this elsewhere – for a fuller account, see Porter 2006a). Here, a local planning manager responded to a deeply felt division within the local Indigenous community, and between those diverse communities and the Victorian government department then responsible for land management in the region. She established a closed forum, only for native title claimants (and later to include cultural heritage officers) to work closely with planners and land managers so as to address native title interests at an early stage.

Many other kinds of responses are being developed across settler states in response to the challenge that Indigenous rights claims mount to modern planning systems. Most are bureaucratic, and sometime legal, responses to those challenges. All seek to 'include' Indigenous people in various ways, such as through representation on boards or decision–making committees, through increased opportunity for consultation or participation, or through employment schemes. In Chapters 4, 5 and 6, I turn to some particular examples of these responses and the enduring (post)colonial politics of identity, meaning and power that they expose. In the next chapter, I take a historical look at where those politics might have come from.

Conclusion

To explore how planning might treat with Indigenous peoples in more just ways, it is fundamental to develop a critical conceptualization of just what kind of challenge Indigenous claims make to planning. I have tried to show in this chapter that the presumptions of modern liberal democracies are unsettled when Indigenous people present different ontological and epistemological understandings of place, and differently oriented spatial practices. As expressions of a different source of sovereignty in place, they challenge at least the ability of planning processes to deal with Indigenous interests as one of many other interest groups. At most, they challenge the very authority and power of modern planning systems. How, then, do we understand these challenges?

In this chapter, I have tried to establish some of the elements of what I see as a necessary critical conceptualization: the politics of identity and difference, the effects of a discourse of dispossession (in Chapter 3 I will look closely at how colonialism does its dispossessing work), and the insidious colonial stereotype of primitivism. This beginning of a framework will help us analyse, through the rest of the book, the mobilizations of truth and knowledge in the politics of place. It is to the constitution of the spatial cultures that are part of the activation of truth and knowledge, that I turn in the next chapter.

Chapter 3
A Colonial Genealogy of Planning

...bringing anthropology home from the tropics.

(Latour 1991, 97)

The 'origins' of modern planning in British settler states are not to be found in Britain alone. Colonies were the places where European ideas traveled to and then sought to dominate Indigenous ideas and systems. Yet as 'laboratories of modernity' (Stoler 1995, 15), colonies were also the places where those ideas either found their best expression, or were re–shaped, newly moulded, dissolved away, or challenged into obscurity. Colonies, then, are a particular kind of 'produced' space in Lefebvre's terms. It is the production of a new experiment with space, the attempted inscription of particular sensibilities (in this case European ones) in a space that is 'new' to those sensibilities. These sensibilities might be seen, from the view of colonizers, as having their purest potential in colonial projects, finding expression in the colonial encounter in a way they could not at 'home'. Colonisers encountered space in the 'New World' in a way resonant with their encounters with the peoples of that space: as radically Othered, not Europe(an).

How did colonial space come to be produced? What rationalities, technologies, desires and modes were present and shaping forces in the production of colonial space? These are the framing questions of this chapter, where I make some initial exploratory remarks about how space in colonies came to be produced, and how this productive work might in fact be some of the early stirrings of modern planning. Moreover, the chapter will set out the historical colonial roots of those rationalities, technologies, desires, and modes that continue to structure the spatial ontology and epistemology of modern planning in settler states.

I am going to call these elements and activities, this spatial ontology and epistemology, 'spatial cultures', and use this notion as an organizing framework for the historical analysis that follows. 'Spatial cultures' intends to capture the range of ways of thinking about, and living, space (including their contradictions and fragmentations). Through this term, I want to explore the many different modes of this thinking and living – not in a gesture toward a comprehensive theory of spatial cultures, but because this range of modes appears to be meaningful, or so the evidence suggests, in the making of colonial space. Huxley's work (2006 and 2007) has been instructive in developing this vocabulary, and I have used her development of governmentality theory in planning that she names 'spatial rationalities' as a point of departure. Her project is concerned with the modes of thinking (the rationalities) of government that 'have made spaces and environments amenable to calculative thought by mobilizing certain "truths" of causal relations in and between spaces, environments, bodies and comportments' (2006, 772).

Those rationalities are also my focus, but only as one part of a broader suite of 'calculative thoughts' and actions. The other instructive source for my vocabulary and framework is Stoler's work (1995 and 2004), particularly her historical reading of sensibility and disposition in the production and maintenance of colonial social moralities. She argues that much of the work of colonial government was not driven by rationality at all, but the opposite: sentiment, affect and sensibility. In so arguing, she criticizes a 'conceit of reason' (2004, 4) in the analytical tendencies of scholarship, that tends to produce a myopia especially in critical postcolonial studies. If the aim of government in colonies was a 'preoccupation with the making of virtuous selves' (2004, 9), then this directed government attention to feelings and passions, not (or at least not only) to reason and rationality. Stoler argues, then, for a different kind of genealogical tracing of colonial power – not one tracing reason (or at least not on its own) and certainly not one that sets out with the supremacy of reason as its starting point. Instead, she suggests historical analyses of colonialism must see the 'culture of sensibility' of colonial government and relations, and in doing so 'register that sustained oscillation between reason and sentiment rather than the final dominance of the one and their definitive severance' (2004, 11).

The spatial cultures that I aim to explicate here, then, schematize *both* spatial rationalities and sensibilities. In that sense, spatial cultures includes the following: spatial ontology, or the view of the existence of space and the human–environment relationship; spatial desires and sensibilities, or the comportments of people in relation to space; rationalities of space, or the mobilization of knowledge toward spatial order and regulation; and technologies of space, or the modes of activity which operated within and upon space.

I deploy this term 'spatial cultures' (rather than rationalities or ontologies or governmentalities) for a specific reason. This book aims to show how the particular spatial activity of government that we know as planning is a culturally specific and bounded activity. It arises as an activity and set of practices from a locatable and cultural world–view: from a spatial ontology and epistemology. My language, then, is for both argumentative and political purposes: 'spatial cultures' helps remind us that the subject of our analysis is not a view from nowhere.

In the next section I discuss the theoretical premises that are important to my organizing framework of 'spatial cultures'. This is followed by a discussion of an important influence on the implementation of colonial practices, as well as modern planning: the labour theory of property developed by John Locke. Using this rather diverse set of philosophical ideas, the chapter then sets out to find how these spatial cultures were made manifest in the actuality of colonial sites in British settler states. In particular, I will look at how space was seen to exist and how it could be known, as well as what I will call (following Young 1990) the 'scaling of bodies' in space to justify and serve colonial appropriation of territory. In the final section, I will explore in more detail the particular technologies of power that made colonial spatial cultures materially manifest. These technologies will be recognizable as the forms of spatial ordering we now call the practice of planning.

Theoretical Premises

To take a position that space is socially produced is not to deny that something called space, as a physical element, exists. Physical space, as it is conceived in the terms that geometry, cartography and physics structure for us, is 'there' in the sense that matter is spatial – it exists some*where*. Equally, the physical presence of land, its matter, is not under dispute. Yet, Lefebvre's theory of the production of space offers a way of undoing the hegemony that the absoluteness of physical space tends to attain in the Cartesian view. The actuality of space remains at the centre of my analysis – because the dispossession of land and incarceration of Indigenous peoples is a material reality – and the framework Lefebvre provides organizes how we might see the active 'productive' work required to make this dispossession an ongoing reality. To restate Lefebvre's (1991) triad of the social production of (social) space:

1. Spatial practice, or 'perceived' space,
2. Representations of space, or 'conceived' space,
3. Representational space, or 'lived' space.

As stated in Chapter 1, the work of colonialism could be analysed as the violent imposition of a dominant European conceived space upon the lived spaces of Indigenous peoples. Given my deconstructive predilection, I read Lefebvre's framework as intrinsically able to accommodate an analysis of Indigenous societies and the spaces they produce, though of course that is not at all what this book is aiming to achieve. I say this to point out that conceived space is not only available to Europe, and of course Europe has its own lived spaces: I do not wish to tie Indigenous–coloniser relations into an essentialized hierarchy. But my aim here is to look at the production of colonial space, and how planning is part of that story. For that reason, my focus is on the perceived and conceived spaces of British colonial thinking and action, as this became, through colonial invasion, the dominant space of colonial society. In this chapter, I will be attempting to apply the notions of perceived and conceived spaces to colonial sites: to see how spatial cultures crystallized the relationship between colonial society, its spaces and Indigenous societies, and actualized colonial (dis)possession.

That framework also, and importantly, enables this work without reducing every account of space to relativism: as only the some*where* of some*one's* perspective. Neither does it reduce all analytical effort to discourse. A significant emphasis in the triad is on spatial practices – the physical spaces that actually exist. I want to construct here an anti–essentialist reading of space, one that wants to account for the relations and practices that bring space into being. Not in the physical sense of 'into being', as an original moment of birth or discovery, but in the social sense. Space becomes, because it becomes some*thing* in social terms. It attains names, uses, meanings, structure, activity and value. Space becomes drawn into, literally and figuratively, social relations.

As these are inherently cultural elements, socially produced, it is self–evident to conclude that 'once one begins to describe land, to talk about space, one is involved in a cultural and linguistic activity that cannot refer outside itself to an unmediated reality' (Ryan 1996, 4). Yet I see this as more than a description, a bringing space into being through talk. As this chapter will explore, space can be actively produced and re–produced through a variety of technologies and practices that are not only unable to refer to an unmediated reality, as Ryan observes: they actively produce their own mediated realities. None of which, of course, is innocent. Certainly not in the imperial context. Enlightenment theories of absolute space, the Cartesian spaces that have come to be naturalized as the reality of actual space, were fundamentally important to imperial processes. Empire's space, as Ryan observes, is 'universal, Euclidean and Cartesian' (1996, 4) and it is so because producing notions of space in this way 'allows imperialism to hierarchise the use of space to its own advantage' (ibid, 4).

It is that colonial process of producing space for a certain ends, to favour certain people (their cultural lifeways and economic systems) that is my focus here. In this chapter, I want to explore this process in historical terms, looking back in time to a series of periods in colonial histories and places, and asking how this production of space occurred. In doing so, I will look not only at the colonial discourses operating, but also at the range of other powers and strategies that were wielded and shaped in actual colonial settings, as Harris (2004) suggests critical histories of colonial sites must. Moreover, for the purpose of this book is to excavate the colonial history and culture of *planning*, this chapter looks carefully at the location of planning within the relations and practices that produced colonial spaces.

To speak of spatial *cultures* requires an investigation of the various forms of cultural materiality that go to make up the relations and practices by which colonial space was produced. Ontologically speaking, I see culture as 'not only *part* of social life but also of its production and reproduction' (Helms 2008, 55, original italics). In other words, culture is an element of life, as well as a constituent process within the formation and re–formation of that life. As my aim is a contextualized and historicized exploration of colonial moments, the approach I adopt is a 'study of relationships between elements in a whole way of life' (Williams 1965, 47). Culture, then, is not to be 'found' in a reading of a series of symbols, though the semiotic is clearly one of the important elements in that whole way of life that Williams suggests should be an empirical focus. What I will attempt to do in this chapter is to explore how different elements of the colonial spatial 'way of life' – spatial cultures – clashed, coalesced, dissolved, and fragmented: but ultimately produced the space of colonies. Let me again clarify my meaning here. By colonial spatial cultures, I do not intend to describe the daily habits, desires and practices of colonists. I am not setting out to document 'what it was like' to be a colonist, explorer, squatter, or colonial Governor. Instead, spatial cultures are the activities, readings, desires, philosophies, technologies and regulatory methods that the historical record shows actively and materially constructed colonies.

In undertaking this daunting task, I have turned to a range of source materials. Primarily, those sources are textual: the journals and letters of those actively involved in space production in colonies, including explorers, colonial governors, colonists and squatters, and the politicians and administrators of the Colonial Office in London; and the texts associated with legislative and regulatory regimes concerning colonial lands. I have also tried to incorporate an analysis of actual social practices in colonies alongside this reading of texts. For example, the chapter discusses the use of a variety of survey and measurement techniques, and mapping principles. It also includes an analysis of the various means and technologies of space production by which Indigenous people were encountered and dispossessed.

These social practices are themselves, of course, primarily accessible through text – the written accounts of who did what, how and where. In that sense, an account such that I am trying to give here, can never alleviate itself of its boundedness within text, and that accessibility to those practices is many times removed. The representational production of colonial subjects, spaces and encounters have been a main foci of postcolonial studies. Said's (1978) careful examination of literary text in *Orientalism* and his theorization of colonial encounters as a material effect of a representation of fundamental Otherness, has been a central approach around which a vast array of intellectual effort in postcolonial studies has circulated. As Said observed:

> The main battle in imperialism is over land, of course; but when it came to who owned the land, who had the right to settle and work on it, who kept it going, who won it back, and who now plans for its future – these issues were reflected, contested, and even for a time decided in narrative. (Said 1993, xiii)

Said's 'narrative' here is the specific domain of literary text, which is not my source material here, yet the message of a certain representivity of encounter is still pertinent.

I have tried to think and write through this by focusing on the current sociospatial material reality of (post)colonies. To this end, Foucault's archaeological technique of discourse, and the theoretical development of this technique within critical geography, has been instructive. Foucault (1972) denied the possibility of relieving texts of their situatedness in material practice as he developed this technique. Critiques within and about the postmodern turn to textuality in geography have served to highlight the 'contact zone of materiality, bodies, objects and practices' (Legg 2007a 273) as especially important theoretical and empirical orientations for (post)colonial geographies (see Jacobs 1996; Clayton 2000; Harris 2002 and 2004; Legg 2007a) and other kinds of geographies as well (see Harvey 1989; Smith 1990). Foucault's own theorizations and positionality are heavily critiqued as Eurocentric and as a reinscription of colonial forms of power (Spivak 1988, Said 1983), nevertheless his writings have become extremely influential in colonial histories and (post)colonial criticism (Chatterjee 1983; Legg 2007b; Rabinow 1989; Young 2001; Stoler 2004; Edwards 2006) as well as in theorizations of planning as a form of governmentality (see in particular Huxley 2006). Debate within postcolonial studies has become concerned with a too–dominant literary and cultural emphasis (Slemon 1994; Harris 2004), and actually missing Said's own attention to discourse as material practice (see Legg 2007a).

While cultural analyses of states, colonies and empires (Stoler 2004; Dirks 1992; Thomas 1994; Sharma and Gupta 2006) have sharpened and deepened structuralist explanations for colonies, my view is that colonial studies will be most useful when representation, materiality and practice are enrolled together:

> One might say that imperialism entails an ideology of land on which colonialism (the actual taking up of land and dispossession of its former owners) depends. One might equally say that imperialism constructs particular kinds of knowledge and representations of land by means of which colonial dispossessions proceed.
> (Harris 2002, 48)

Like all social practices, colonialism should be seen as an interweaving of textual, ideological, semiotic and practical/material work. Discourse analysis, therefore, must be situated historically, spatially and socially within that 'contact zone' Legg identifies, because discourse is already about social practice and cannot be limited to the realm of representation.

This is critical. Land reserved for Indigenous peoples, for example, was a form of dispossession and containment that was certainly figuratively constructed as a 'final solution' to the 'Indigenous problem'. And the concomitant semiotic currency that had Indigenous people exiting stage left as the tragic, but primitive, 'dying race' are surely all part of that story. Yet reserves and mission stations *exist*. They were given material effect. People came to live their lives out in them: they *became* spaces and places. In keeping this in view, I hope to construct an analysis here that does not reduce all of those colonial realities to text, nor to alleviate text of its situatedness, nor to deny the importance of text as a social practice in itself. By looking at the locally contextualized and historically specific spatial cultures used to produce colonial space, my hope is that we open up new modes of thinking about culture, colonialism, and planning.

Such an approach also helps methodologically, by contextualizing what might become an over–reading or over–interpretation of early colonial texts. That analysis cannot uncover how colonists 'felt' about space, neither in relation to specific moments and individuals or in an archetypal sense as 'these experiences are not extricable from history and language' (Edwards 2006, 11). We do not live in texts, though we surely interpret our worlds through texts. We live in social space, as Lefebvre shows, and so I use 'spatial cultures' here to bridge 'the gap between the theoretical (epistemological) realm and the practical one, between mental and social, between the space of the philosophers and the space of people who deal with material things' (Lefebvre 1991, 4).

On a methodological note, I would caution that my explorations here are just that, and hardly final conclusions. In some cases, I have been able to read the 'actual' (copies of) journals and letters of explorers, governors, colonists and settlers. In other cases, I have been using secondary sources which quote a range of primary sources that I would have liked to access but was unable. Where possible, I have tried to piece together significant primary accounts from these secondary sources, but am aware that they are nonetheless already interpretations of those journals and textual accounts.

Further, I am cognisant of the very considerable time frame across which an undertaking like this is inevitably moving. 'Constraining' my focus in this book to the British settler states of Australia, Canada, Aoteoroa–New Zealand and the USA may have 'contained' the spatial and temporal focus to a degree. Nonetheless, to attempt any *coherent* kind of account of how space was produced in these settler colonies is impossible and, I would suggest, undesirable. We are talking about a space–time of billions of square kilometres, millions of human settlements, and at least three centuries of human history. Comparing the technologies, practices and philosophical underpinnings of British settler colonialism on the east coast of the American continent in the 1620s with those of British settler colonialism in Aoteoroa–New Zealand in 1840 looks a doubtful endeavour in light of the tectonic social shifts that occurred between these space–times. I have endeavoured not to fall into a gross comparison of that kind.

However, I do attempt to read alongside one another a variety of accounts from different space–times to explore the colonial practices of space production that seem to me to be critical. In deconstructing texts and their practices I have structured my analytical thoughts around a series of questions that try to access the spatial cultures at work in producing colonial space. What becomes invested with meaning and what doesn't in colonial settlement? Towards what ends are activities directed and how are they directed? How are humans, nonhumans, and their relations with space defined and understood? What forms of spatial arrangement and use have meaning and how are they made? In short, I am exploring the possibility of a cultural genealogy of planning in settler colonies.

Planning's Colonial Constitution

Accounts of the origins of the modern town planning movement can be conceived in two broad categories. 'Progressive development' histories argue that the central tenets of modern planning systems arose out of the pressures and challenges of rapid urbanization, particularly in the late nineteenth and early twentieth centuries (see Sutcliffe 1980; Hall 1996). A 'political–economy' strand of analysis sees planning as arising out of the underlying conflicts inherent within capitalist urban development as the state's mechanism for resolving those conflicts (in the interests of capital) (see Foglesong 1986; Harvey 1985; Dear and Scott 1981). Those writing specifically about planning and urban development in colonial contexts usually highlight how ideas and expectations of Europe were transported and modified for use in the 'New World' (see Foglesong 1986; Reps 1979; Sandercock 1976; Sutcliffe 1980).

Histories of planning also consistently point to the early 1900s as the time when the 'machinery' of planning (the legislation and ordinances for example) was first set in place. Booth (2003) explores the medieval origins of planning law in England particularly, and the sensibilities and desires for particular building forms, techniques and materials that travelled between England and continental Europe. The cities of Europe, including what is now the UK, had long–evolved systems of urban regulation to (attempt) control of population growth, fire risk, sanitation and transport (see Booth 2003).

Yet the historical record in settler colonies demonstrates that the machinery of land use planning in its strategic sense, and the spatial cultures that allowed its performance, was in existence long before. As Europe continued to attempt to perfect the regulation of urban development, it found new opportunities in the colonies to try out experiments of town layout, land use formation and patterns, that were not available at home. The *Virginia Act of 1662*, for example, specified sites in this part of America where towns should be built, the method of land acquisition and valuation, how the towns should be laid out and how lots would be disposed.

Behind this early land regulation lay the understanding that the ordering of settlement was integral to the success of colonial endeavours. Town life was 'the best means of stimulating the development of...colonies and the wish to control trade and customs collections for the benefit of the mother country' (Reps 1965, 95). In French colonies, there was far–reaching legislation both controlling built form and requiring plans to guide future development ever before France developed modern town planning laws (Wright 1991, 11). Indeed, Rabinow contends that it was in Morocco where 'France's first comprehensive experiments in urban planning took place' (1989, 277). It was in the colonies, Rabinow shows, where the work of imposing order and regulating the relationship between people and environments could best work. He writes:

> A 1931 Conference on Urbanism in the Colonies summed up the state of the art. The mood in Paris was confident, contrasting with a growing pessimism about the possibilities of urban planning in France itself, as well as Lyautey's bitter realization that his colonial dream was over. The Congress agreed on twenty–one points. It called for the mandatory institution of *plans d'amenagement et d'extension* for all agglomerations, requiring that these plans be approved by those competent to do so, that the designs respect the practices of the 'races' involved but not exclude contact between them, that the cities be airy and well planted,

that architectural pastiche be avoided, that local arts be used as much as possible in ornamenting these cities, that modern arts be used for modern necessities, that hygiene be the norm in all dimensions of the plan, that historical monuments be preserved, and that aerial photography be used in planning. (1989, 318–319)

European sensibilities, theories and perspectives did of course fundamentally shape the development and settlement of colonies. Yet a far more creatively constitutive process was at work in colonial settings, not only concerning the allocation of land use and the spatial arrangement of activity, but across a whole raft of economic, cultural and political aspirations. Colonies are far more than merely 'sites of exploitation' (Stoler 1995, 15), they are 'laboratories of modernity' (ibid), where a deepening of the work of 'home' became possible (Dirks 1992, 4).

Critical thinking about the role of planning in these histories has made a significant contribution to planning theory and planning history in recent years. Revisionist histories have highlighted the various omissions and silences of these foundational histories particularly with regard to their gendered and racialized silences (see contributions to Sandercock 1998; Boyer 1994; Wilson 1991). In this vein, another seam of critical scholarship has moved planning theories and histories away from the imperial centre to focus on the operations of modern land control as a function of territorial and colonial power (see Yiftachel 1996; Yiftachel and Fenster 1997; Alexander and Yiftachel 1997; Jackson 1997 and 1998; Roy 2006; Jacobs 1996; Porter 2006a). This very important strand of analytical work in the planning field has very clearly showed the critical nexus between planning and Indigenous dispossession. Land was fundamental for the success of colonization in making new territories by securing imperial state rule and creating economic growth in those territories. Land use planning was the principal instrument of state control of land, and therefore of state rule and economic growth, in those territories. In the context of settler states this has meant that planning has been, and remains, integrally involved in dispossession.

Looking at the various activities that colonists and colonial authorities did when they 'got there' highlights not how much of Europe got transported but instead how the actual processes of colonization – the locally contextualized and historically specific activities of settling land – are in fact *constitutive* of the practice that today we call 'planning'. Colonialism may have produced the conditions for modern planning to emerge: and if that is the case, planning itself has a colonial constitution. This claim requires some further exploration.

In his book *Seeing Like a State*, James C. Scott describes medieval Bruges. It is a town, he says with 'no abstract form' but instead 'resembles the intricate complexity of some organic processes' (Scott 1998, 53). Bruges in this era, Scott claims, is essentially 'unplanned' – no particular subject authority has laid out a city form or function in advance. Streets and paths have been made by the people who traverse them, homes and marketplaces exist where people have built them. It is a town, Scott claims, that privileges local knowledge (1998, 53) because it has literally formed from the spatial practice of that knowledge by its inhabitants, day in and day out, over a long period of time. The 'lived space' of Bruges, in Lefebvre's sense, is very present.

This is not to suggest that towns weren't designed in Europe, in other words that conceived space, in Lefebvre's terms, was not present. Philosophies of urban form and function, spatial arrangement and design – in short, the desire to conceive of an abstract space amongst the elite – have been identifiable for as long as dense human settlements have existed. More's *Utopia*, Andreae's *Republicae Christionopolitanae Descriptio*, Campanella's *City of the Sun* and the work of early architects Alberti (*De Re Aedificatoria*, published 1485) and Palladio (*I Quattro Libre dell Architettura*, published 1570) were all influential in the laying out of human settlements in Europe and its colonies.

Yet the distinctly modern forms of controlling and regulating space and population – the production of what Lefebvre (1991) calls 'abstract space' – were influenced by colonial processes. Compare Scott's medieval Bruges with the settlement of early Spanish colonies in the West Indies. Spanish officials furnished Governor Nicolas de Ovando with orders to establish the town Santo Domingo, in the Isles of the West Indies, in 1501. While only the most general instructions were given, the town that Ovando ultimately laid out 'with ruler and compass' had wide, straight streets and an orderly layout that marked a substantial difference with towns of Spain at the time (see Reps 1979, 35). In 1513, as Pedrarias Davila set out with instructions from Ferdinand V to set up new colonies (ultimately Panama City) he was given very specific instructions concerning the use of regular city lots, the allocation of space for plaza and church, and a sequence to streets, that were probably influenced by Ovando's work:

> in places newly established, proper order can be given from the start, and thus they remain ordered with no extra labor or cost; otherwise order will never be introduced. (quoted in Reps 1979, 35)

As a colonist, or a colonial governor, you stood and surveyed territory that was not yet known to Europe, not yet given European shape, sensibility and function. There was no existing modern pattern of settlement: the natural topography, features and perhaps climate were the local conditions to which you adjusted your arrangement of settlement. That particular sense, then, of perceiving a 'blank slate', a *tabula rasa*, a *terra nullius*, on which to dream and build your ideal human settlement is a peculiarly colonial phenomenon. That ability, to survey a place as new and 'empty' to Europe, did not exist in the metropole, not even in the Home Colonies movement. It was the far far away colonies that could become laboratories, the 'unadulterated primitive lands where one could carry out controlled tests' (Wright 1991, 12). Those tests and their results would give rise to the peculiar modern assemblage of spatial sensibility, legal and administrative technology and materiality (in short, spatial cultures) that we now recognize as planning. It was in the colonial moment that Europe realized it could determine the arrangement of space on its own abstract terms, as Scott's Bruges could not.

Lockean Theories of Property

A significant influence on the work of colonization and also the development of laws, regulations and social practices in relation to achieving spatial order was the philosophical writings of John Locke. Locke was an English natural law jurist and liberal political theorist, writing during the late seventeenth century. As a significant Enlightenment thinker, Locke expounded some radical views. His 'Two Treatises on Government', written in the late 1680s (see Laslett 1988 on the debate concerning datings of Locke's work and their relationship to the Glorious Whig Revolution of 1688) are an attack on arbitrary, absolutist and monarchical government, where he asserts 'a radical constitutionalist theory of popular sovereignty and an individualist theory of resistance' (Tully 1980, 54).

At the time of Locke's writing the huge social transformation of Enlightenment Europe was stirring. Feudal tenure is one of the social and spatial relations being revolutionised in England at least, at the time of Locke's writing. In the English feudal property system, there was no proprietor in land other than the Crown. While the Crown handed on land to nobles, who then became 'tenants–in–chief' and allocated their own tenancies to that land, the Crown was the only source of property right. Occupancy required an agreement with the Crown in return for service, such as domestic or military service, though by the thirteenth century, well before Locke's writing, 'service' had virtually entirely been incorporated into monetary payments (Booth 2003, 30). This is the system Locke and other European jurists at the time were writing in and against.

Locke's thinking, deeply religiously rooted, overturned the notion of ultimate sovereign property and rights and saw instead that the earth had been given to humanity by God, and that no one person had any more right than another to reap the abundance of God's creation. For Locke, all persons ('men' in his terms and I will use that term throughout this section) had dominion over and rights to the natural world, not just the Crown.

Locke's theory of property (rights) or theory of rights is rooted in his understanding of the relations between God and man, what Tully identifies as the 'workmanship model' (1980). Here, the servant–master relation of man to God bestows on the servant certain rights and obligations (Tully 1980, 34). The relation has a one–way dependency (man to God), as God is the original maker and creator. Consequently, man's natural law obligations flow from this dependency (Tully 1980, 36). The principal aspect of this natural law and obligation is that mankind must act to preserve itself. This arises in the First Treatise on Government, where Locke states:

> God having made Man, and planted in him, as in all other Animals, a strong desire of Self–preservation, and furnished the World with things fit for Food and Rayment and other Necessaries of Life, Subservient to his design, that Man should live and abide for some time upon the Face of the Earth…[and make] use of those things, which were serviceable for his Subsistence, and given him

> as means of his *Preservation*...And thus Man's *Property* in the Creatures, was founded upon the right he had, to make use of those things, that were necessary or useful to his Being. (Locke 1988, I:86,[1] original italics)

Further, that right and obligation extends to a relationship between individuals within society, such that not only is it a God–given duty for man to act in self–preservation, but that those same men should not act to limit the self–preservation of anyone else:

> Every one as he is bound to preserve himself, and not to quite his Station wilfully; so by the like reason when his own Preservation comes not in competition, ought he, as much as he can, to preserve the rest of Mankind, and may not unless it be to do Justice on an Offender, take away, or impair the life, or what tends to the Preservation of the Life, the Liberty, Health, Limb or Goods of another. (Locke 1988, II:2.6)

Kramer asserts the conclusion of the logic thus

> because self–preservation could not succeed without the use of materials that derived from the natural world, everybody had a general entitlement and a general duty to exploit nature's resources. Conversely, everyone had a duty to accept other people's dominion over parts of the earth's abundance. (1997, 99)

For Locke, then, the rights of individuals are always contextualized by, and contained within, the interests of a wider community, or public good. The continuing notion of the commons is fundamental to Locke's thinking and scholars of political philosophy have contended this is a much misread aspect of his work (see Kramer 1997, Tully 1980). Without a strong sense of the commons, obligations and indeed natural law itself would, for Locke, 'disappear and a kind of egoism would prevail. If man were independent he would be under no law but his own will and this implies that he would consider no end but himself' (Tully 1980, 57).

In theorizing common property, Locke approaches two issues – first, that common property (common rights, in the wide view that Locke takes of property) exists, and second the principles that will specify how those common rights should be used (to what ends). This is certainly for preservation, given the natural law that Locke posits in man's relation to God, he also hints at convenience and enjoyment (Tully 1980, 64).

It is in his Second Treatise on Government where Locke deals with the legal and philosophical problem of getting from common property to private property. If, as Locke has it, the world is a gift from God to mankind in common, then the

---

1   I will give references to Locke's writings in this section as 'I' or 'II' for the First and Second Treatise on Government respectively, followed by Locke's paragraph numbering system.

question becomes 'how any one should ever come to have a *Property* in any thing' (Locke 1988, II:2.25). It is here that his labour theory of property is explained:

> Though the Earth, and all inferior Creatures be common to all Men, yet every Man has a *Property* in his own *Person*. This no Body has any Right to but himself. The *Labour* of his Body, and the *Work* of his Hands, we may say, are properly his. Whatsover then he removes out of the State that Nature hath provided, and left it in, he hath mixed his *Labour* with, and joyned to it something that is his own, and thereby makes it his *Property*. It being by him removed from the common state Nature placed it in, it hath by this *labour* something annexed to it, that excludes the common right of other Men. For this *Labour* being the unquestionable Property of the Labourer, no Man but he can have a right to what that is once joyned to, at least where there is enough, and as good left in common for others. (Locke 1988, II:2.25 original italics)

Private rights in property become so when someone invests labour, thus transforming common property into something else. It is *'labour* [that] put a distinction between them and common' (II:2.28 original italics). It is widely held that Locke therefore sees that unowned objects (including land) become property simply by mixing labour with them. For Tully (1980, 116), however, this begs the question of how that right comes to be extended to the whole object and not just the part with the added labour value? Tully answers this in relation to the principles Locke set out about the relation between God and man and 'workmanship'. The labourer is making the object into an object – the raw material is provided by God, it becomes an object through labour, and thus becomes an object as property. Thus '[l]abour transforms the earthly provision provided *for* use into manmade objects *of* use' (Tully 1980, 117, original italics).

Locke applies a similar logic to the question of property in land itself, where God gave the land to 'the Industrious and Rational' (II:5.33) to be worked for the fulfilment of humanity's self–preservation, therefore:

> *As much Land* as a Man Tills, Plants, Improves, Cultivates, and can use the Product of, so much is his *Property*. He by his Labour does, as it were, inclose it from the Common. (Locke 1988, II:5.32, original italics)

Consequently, the logic is that 'God, by commanding to subdue, gave Authority so far to *appropriate*' (II:5.35, original italics). It is by this logic that the theory of waste lands, or pure nature, came to be structured. Locke draws a distinction between history and pre–history, between the time of society and the time before the development of a social polity: that of pure nature and natural law, and the existence of an entire commons. It is the social polity (the European one, ultimately) that gives rise to the will to labour and therefore the right to property. Prior to that polity, or rather prior to the social practice of cultivation for the fulfilment of self–preservation, any land can be called 'waste' or pure nature:

...Land that is left wholly to Nature, that hath no improvement of Pasturage, Tillage, or Planting, is called, as indeed it is, *wast* (sic); and we shall find the benefit of it amount to little more than nothing. (Locke 1988, II:5.42, original emphasis)

Not only, then, does property arise from the labour applied to objects and land, but the same land that has had no recognizable (industrious and rational) labour applied is entirely lacking in value. The distinguishing feature of the Lockean theory of property rights, then, is labour. In addition, is the notion that a property right is ultimately defined as a moral right (God given) and able to be defended against others. If labour has been bestowed on an object or land, and therefore private property, or rights, can be identified, then that property cannot be taken away from its private owner without consent. This is Locke's 'Fundamental Law of Property' (Tully 1980, 115): the definition of property requires that it cannot be taken without the owner's consent.

In democratising the right to property by wresting it off the Crown as the sole proprietor, Locke, and others like him, revolutionised land tenure and social structure. Instead of coming about through 'birth right', private property can be recognized through the application of labour (a particular kind of labour, as was soon to be shown in the colonial context) to land and its resources. Land or resources that were not improved through labour remained 'waste', which in Locke's terms meant unfulfilled by the terms of man's natural law duty to God to self–preserve. Waste lands, then, can be seen as an unfulfilled duty to God, and as waiting and available (common) for the application of labour. These important and radical ideas about property were intrinsic to the work of colonialism as we are about to see.

Seeing Space and Scaling Bodies

How, then, did colonialism dispossess, to borrow a phrase from Cole Harris (2004)? On 27 May 1634, an early colonist wrote in his journal about his experiences in Maryland, America:

Our Town we call Saint *Maries*: and avoid all just occasion of offence, and colour of wrong, we bought of the King for Hatchets, Axes, Howes and Clothes, a quantity of some 30 miles of Land, which we call *Augusta Carolina*. And that which made them the more willing to sell it, was the wars they had with the *Sasquesa–hanoughs*, a nigh bordering nation, who came often into their Country, to waste and destroy, and forced many of them to leave their Country... Yet seeing we came so well prepared with arms, their fear was much less, and they could be content to dwell by us: yet do they daily relinquish their houses, lands and corn–fields, and leave them to us. Is not this a piece of wonder, that a nation, which a few days before was in arms with the rest against us, should yield themselves now unto us like lambs, and give us their houses, lands and livings for a trifle?...surely some great good is intended by God to this Nation. Some few families of *Indians* are permitted yet to stay by us till next year, and then the land is free. (White 1634, 4–5, original italics)

This extract from a colonists journal offers some hints toward the actual work of colonial (dis)possession. The work of the colonist is to extend the frontier with the moral authority of God and 'civilization', if not the legal sanction of the British Crown. The extract exposes ambivalent perceptions of the relations between Indigenous peoples and colonists. While land can be recognized as native land in the first instance (hence the transaction of 'sale' with the King), ultimately 'the Indians' are only there by permit and there are clearly unspoken plans for their forced eviction in the next year, after which the land becomes 'free'. Relations between Indigenous groups are also shown as critical, where tribal politics come to serve the colonists well in this instance. The violence of territorial conflict and the power of the presence of arms is ever present.

Europe had long been fascinated by the lands it did not yet 'know', and had not drawn into productive ownership in the way Locke came to identify. Writing in the fourteenth century, long before Locke, Ranulf Higden writes about those places considered still in their pure state of nature:

at the farthest reaches of the world often occur new marvels and wonders, as though Nature plays with greater freedom secretly at the edges of the world than she does openly and nearer us in the middle. (quoted in Ryan 1996, 107)

The spatialization of extremeties – over there, as opposed to here with 'us in the middle' – was a core structuring component of imperial attitudes. Empire is the centre, everywhere else is spatially 'over there', and in being so is utterly different. Such tropes have remarkable persistence. As a white Australian living in the UK, I am constantly struck by the number of Europeans I meet who exclaim, when they hear that Australia is my birthplace, that they have always wanted to go 'out there' (never just 'there').

These 'out there' lands were seen as empty, of land waiting to be filled with Europe, and emptiness is a central trope of colonial writings. Emptiness is also the legal fiction upon which colonization depends. Here is an extract from the Act of British Parliament that established the colony of South Australia:

Whereas that part of Australia which lies between the meridians of the 132d and 141st degrees of east longitude, and between the Southern Ocean and 26 degrees of south latitude, together with the Islands adjacent thereto, consists of waste and unoccupied lands which are supposed to be fit for the purposes of colonization. (quoted in Bell and Morrell 1928, 205)

James Cook, who I was taught as a school–child 'discovered' Australia in 1788, saw Australia as a continent existing in a 'pure state of Nature' (quoted in Ryan 1996, 160). After Cook's invasion of the eastern seaboard of that continent on behalf of the British Crown, the Colonial Office sent and funded explorations and surveys of the land. Major Thomas Mitchell, a Scottish born explorer, was appointed as the New South Wales colony's Surveyor–General in 1826 to comprehensively survey and map the territory of both New South Wales and Port Phillip (now Victoria). While Mitchell clearly acknowledged the presence of Indigenous peoples, and at times actually recognized forms of property ownership and cultivation, his view was that the land was empty:

> Here was an almost boundless extent of the richest surface in a latitude corresponding to that of China, yet still uncultivated and unoccupied by man. A great reserve, provided by nature for the extension of his race, where economy, art, and industry might suffice to people it with a peaceful, happy, and contented population. (Mitchell 1848 quoted in Ryan 1996, 164)

Robert Brown, an explorer of Vancouver Island in the 1850s undertook similar explorations in Nuu–chah–nulth country, in Canada's Pacific northwestern islands and reflected on the exploration's purpose:

> It was the intention...that we should strike through the unexplored sections of the Island, carefully examine that tract as a specimen, and thus form a skeleton to be filled up afterwards. (quoted in Willems–Braun 1997, 13)

More than empty, land was waiting for the kind of European labour that could make it productive and yield its value. Surveys and explorations were universally applied activities of documenting land and securing its ownership in British settler colonies. In Canada, the Geological Survey of Canada was established in 1871 to survey lands that were to become part of the Dominion of Canada. George Dawson travelled with the Geological Survey team along the Pacific northwest coast fifteen years after Brown. He saw lands and resources in the area, particularly the Queen Charlotte Islands as waiting for use in the new Dominion and predicted that

> before many years extensive saw–mills will doubtless be established...The quality of the spruce timber is excellent, and beside the immediate shores of the harbour, logs might probably be run down the Naden River from the lake above. (1880, 38, quoted in Willems–Braun 1997, 13)

Seeing land as awaiting occupation and use in this way highlights the Lockean–inspired 'instrumentalist gaze' (Ryan 1996, 71). This gaze was active ever before the ships set sail. Emmanual Bowen, a British map maker, produced a map of the continent then known as 'terra Australis' in 1744, well before Cook's voyage, which clearly proscribed the possibilities of its land:

> It is impossible to conceive a Country that promises fairer from its Situation, than this of Terra Australis; no longer incognita, as this map demonstrates, but the Southern Continent Discovered...whoever perfectly discovers and settles it will become infallably possessed of Territories as Rich, as fruitful, and as capable of Improvement, as any that have been hitherto found out... (quoted in Ryan 1996, 116)

Discovery and settling are long and difficult processes and yet attempt to crystallize the possibilities that are predicted for these 'new', exotic and 'empty' lands. These are the words of Robert Beverley, a colonist in Virginia, America, reflecting on the work required to construct the town of Jamestown, the first settlement of the Virginia colony:

> Before they would make any settlement here, they made a full search of James river, and then by an unanimous consent pitched upon a peninsula about fifty miles up the river, which, besides the goodness of the soil, was esteemed as most fit, and capable to be made a place both of trade and security, two–thirds thereof being environed by the main river, which affords good anchorage all along, and the other third by a small narrow river, capable of receiving many vessels of an hundred ton...The town, as well as the river, had the honor to be called by King James' name. The whole island thus enclosed contains about two thousand acres of high land, and several thousands of very good and firm marsh, and is an extraordinary good pasture as any in that country. (Beverley 1705, 262)

The utilitarian requirements for human activity, such as anchorage and pasture, of founding a colony are marked. Descriptions of such possibility abound in colonial writings, where land and natural resources are spatially (re)produced with a European utilitarian purpose for their potential in commodity exchange. The explorer John McDouall Stuart, famous for his exploits 'into the centre' of the Australian continent, saw the possibilities in the lands and country he travelled through and wrote about them during the 1860s:

> ...the country in the ranges is as fine a pastoral hill–country as a man would wish to possess...
> ...it is a splendid feeding country for cattle.
> ...[the grass is] fit for the scythe to go into, and an abundant crop of hay could be obtained.
> ...a splendid country for producing cotton.
> (all quotes from Stuart sourced in Ryan 1996, 71)

Similarly, explorers frequently used the word 'adapted' to appraise the potential of land for economic use. Ryan notes that explorers like

> Forrest mentions 'fine, grassy plains, well adapted for sheep runs'; Leichhardt writes similarly of plains and riverbanks which were 'adapted for cattle and horse'; Gosse speaks of lands 'well adapted' for pastoral purposes. Oxley, looking at an area which had a 'fine park–like appearance', writes that he 'never saw a country better adapted for the grazing of all kinds of stock than that we had passed over this day'. That lands are 'naturally' suited for agricultural or pastoral purposes is taken as a sign that such an enterprise is, probably divinely, blessed. (1996, 74)

Colonists attention was drawn to those particular kinds of natural elements and proximities: vegetation becomes free fodder; watercourses become a station's permanent supply of water; grassy plateaus become pasturelands. The work of investigating this was described by a group of squatters in New South Wales in a petition to the Colonial Secretary in January 1846:

> the climate, the probably distance from navigation, the openness or denseness of the forest, the permanence of water, the character of the soil, the grass and the substratum of rock on which it grows, are all matters of anxious investigation. (Bell and Morrell 1928, 236)

Boundaries and timber, density and cultivation, emptiness and grain, Queen and country, ports and gardens, wool and lot sizes, pickaxes and plantations, fisheries and savages – these are the things with meaning in the colonial spatial sensibility toward places not yet home.

Describing such possibilities in explorers journals did not limit the effects of that description merely to text. The work and description of exploration was the work of appropriation and dispossession. When Mitchell travelled across the plains of the Wotjobaluk people in what is now the Western District of Victoria, Australia, he waxed lyrical about their excellence:

> The land is short, open and available in it's present state, for all the purposes of civilized men...In returning over flowery plain and green hills, fanned by the breezes of early spring, I named this region Australian Felix, the better to distinguish it from the parched deserts of the interior country. (Mitchell 1839)

In doing so he legitimated the illegal squatting that was then taking place and 'opened up' the country for further selection. Surveying, map production, exploration and squatting operated as a web of social practices that together focused colonial attention on places and times to produce the spatial rationality of colonial order. I will discsuss these in more detail later in the chapter.

Yet Mitchell admits that it was not really, or at least not only, the practices of exploration and surveying that 'opened up' country and made it possible for expropriation and use by colonists. Indigenous land management practices such as burning were visible to colonists in Australia and widely remarked on, sometimes in a positive way but mostly as a backwards and uncivilized practice. Mitchell, however, recognized how important those practices are to exploration and settlement, stating that if those practices had not been undertaken 'the Australian woods had probably contained as thick a jungle as those of Aoteoroa–New Zealand or America, instead of the open forests in which the white men now find grass for their cattle' (quoted in Ryan 1996, 160). Moreover, Mitchell is able to recognize the effects of white settlement on the landscape as a result of the cessation of burning practices on the area around Syndey where 'thick forests of young trees' have grown up 'where formerly, a man might gallop without impediment, and see whole miles before him' (quoted in Ryan 1996, 160). Land, then, is not 'empty' as such, but Other because it is occupied by Othered peoples. It is empty of familiar, European use patterns and empty of a form of cultivation recognizable to European eyes. This question of improvement, and what can be considered improvement, was fundamental to dispossessory activities in colonies, and was also fundamental to the colonial property relations between settlers and state.

In addition to 'opening up' colonial territory to supply raw materials to the expanding capitalist markets of Europe, settler sensibilities to landscape were powerfully shaped by romantic traditions. This came to construct a peculiar relationship between colonists and the landscape, one shaped by the interplay of a desire to conquer based on fear and hostility, and a sense of wonder emanating from the pre–existing ancientness of nature. Bonyhady describes how in Australia

> colonists came to feel deep affection for particular places that satisfied their taste for the picturesque and the sublime. Rural settlers identified with fern gullies, waterfalls or mountains in their local areas and many First Fleeters lauded the gum tree [eucalypt] for its distinctiveness. (Bonyhady 2000, 3–4)

Wilderness in both Australia and North America came to be prominent in a developing national identity.

Such thinking was related to a European 'planetary consciousness' that was developing as the scientific world became increasingly interested in classifying the elements of the natural world (see for example the influence of this in Clayton's reading (2000) of James Cook as an Enlightenment figure). Combined with a fervent desire to draw all things on the planet into that schema, by the end of the eighteenth century all imperial expeditions were accompanied by a scientific or natural historian (Pratt 1992).

Romanticism drew from this 'planetary consciousness' but reacted vehemently against the classificatory schema and empiricism that was enacted through natural science. Producing wilderness was a reaction to this empiricism, a search for a sense of the sublime, for contact with the divine (see Spence 1999, 11).

Publication in 1864 of George Perkins Marsh's book *Man and Nature* was influential in this regard, calling up Rousseauian notions of original nature as the existential touchstone of human society. Marsh called for a 'return' to that touchstone, a negation of the pollution of modern urban life (Hall 1992;

Powell 1993) and sparked the beginnings of the modern conservation movement. Regulatory practice toward places valued for their wild, romantic qualities emerged with Yellowstone National Park in America designated a protected area, the first of its kind, in 1872. In spite of this area having been continuously occupied for at least 11,000 years (Stevens 1997), the park was seen as a wilderness, untouched by human agency and thus valuable not only for the potential consumption of its sublime aesthetic, but also for what secrets it might offer up to natural scientific enquiry. Mitchell also wrote in this vein:

> At this time, the outlines were wild, the tints sublimely beautiful. Mighty trees of Casuarinae...contrasted finely with erect Mimosea, with prostrate masses of driftwood, and with perpendicular rocks. The hues of the Anthistria grass, of a red–brown, contrasted most harmoniously with the light green bushes, verdure, driftwood and water – were so opposed to the dark hues of the casuarinae, Mimosae and refted rocks, that a Ruysdael, or a Gainsborough, might there have found an inexhaustible stock of subjects for their pencil...May the object of our journey be successful, I thought then; and may we also hope that these beauties of nature may no longer 'waste their sweetness in the desert air'; and that more of her graces may thus be brought back within the reach of art. (quoted in Ryan 1996, 59)

In his book about the colonial Cartesian spaces produced by the explorer's gaze in Australia, Ryan (1996) discusses what he sees as an important disjuncture between the sublime or in his terms 'picturesque' ethic in explorers writing as against the utilitarian views of land as open for cultivation. It is a split that circulates around two relations with space that in my terms might be described as 'rationality' and 'sensibility'. For Ryan, it is a split between the poetic language used to describe an aesthetic landscape and the scientific language used to document, in utilitarian terms, the objects within that landscape. By analysing the journals of a number of explorers on the Australian continent in the early years of colonization, Ryan notices that this fissure occurs around the type of object being described. Things, or discrete elements, are documented in the language of science because such a language exists and is readily to hand to categorize and classify. Landscape, conversely, was harder to scientifically classify because a sufficient vocabulary did not exist. The result was a turn to the tenor of the picturesque or aesthetic poetry to capture what was seen (Ryan 1996, 56–7). Such disjunctures of language, vocabulary and purpose were not lost on the explorers. The needs of clients and sponsors, and the requirement to communicate items of both scientific interest but also journalistic 'interest' was keenly felt.

The result is a fusion as well as disjuncture within the writings of explorers. Most importantly for my purposes here, Ryan concludes that these two apparently opposing elements (rationality and sensibility, as I have called them) were in fact contained within the same agenda. He argues that proprietorial attitudes came with the explorers and that the picturesque language attempts to transform the country into something exploitable, appropriatable, containable – fit for habitation by colonial powers (73). Read like this, the picturesque accounts by explorers and others are understood as the production of nature for a sole, utilitarian purpose: as 'an object to be valued according to its ability to please and serve human beings' (Ryan 1996, 57). In the colonial context, of course, the human beings to be served and pleased are the colonists. Space, then, is becoming valued – whether for its utilitarian, scientific or instrumental purposes or for its (equally instrumental) sublime and picturesque qualities. Both offer to the colonial effort a ripeness of space for inscription within the colonial order of things. Those lands seen as lacking in cultivation are waiting for European improvement. Those that are pleasurable to look at can be saved from waste by the presence of appreciative European eyes upon them.

But when it comes to the progress of town building, those same picturesque landscapes make way for something even more sublime – human use and settlement. Ryan writes: 'Picturesque landscapes are described in such a way as to invite colonization; once a colony is implanted, however, the land is then constructed according to the "gloomy, melancholy and monotonous" paradigms of description' (1996, 80). Here is an extract from Sturt's 'Two Expeditions' into the interior, where Sturt is describing the progress of Sydney as an achievement over that gloomy bush:

> A single glance was sufficient to tell me that the hills upon the southern shore of the port, the outlines of which were broken by houses and spires, must once have been covered with the same dense and gloomy wood which abounded everywhere else. The contrast was indeed very great – the improvement singularly striking… success has been complete: it is the very triumph of human skill and industry over Nature herself. The cornfield and the orchard have supplanted the wild grass and the brush; a flourishing town stands over the ruins of the forest; the lowing of herds has succeeded the wild whoop of the savage; and the stillness of that once desert shore is now broken by the sound of the bugle and the busy hum of commerce. (quoted in Ryan 1996, 80)

A sensibility to a particular meaning of progress (buildings, order, human–induced change) underpinned perspectives on place. It crucially determined ownership and usufructary rights in Britain, heavily influenced by Lockean theories of property. Land devoid of obvious human activity was considered 'empty' or unsettled and thus 'unimproved'. Human (European) activity had not (yet) shaped its form and function.

Types of human activity on land enabled a classification of land as either 'settled' or 'unsettled', 'improved' or 'waste' according to an Order in Council on Squatting in New South Wales dated 9 March 1847 (Bell and Morrell 1928, 242). The improvement of land in European terms was the hallmark of progress in a colony. The 'waste' lands of the colonies, which at that time carried Locke's meaning of surplus or not yet being recognizably improved, were the source of considerable consternation of the British Imperial government. Numerous select committees, royal commissions and letters and despatches to colonial Governors discuss such issues as how to control, manage, distribute and allocate 'waste' lands. In his 1839 report on the administration of public lands in the British colonies, Lord Durham noted that such an activity is

> an operation of Government, which has a paramount influence over the happiness of individuals, and the progress of society towards wealth and greatness...Upon the manner in which this business is conducted, it may almost be said that everything else depends. (quoted in Burroughs 1967, 1)

At the colony of Victoria's first Exhibition, the Governor confidently announced that the colony was making 'steady progress, and advances day by day towards a higher stage of material prosperity' (Archer 1861, 33) through the use of waste lands. This was illustrated through counts of people, sheep, grain and civic building. Reporting on his travels through his new jurisdiction of Queensland, Sir George Ferguson Bowen (then Governor of Queensland) described in a letter to the Duke of Newcastle on 7 April 1860 his own sense of progress:

> Not only have I seen vast herds of horses and cattle and countless flocks of sheep overspreading the valleys and forests, which, within the memory of persons who have yet scarcely attained to the age of manhood, were tenanted only by wild animals and by a few wandering tribes of savages; not only have I travelled over roads beyond all comparison superior to the means of communication which existed less than a century ago in many parts of the United Kingdom; not only have I beheld flourishing towns arising in spots where, hardly twenty years back, the foot of a white man had never yet trodden the primaeval wilderness; not only have I admired these and other proofs of material progress, but I have also found in the houses of the long chain of settlers who have entertained me with such cordial hospitality all the comforts and most of the luxuries and refinements of the houses of country gentlemen in England. (Bowen 1889, 127–8)

Improvement of land was the material expression of imperial authority and cultural sensibilities in the colonies, and was considered a 'moral duty', as this extract from the New Zealand Parliamentary Debates of 1862 attests:

> It is our duty to bring the waste places of the earth into cultivation, to improve and people them. It was the law laid upon our first parents – to be fruitful and multiply, and replenish the earth and subdue it – to restore the wilderness to its original gardenlike condition. In doing this work we are fulfilling our mission. (quoted in Banner 1999, 837)

Without the control of land, its settlement and 'civilization', its turning to pursuits deemed valuable in European terms (town building, cultivation, agriculture, wool production), the colony would fail. Land was a commodity, certainly, but it was also something else.

Certain kinds of 'unimproved' land had unique qualities as raw natural resources that benefited from remaining unimproved. Timber production in the Canadian forests and the wool production from grazing native herbage on the Australian pasturelands are good examples. Sir George Gipps, then Governor of New South Wales, partially defends the unimproved state of lands in the New South Wales colony in a despatch to Lord Stanley on 17 January 1844. This was in response to new regulations issued in 1840 to ensure land in Port Phillip was disbursed through sale at a uniform price. He argued that

> instead of complaining that three acres of unimproved land are required to feed a Sheep, we ought to be thankful that, from nearly every acre of land, a pound of Wool can be annually produced, without the necessity of improving it. (Bell and Morrell 1928, 231)

Conversely, exclamations of disappointment are also common as landscapes and conditions proved different from expectation and stubbornly difficult to 'improve'. In the early years, the New Zealand Company faced serious civil unrest amongst the labourers it had convinced to take up settlement in Aoteoroa–New Zealand, who complained that far from the great fertile pastures they had been promised, what they had found on arrival was a 'flax tree in a Swampy piece of Ground' (quoted in Mahar 2005, 71).

All of this effort and work in implementing and building spatial cultures into lands not yet European, however, continued to strike up against the lived reality that these were lands already owned and occupied. Far from being a straightforward or clean affair, colonialism is violent, messy, incomplete, and contradictory. Indigenous peoples especially in the early years of colonialism in British settler states, actively reshaped the intentions and plans of colonists, forced withdrawal and the quitting of settlements and expeditions. By way of one small, but significant example, the Cherokee nation fought against colonisers in their country (now North and South Carolina, US), disrupted colonial efforts at town building, and performatively reshaped the possibility of the colonial project. Violence between settlers and Cherokee led to efforts at peaceful settlement, and it was through a variety of congresses where the British eventually agreed to a physical boundary on settlement in return for Cherokee ceding lands. This culminated in Governor William Tryon's proclamation in 1767 for 'any and all persons living beyond the line to vacate' and a cessation of colonial land grants within a mile of the boundary (Alden 1944, 221). The Cherokee had successfully limited, albeit only for a time, the colonial theft of their lands. The presence of Indigenous peoples could not then, in reality, be ignored. Significant to the colonial work of appropriating land to the empire was how the reality of Indigenous presence and ownership would be dealt with.

Questions of Indigenous property rights and the legality or otherwise of colonization were subjects of some debate in Europe during the seventeenth and eighteenth centuries. Central themes of those debates were both the 'method' of colonization (conquest, discovery and so on) and the 'nature' of the people colonisers found upon arrival. Such questions were inextricably linked. The Doctrine of Discovery, as I discussed in Chapter 2, rested on the assumption of 'empty lands' and answering that question very much depended on whether Indigenous peoples came to be counted as people in the colonial scheme of things. It was entirely convenient to simply classify Indigenous peoples as too 'primitive' to own land, and therefore see a land as 'unpeopled', and this was of course a widespread, though by no means universally held, view.

To say that such questions were settled in law at the time would be to radically overstate agreement amongst jurists on these questions. Lockean theories of the labour value of property were widely institutionalized – land could not be owned unless it was being improved. Yet many jurists disagreed with this comportment of law, and there is a long lineage in 'international law' (which is of course European law imposed on other places) that saw the possibility of Indigenous ownership of land and property, albeit in a different structure. The jurist Emerich de Vattel held both the Lockean view that the earth should be subdued according to man's duty to God, but also that native people have rights to land. Others viewed that permanent cultivation was not a necessary precondition for land ownership (see Reynolds 1992). The argument was a convenient one for settlement: 'settlers may alienate sections of land to their use, restricting natives within certain bounds, but have no right to appropriate the whole of the land' (Ryan 1996, 156). It would also ignore the fact that despite what jurists might be debating back home at the centre of empire/s, colonists themselves were getting on with whatever work was required to steal land for themselves.

Consequently, it is impossible to summarise a general viewpoint on Indigenous peoples and the question of land ownership in British settler colonies. While some colonists were convinced that those people they came into contact with had sovereign and propertied rights, others considered this laughable. The explorer Edward John Eyre wrote of his personal concern about the widely held belief in Australia that 'the natives have no idea of property in land, or proprietary rights connected with it'. Eyre considered this 'a great injustice, as well as incorrectness' (quoted in Ryan 1996, 159). The writings of colonists, explorers and governors reveals tensions within individuals themselves, one moment expressing recognition of, sometimes even respect for, Indigenous systems of land law, and at other moments in the same accounts writing about land as 'empty'. I do not wish to try and settle these debates here. Instead, I want to focus briefly on the central question of identity politics I discussed in Chapter 2: the 'scaling of bodies' (Young 1990) to refer to the work of particular forms of discourse that classifies difference into a hierarchy of power and subordination.

This scaling work in the colonies is intrinsically important to colonial dispossessory desires and activities, and for that reason 'scaling bodies' (Indigenous ones particularly) is also spatializing work. The contingent and shifting hierarchies of colonial moral order – pastoralist, governor, savage, half–caste, squatter, convict, entrepreneur – were intensively spatialized. The tropes that circulate around this scaling and spatializing work – deciding which bodies belong in which places – are highly persistent. They have also been extensively dealt with in previous studies and literature, and for that reason I only want to dwell briefly on them here to set out some key points that will be encountered in later chapters.

The first method of scaling and spatializing bodies in colonies is to determine certain kinds of people as too primitive, 'pre–historic' and thus 'pre–social', to be able to own land. Such a fiction was the founding myth of the invasion of the continent now known as Australia, but also appeared in other times and places. Indigenous peoples in Australia were cast as the complete savage, the absolute other to European civilization and sensibility. Lord Stanley, then Britain's Secretary of State for War and the Colonies described 'the aborigines of New Holland' in a despatch to Captain Robert Fitzroy, then Governor of Aoteoroa–New Zealand, as

> …feeble and perfectly savage migratory tribes, roaming over boundless extents of country, subsisting from day to day on the precarious produce of the chase, wholly ignorant or averse to the cultivation of the soil, with no principles of civil government, or recognition of private property, and little, if any, knowledge of the simplest forms of religion, or even of the existence of a Supreme Being. It is impossible to admit, on the part of a population thus situated, any rights in the soil which should be permitted to interfere with the subjugation by Europeans of the vast wilderness over which they are scattered. (quoted in Bell and Morrell 1928, 572)

This assumption was so deeply entrenched in British thinking about Indigenous peoples in Australia that the continent itself was classed '*terra nullius*', or empty land: a bizarre foundation given the prominence with which colonisers, colonial governments, and the Colonial Office in London afforded discussion of the 'native problem'. The legal assumption of *terra nullius* persisted in Australian law right up until the early 1990s, when it was finally overturned by the High Court of Australia in the landmark Mabo cas. *Terra nullius*, however, casts a long shadow over spatial cultures in Australia (see Chapter 2).

By contrast, the Maori people of Aoteoroa–New Zealand were considered 'less primitive' than Indigenous Australians. The Treaty of Waitangi officially recognized the sovereignty of Maori people in respect of their lands, and there was widespread recognition in the colony that Maori property rights were distinct and legally identifiable, if different from British property systems (Banner 1999). This consideration gives rise to the second trope around which colonial scaling of bodies occurred and it is here we come right back to Locke. Maori were considered to be 'farmers' whose well tilled grounds and apparently 'settled' lifestyle and culture were more recognizable to a spatial culture that considered its duty to God to improve the earth and possess its resources.

Yet even where there was 'recognition' of either legal tenure or land improvement, colonialism always sought to dispossess and appropriate land for itself. Colonists, governors and the British government quickly began to abrogate the Treaty of Waitangi, sparking a series of land wars in Aoteoroa–New Zealand during the 1860s. Sir George Ferguson Bowen, then Governor of the colony of New Zealand, addressed the Ngatihaua clan at Hamilton in the Waikato region of Aoteoroa–New Zealand on 21 May 1868. He stated:

> those who rebel against the Queen and the law, would be punished by the loss of their lands. But large reserves of land have been made in the Waikato, and also at Mangere near Auckland, and in many other districts, with the object of rewarding the loyal, and of providing homes and subsistence for all those who desire to return to the paths of peace and quietness. (Bowen 1889, 315)

Colonial encounters in the Pacific northwest also recognized Indigenous sovereignty and legal right to territory, yet continued to enforce a violent interpretation of the notion of sovereign nations treating with each other in land negotiations. After Robert Brown's declaration of the colonial possibilities inhering in Nuu–chah–nulth country, colonists and entrepreneurs were keen to afford themselves of those possibilities. The English businessman Gilbert Sproat travelled to Nuu–chah–nulth country in 1860, seeking to start a sawmill on the western coast of Vancouver Island. Sproat 'purchased' the land from the Nuu–chah–nulth people and requested that they move out of the area the next day. But Nuu–chah–nulth neither recognized the sale nor were interested in selling and refused to move. Sproat returned a few days later with 'ships armed with cannon' to enforce his transaction (Harris 2002, xv).

A final important trope in constructing a hierarchy of appropriate bodies in appropriate spaces is the notion of the dying race. Here is Major Mitchell again, describing Australian Indigenous burning practices:

> The extensive burning by the natives, a work of considerable labour, and performed in dry warm weather, left tracks in the open forest, which had become green as an emerald with the young crop of grass…how natural must be the aversion of the natives to the intrusion of another race of men with cattle: people who recognize no right in the aborigines to either the grass they have thus worked from infancy, nor to the kangaroos they have hunted with their fathers. (Mitchell 1848 quoted in Ryan 1996, 161)

If Indigenous people can be recognized, then it is often through a lament for a time and culture being 'lost' through the imposition of modernity.

Colonial Spatial Technologies and the Foundations of Modern Planning

The colonial work of (dis)possession was not only located in the direct encounter with Indigenous peoples, or the practice of squatting land and defending your boundaries. Land got settled, (dis)possessed, by the busy pursuit of a range of other spatial cultural practices that are recognizably part of the suite of spatial practices that we now recognize as planning. This final section discusses the very specific work these practices intended and achieved. They are the dispossessory activities of planning.

One of the early, significant and universally applied activities of British colonialism was the cadastral survey. Upon arrival in lands new to them, the British government quickly funded exploration teams and surveyors to generate useful knowledge about the territory – its extent, its features, its possibilities and opportunities. Particular instruments were used for this purpose, for example Ryan notes that Philip Parker King, a surveyor on Australia's coast, 'carried with him a sextant for fixing his position at sea, a theodolite to measure the earth when on inland surveys, and a magnifying glass' (Ryan 1996, 128). The cadastral survey was a powerful instrument in land allocation, and surveyors were consequently powerful men (Home 1997, 37). As a social practice, it performed two functions. First, it enclosed territory as European space by literally marking it as known, legible and available for settlement. In the words of Major Thomas Mitchell, surveyors had 'encompassed those wild recesses' (quoted in Ryan 1996, 97). Second, it produced a particular set of knowledges about land. Natural features were measured, classified and described. Scientific method performed the production of such things as water supplies and topography, drainage systems and pastureland. In other words, surveying was the first part of the work of producing abstract space in colonies. Again, here is how Mitchell describes his activities: 'I made the most of each station when it had once been cleared by taking an exact panoramic view with the theodolite, of the nameless features it commanded' (quoted in Ryan 1996, 97).

Once known and measured, that land could not only be 'encompassed' as Mitchell writes, but could in fact be appropriated. If initial settlement, the 'landing moment' was the first moment of an ad hoc (dis)possession, surveying, then, was when that (dis)possession became strategic and sought comprehensiveness. One of the methods of staking a claim to land was to make marks in the landscape that signified presence and ownership. When Stuart's expedition party eventually succeeded in making it into the 'interior' of the Australian continent, he described in his journal what they did when they got there. He built:

> a large cone of stones, in the centre of which I placed a pole with the British flag nailed to it. Near the top of the cone I placed a small bottle, in which there is a slip of paper, with our signatures to it, stating by whom it was raised. We then gave three hearty cheers for the flag, the emblem of civil and religious liberty, and may it be a sign to the natives that the dawn of liberty, civilization, and Christianity is about to break upon them. (Stuart quoted in Ryan 1996, 153)

Through this startlingly simple, thoroughly arrogant, but utterly culturally constructed act, Stuart thinks he and the British Empire have appropriated a land. Indigenous people are 'there' but unseen in Stuart's gaze, passive peoples waiting to be made subjects of the Crown, of the liberty and civilization that 'is about to break upon them'. The building of a cone of stones, the placing of things in the landscape (a flag, a written note, the hearty cheers), these are the signifiers of first attempts at dispossession.

The 'discoveries' of surveying were recorded on cadastral maps, often with accompanying journals and notebooks. The construction of maps performed the 'reinscription, enclosure and hierarchization of space' (Huggan 1989, 115) and thus became a representation of territorial control, of conquest. Here is the explorer Stuart again, describing his anticipation of his explorations in the mid 1840s into central Australia:

> Let any man lay the map of Australia before him, and regard the blank upon its surface, and then let me ask him if it would not be an honourable achievement to be the first to place foot in its centre. (quoted in Ryan 1996, 100)

Through maps, territory became navigable, legible, known and ultimately conquerable (Harley 2001). Their construction rested on the suite of colonial tropes explored earlier in this chapter – of emptiness, and lurking savagery. Mitchell in his journal describes the work of maps and names on 'empty' lands: 'Those beautiful recesses of unpeopled earth, could no longer remain unknown. The better to mark them out on my map, I gave to the valley the name of Salvator Rosa' (quoted in Ryan 1996, 61).

As a number of scholars have shown, maps are created as innocent representations of the real world, of actual space (see for example Harley 2001; Edwards 2006; Ryan 1996; Huggan 1989). Critical re–readings of maps exposes how maps are instead a technique of power, of the power/knowledge nexus, where the authority to represent the world resides in the (colonial) power producing the map and claiming its truth. Maps helped perform discovery and in doing so, helped perform dispossession. The authority of the map resides in its accuracy, its ability to be a truthful and real account of actual space, such that the 'founding assumption of cartography is that it presents the user with a view of the land from above' (Ryan 1996, 102).

Particular positivistic mapping techniques enabled this to occur: the 'conventions of shading, colouring and iconographical codes for objects as seen from above' (ibid, 103). Codes, such as colours, symbols or types of shading signify objects or elements in a landscape – they signify the presence of these objects and their 'where' quality. Through maps, 'emptiness' is converted into a landscape populated by the kinds of things European spatial cultures can see and use. Yet maps, as Edwards (2006) shows, operated rhetorically as only one kind of social practice in time–space. Maps had meaning only when they were themselves employed within a web of other spatial practices. I showed earlier in this chapter how the production of maps through the activities of surveying 'opened up' land for settlement. Maps existed momentarily as a textual representation of colonial possibility, and then gave impetus to the material work of colonial dispossession. Exploration and surveying produced colonial space by rendering it intelligible to the colonial gaze through what Jackson (1998) terms 'exploration epistemologies'. Geographical knowledge, implemented through the scientific technologies of surveying and cartographic mapping, and the discursive strategy of naming (see Carter 1987) rendered places known, ordered, rational, and ultimately 'settled'. Exploration rested on the assumption of being the 'first' to discover hitherto 'unknown country', the racial assumption upon which the legal fiction of *terra nullius* ultimately came to rest.

The early work, then, of surveying, mapping and naming created in a representational sense (at least for a moment), the opportunities for colonial dispossession. As settlement proceeded, surveying, mapping and naming continued to be critical technologies by which space was produced for colonial possession. Surveys became useful in a different way, for the parcelling of land to create settlements and townships. Roads and building lots were determined, spaces allocated for parks, customs houses, piers and drainage systems. Again, the representational act of surveying (the drawing of plots on paper and then transferring that drawing onto the land itself) made the land available for 'civilization' through improvement as houses, huts, roads, fences and gardens were built.

Particular forms of spatial order came to be considered 'good' in settler colonies, at least from the perspective of those privileged to be able to write about their sentiments or their experiences at the time and whose records have survived. The gridiron pattern of town platting was prevalent, almost ubiquitous, in American colonial towns as it was 'easy to design, quick to survey, simple to comprehend, having the appearance of rationality, offering all settlers apparently equal locations for homes and business within its standardized structure' (Reps 1979, x). The gridiron pattern was particularly useful to bring standardized land parcels as commodities to the land market:

> [l]ike Jefferson's scheme for surveying or the Torrens system for titling open land, the grid creates regular lots and blocks that are ideal for buying and selling. Precisely because they are abstract units detached from any ecological or topographical reality, they resemble a kind of currency which is endlessly amenable to aggregation and fragmentation. (Scott 1998, 58)

Such standardization, as Scott points out, is a key feature of statecraft. Yet in this case, it was rarely activity by the state (local or imperial) that employed this particular measure. Towns in British America were settled and laid out predominantly by private entrepreneurs and colonial companies who came to hold large tracts of land either by Crown grant, squatting, war or negotiation with Indigenous peoples. The Plymouth and London Companies, for example, together founded Virginia having been granted 'settlement rights' in the early 1600s (Reps

1965, 88). Similarly, in Pennsylvania, William Penn had been granted a vast tract of land (now the states of Pennsylvania, Delaware and a part of New Jersey) by the British Crown to square a family debt, and he had sole authority, in colonial terms, to determine the layout of settlements (Foglesong 1986).

Township building had a significance beyond the immediate occupation of space and the performance of a disposition toward space for order out of chaos. Towns were a military strategy in the wars with Indigenous peoples. Townships afforded protection to colonists by the proximity of assistance from neighbours, and allowed easy policing and patrol of town boundaries to restrict the movement of Indigenous people. The use of settlements as military strategy was prevalent in early Hispanic America. Forts or *presidios* were built as garrisons to protect Spanish settlements and were

> intended to safeguard the occupants of religious and civil communities from Indian attack or invasion by other colonizing powers...The task of defending the frontier against Indian attack – the principal function of the presidio garrison – was made easier by the work of the missionaries and the gathering of the natives into the missions settlements where their activities could be observed and directed. (Reps 1979, 42)

Those mission 'towns' were laid out according to the same principles as other early towns with ordered lot sizes, allocated spaces for open space, church and market, and regularized street patterns. Ultimately, these missions were intended to become self–governing civil settlements 'once their Indian inhabitants had been converted to Christianity, learned useful trades, and adjusted to European social and political institutions' (Reps 1979, 41). Buildings and settlements constituted the proper curatorship of land and it was this disposition toward appropriate activity upon land that marked authority and ownership. Buildings were quite literally stakes in the acquisition and control of land, the physical manifestations of colonial (dis)possession.

The work of settlement, whether it be in towns, pastoral runs or farms, was also predicated upon a variety of land policies. If the early years of colonization were marked out by speculative and privately–driven efforts toward settlement, at some point this needed to be reined in by the state. A key question concerning colonial authorities, including the government's Colonial Office, was the question of disbursement of lands to private individuals. When the Crown assumed appropriation of land in colonies, what did this mean for its actual occupation and settlement? British colonial land policy was heavily influenced during the 1830s and 1840s by the thinking of Edward Gibbon Wakefield, a British politician, diplomat and entrepreneur. Wakefield's theory was that the success of British colonialism could only be realized by creating monetary value in land, as well as supporting the emigration of colonists to new land. He devised a system of colonial land sales to deal with both these problems simultaneously: the sale of lands newly 'discovered' would create funds to support the emigration of more people to colonies. That emigration effort was particularly targeted at labourers and women – two categories of people upon which social reproduction in the colonies depended. At the heart of this thinking lay the premise that if imperial government could control the land price and the rate of emigration simultaneously, it could establish the value of land, labour and reproduce a social hierarchy in the colonies (Harris 2002, 5).

The first application of Wakefield's ideas was the introduction of a uniform price for land per acre into the land system of the colony of New South Wales (Australia) by then Under–Secretary for the Colonies Lord Howick. Wakefield wanted to do a lot more than introduce the land sales system, including establishing an entirely new colony based on his principles, but his principles were so at odds with the Colonial Office that he was initially unsuccessful. In 1836 Wakefield extensively lobbied a House of Commons Committee on Colonial Lands for 'central control of the lands of the whole Empire in the interests of a comprehensive policy of Empire settlement' (Bell and Morrell 1928, 195). In other words he wanted to reserve the power over land disbursement and sale to the British government, rather than to the local authorities and governors. Asked by the Committee whether he considered the land disposal system operating in the colonies of NSW and Van Diemen's Land to be sufficient, he replied they were not because of their insecurity in the regulatory regime. He recommended the principle of price and land purchase to be guaranteed by an Act of the British Parliament to provide that certainty. This followed the model then gaining ground in America, where an 1820 law provided for the sale of land at a set price per acre.

Wakefield's proposals finally found favour and were applied to the Australasian colonies in the form of the *Australian Land Sales Act of 1842*. This established a uniform land sales policy throughout the colonies on the continent of Australia, whereby no transfer of land could occur without a sale at a set price. This required a survey prior to sale to determine lot size and shape. He also attempted, with limited success, his own initiatives in colonization through the establishment of his New Zealand Association (later to become the New Zealand Company) which funded the emigration of settlers and their take–up of land particularly in the Otago and Canterbury districts of Aoteoroa–New Zealand.

Wakefield's ideas were highly controversial, not just in London where it took some time for them to be received favourably, but in the colonies themselves. Lord Sydenham, then Governor of Canada, wrote in a letter on 23 November 1840 stating that 'Wakefield's plan of bringing out labourers by the sale of lands is utterly impracticable in these colonies. Land is worth nothing except through the labour bestowed upon it' (Bell and Morrell 1928, 219). Value in land (exchange value in this case) is derived from use, from human activity. This was why Wakefield's ideas were so contentious: disposing of land through sale had the possibility of effecting value, but because lands were 'empty', and the colonies distant, it was very difficult to implement. Moreover, granting (rather than selling) small lots of land to poor settlers was absolutely essential to the survival of the colonies and the forms of social reproduction critical in a new colony. In 1824, Lord Falkland received a despatch from a colonial governor in North America, stating:

> I cannot but believe that the unqualified doctrine of never giving away Land has done much mischief in British North America, and has driven away many thousands of Immigrants who would have at least have maintained themselves, and whose children would have lived in the Queen's Dominions in a state of Comparative Wealth. (quoted in Bell and Morrell 1928, 221)

A more successful form of ensuring improvements was through taxes and the threat of revocation of grants if land improvement was not in evidence in a specified time after the grant was made (Foglesong 1986).

The other question that colonial land policy had to address was that of Indigenous peoples. Successfully implementing land policy whether by grant or sale, literally depended on freeing land of Indigenous interests and presence. Apart from mass slaughter and frontier violence, land policy offered a different way to achieve this, best exemplified and practiced through land reservation. This was a form of spatial ordering of racialized bodies in its most extreme form: to 'contain' Indigenous peoples in a system of land zoning. Reserves became one of the fundamental costs of colonial space, and remain key sites for Indigenous land claims and policy as we shall see in later chapters. Missions and reserves, while heavily influenced by the emancipationist movement in Britain, entailed other forms of material practice with Indigenous peoples in the colonies. A juxtaposition of patronizing concern for the 'dying aborigine' in Britain and the realization that confinement of Indigenous peoples presented a certain kind of colonial solution, gave rise to a system of reserving land for Indigenous use, which effectively 'cleared' other lands of the encumbrance of Indigenous rights. This was a kind of somewhere–in–between point in amongst the European legal arguments about whether Indigenous peoples could be recognized as holding property.

One manifestation of this was the mission station: staffed by missionaries, funded by churches, implementing the assimilation policies of colonial governments. This was a distinctly spatial policy of dispossession and assimilation. Indigenous people were variously forced, tricked or cajoled onto mission stations and kept there to be 'taught' the values and customs of civilization and Christianity (for excellent examinations of the role of missions in colonizing processes, but also the reinscription in contemporary Indigenous thinking of reserves and missions as home or representations of sovereignty see Critchett 1980; Clarke and Chance 2003; Hibberd 2006). Assimilation, differently from other practices of dispossession, was based in universalist Western liberal thinking. It sought to obliterate the cultural difference that Indigeneity represented to the Eurocentric view.

Another manifestation of this was the land reservation (see Harris 2002), a form of spatial containment of Indigeneity (and more importantly the revocation of rights) which underpins legal relationships between Indigenous nations and modern nation–states today. Creating unfettered access to land became the central object of colonial endeavour throughout the nineteenth century as industrial capitalism sought to produce space as an image of its own relations of production, and as the circulation of a shifting sensibility to the 'Indigenous plight' began to take hold. A juxtaposition of racialized mindset, economic self–interest and the intricate power of industrial capitalism brought colonial land policy to the centre of attention of colonial Governors, and London's Colonial Office.

Reserving land for Indigenous peoples became one of the mainstays of those policy practices. In the United States, the reservations sprang out of a legal doctrine and historical set of relationships that recognized (partially at least) sovereignty of Indian nations. An intricate and fundamentally contradictory legal argument and practice developed in postrevolution United States, particularly through a sequence of Chief Justice Marshall's legal rulings, as discussed in Chapter 2. This formally recognized Indian property rights, yet simultaneously practised a form of land policy that safeguarded what were technically illegal Crown land grants as well as the acquisitions of territory west of the settlement prohibition line that was drawn by King George III in 1763 to keep the military might of the Iroquois and Muscogee Creek Indian confederacies on his side (Churchill 1992, 141). Reservations for Indian nations 'respected' a limited form of Indian sovereignty by holding that native Americans could treat with the US government (in order to cede territory), but were not sufficiently sovereign to disallow the US government to abrogate those treaty agreements when they didn't suit (Churchill 1992, 143; Hibberd 2006, 90). Over time, Indigenous peoples in America were spatially contained within about two and a half per cent of their original two billion acre land base (Churchill 1992, 144). This not only represented, but materially produced a radical geographical restructuring, and created the opportunity for using reservations as social laboratories to transform Indians into 'good citizens'.

The spatial containment of Indigeneity was a basic technology of colonial practice, brought about by violence, legal argument, and the steady, often violent, encroachment of colonial activities upon Indigenous places. Reserves also served to fit those lands into the grid of calculation and surveillance necessary for government in the colonies:

> Indian reserves were mapped, named, usually numbered, and surveyed, and, so treated, entered a grid of calculation…The reserve acquired a fixed place in the Cartesian space of the survey system and in the minds of officials and settlers… [and] situated the reserve within an official ambit of sovereignty, surveillance and management. (Harris 2002, 271)

Reserves were a spatial mechanism for containment and regulation of the native problem. This policy was 'successful' in colonial terms. By the late nineteenth century, Indigenous peoples in those parts of settler states where the efforts of industrial and agricultural capitalism were most keenly employed, were significantly dispossessed of the legal and material rights in their land.

Conclusion

Producing space in settler colonies was the enactment of a politics of (dis)possession. Dispossessory activities were the work of erasing the lived space of Indigenous peoples. That lived space, and the peoples that occupied them, were the difference Europe encountered in its colonies. As Europe encountered its Others and Othered spaces, peculiarly colonial spatial and social cultures emerged. The social spaces of colonies, and ultimately the spatial cultures that emerged, were produced through this struggle, by the necessity of settling and remaking Indigenous place in European terms.

The spatial cultures of colonists produced social spaces according to their use and exchange value. Simultaneously, they spatialized the scaling of bodies that were part of the social relations of production: women belong in dwellings, labourers on the land but not in the town hall, natives must stay on the other side of the fence, or inside the reserve. Such practices had the triad of effects Lefebvre suggests arises out of the production of modern, abstract space: homogeneity, fragmentation and hierarchy (2003, 210). A formation of spatial categories (improved or waste lands, the use value of natural features) homogenized space into a schema of general but fragmented characteristics. All open plains became potential pasturelands, all rivers potential trade routes. In providing the schema, a spatial hierarchy emerged based on racialized ideological formations of progress, utility and beauty. This was underpinned by a relation between knowledge and power that was necessarily both productive and repressive and was oriented to space and the peoples who occupied it (Said 1978).

Such was the production of space in British settler colonies, with the early practices of spatial ordering at its heart. Spatial cultures – the knowing, categorizing, seeing and naming of space – helped establish a more systematic, though always contingent, geography of knowledge about a colony (Carter 1987; During 1991; Jackson 1998), and in turn a more systematic dispossession from Indigenous peoples. Such spatial cultures in settler colonies were shaped and articulated through the early practices of spatial ordering, or planning: surveying and selection, mapping, (re)naming, town building, and the various and widespread intricacies of land policy. The early formative activities of planning were a part of the politics of (dis)possession in colonies. And those formative activities, the moments of planning's modern emergence, were located in those same politics of (dis)possession. Planning is constitutively and culturally colonial.

Chapter 4
Systematizing Space: 'Natures', 'Cultures' and Protected Areas

> Like the gods and totems, being human involves being non–human.
> (Langton 1996, 18)

Colonial space, as shown in Chapter 3, was the production of spatial cultures. I have been looking up until now at a wide range of the practices that achieved this, and in historical perspective. It is important now to closely examine particular manifestations of the production of systematic and hierarchised geographies, to look at how they work but also at what work they do in continuing dispossessory activities. One critical systematic geography of hierarchy that I have already begun to touch on in Chapter 3 is the separation of natural space – the ultimate 'commons' in Lockean theory – and the cultural space of 'improved' place. This is the 'space that *sorts*' Lefebvre identifies (1991, 375 original italics). Such a systematization is exemplified in protected area management, where spaces are classified according to their overarching value, and the extent to which modern, human effects are inscribed in the landscape. That systematization produces two poles around and between which space is structured and hierarchised: utility and the picturesque or sublime. In this chapter, I will explore how this contemporary hierarchisation of space, via the modes of spatial cultures, has particular implications for (post)colonial politics and Indigenous peoples.

Protected areas have become key sites in (post)colonial contests about land rights and custodial responsibility across the globe (Woenne–Green et al. 1994; Jaireth and Smyth 2003; Spence 1999), as well as natural resource rights more broadly (Howitt et al. 1996; O'Faircheallaigh 2008). Further, how protected area establishment and management has come to dispossess Indigenous peoples is well established in the literature (Cronon 1995; Stevens 1997; Palmer 2004 and 2006; Lawrence 2002; Langton 1996). These studies, drawing on significant theoretical ideas about nature as a cultural construction, have opened up new ways of thinking about environmental management and planning. As Cronon (1995) observes, the concept of nature remains 'uncommon ground' between Indigenous and western peoples. Moreover, western conceptualizations of nature, and the enshrining of 'wilderness' as a key concept in environmental management and green politics, has served to continue the colonial work of dispossessing Indigenous peoples from their lands. This occurs by making Indigenous people invisible, because 'nature' is something where people are not, and it is raw, untouched, primeval nature that colonists and their descendants see outside the lands that are settled and 'in use', in settler colonies.

Then there is the problem of where to locate Indigenous relations with land. In recent years, a considerable and powerful public discourse has begun to turn an appreciation of the importance of territory to Indigenous societies (the 'closeness' of Indigenous people to land, a notion which Indigenous people themselves use with great strategic effect) into a new kind of erasure. The 'noble savage' of Rousseau's imagination makes Indigenous people unique in their closeness of relations to land, so close that they are easily rendered 'part of the fauna' (Langton 1996, 18). Langton sets out how we might access an understanding of how this occurs:

> We can deduce what terms like 'nature', 'wilderness', 'landscape' and 'primitive' mean by interrogating the images and texts which draw and write these conceptions, as well as the social forms which give a social appearance to their conception. In manufacturing representations of 'Nature' and 'wilderness', the human mind constructs a relationship with the non–human. It is in this cultural paradox of 'Nature' and 'wilderness' signified as both human and non–human that certain kinds of cultural meaning are found. Like the gods and totems, being human involves being non–human. Locating 'Nature' in this way, enables us to examine it as a contested site of power between Europeans and Aborigines… The valorization of 'wilderness' has accompanied an amnesia of the fate of indigenous peoples. (Langton 1996, 19)

In this chapter, I will turn analytical attention to texts and social forms within the field of planning and land management that give rise to the notions of nature and culture. In doing so, the purpose is to build a contemporary empirical understanding of how the colonial spatial cultures I explored in Chapter 3 live on, in their variegated and changing forms, and how these are important sites of power and struggle.

It must, of course, be acknowledged that much has changed in the procedural, administrative and governance arrangements of 'nature', 'wilderness' and protected area planning in the last 30 years. Models of joint management, co–management, collaborative management, shared ownership and a range of partnership approaches are being adopted in a variety of ways in different places (Craig 1992; De Lacy and Lawson 1997; Smyth 2001; Stevens 1997; Beltran 2000; Lawrence 2002; Davies et al. 2000). Why, then, do we need to keep analysing the twists and turns of planning governance if more collaborative and empowering models of planning are being developed? My view, one that I will explore in greater theoretical and empirical depth in Chapter 6, is that the collaborative turn in planning and management is in danger of missing the key moments of critical transformation unless it is accompanied by a sufficiently deconstructive stance towards its own ontological and epistemological philosophies. In other words, if the spatial cultures of planning – the ones recognizable, from Chapter 3, as constituting the spatial and social manifestations of colonial power relations – remain intact in amongst the reshuffling of management models and procedural rules, then little has changed. Unless we analyse the continuation of colonial spatial rationalities, how they shape the very production of the categories 'natural' and 'cultural' space, the moments for real disrupture, for real change, remain obscured.

In this chapter, I begin by looking at how the global system of protected areas, and environmental planning more generally, produces and spatializes natures and cultures. Following this, I move to an analysis of specific local contexts where that place production can be seen in greater depth and richness. In Gariwerd, Australia, particular kinds of discourses about how natures and cultures can be seen and measured in a national park operate with particular implications for Indigenous peoples. Of particular importance is the way in which that discourse shapes how the place is named, and also used. In Nyah, the story about natures and cultures is all about the western definition of timber as a natural resource. Natures, cultures and their representation became the site of globally significant contests in Clayoquot Sound, in Canada's Pacific northwest region. I will look briefly at the establishment, after a long struggle by the Nuu–chah–nulth people, of the Clayoquot Sound Biosphere Trust and community board. Finally, I will turn to a case from Aoteoroa–New Zealand, where the recognition of Maori land rights through the Treaty of Waitangi process has resulted in the first glimmers of a shift in the division of natures from cultures in park planning at Aoraki/Mt Cook National Park.

The following questions structure the analytical approach to these global and local areas: how do the legislative and policy frameworks that both create and manage the protected area estate, construct and codify natures and cultures? How are these made spatially manifest? How do those same frameworks make nature and culture legible to the state? What kinds of knowledge production are at work in this process? And finally, what are the implications for action within place?

A Global Hierarchy of Natures and Cultures

Protected areas occupy a crucial and visible location in the 'geography of hope', a phrase coined by those championing the cause of nature conservation and wilderness protection (see in particular Stegner 1969; Hall 1992; Brandon, Redford and Sanderson 1998). This geography of hope enlivens protected areas in the industrialized, western public mind as pristine places of natural splendour, places of escape, away from the crowds and pollutants of city life. Protected areas, then, are seen as the

> benchmarks against which we understand human interactions with the natural world. Today they are often the only hope we have of stopping many threatened or endemic species from becoming extinct. (Dudley 2008, 2)

It is a geography that renders those places the romanticized 'somewhere else' of the urban imagination – a space/time radically different from modern, urban life.

The protected area estate is a state–governed system of lands and waters reserved for conservation and natural resource management, through a wide, and globally linked, network of actors and institutions. A protected area, according to the guidelines of the IUCN, is

> a clearly defined geographical space, recognised, dedicated and managed, through legal or other effective means, to achieve the long–term conservation of nature with associated ecosystem services and cultural values. (Dudley 2008, 8)

The World Commission for Protected Areas (WCPA) is a global network of protected area expertise, established to 'promote the establishment and effective management of a worldwide representative network of terrestrial and marine protected areas' (WCPA, no date). That global representative network is structured into a categorization of protected areas:

Ia Strict Nature Reserve – managed mainly for conservation and scientific enquiry.
Ib Wilderness Area – managed mainly for wilderness protection.
II National Park – managed mainly for ecosystem protection and recreation.
III Natural Monument – managed mainly for conservation of specific natural features.
IV Habitat/Species Management Area – managed for conservation through management intervention.
V   Protected Landscape/Seascape – managed mainly for conservation and recreation.
VI Managed Resource Protected Area – managed mainly for sustainable use of natural ecosystems.
(International Union for the Conservation of Nature 1994)

These categories were changed in 1994 to recognize the interests of Indigenous peoples in five of the six protected area categories above (only Category I makes no reference to Indigenous interests). While this constituted a significant change it by no means guarantees Indigenous rights.

The categorization of protected areas performs the modern, gulf–like, division of natures from cultures. Nature is rendered the backdrop to the agency of human sociality, the raw as against the 'culturally cooked' (Bennett and Chaloupka 1993). Protected areas, through this definition, are the imagined places of ultimate (imperial) human civilization:

as that which lies outside [their] historical and geographical reach...A place without *us* populated by creatures (including, surreptitiously, a variety of human 'kinds') at once monstrous and wonderful, whose very strangeness gives shape to whatever *we* are claimed to be...This framing of the wild renders the creatures that live 'there' inanimate figures in unpeopled landscapes, removing humans to the 'here' of a society from which all trace of animality has been expunged. (Whatmore 2002, 12 original emphases)

But there is more at stake, and at work, here. Not only is nature naturalized, but cultures are also silently classified. Indigenous cultures become an object of recognition, interest and regulation in the protected area classification. Non–Indigenous forms of human agency are also present, but silent, in these systems and frameworks. They are presented as the universal norm, the (cultural) backdrop of appropriate human intervention that is never available for recognition or analytical interest.

There is a debate within the IUCN itself about whether the categories imply a hierarchy of 'naturalness' (Dudley 2008 says it doesn't, but Borrini–Feyeraband et al. 2003 declare that it does). A close reading of the categories and management objectives for each expose the spatial cultures at work. Category Ia protected areas are those places deemed very 'strictly' natural, where a purified kind of human scientific interest is legitimate because those places are seen to have remain unsullied by human intervention of a modern, large–scale type. Wilderness areas are recognized as

> large unmodified or slightly modified areas, retaining their natural character and influence, without permanent or significant human habitation, which are protected and managed so as to preserve their natural condition. (Dudley 2008, 14).

The language of wilderness and its associated spatial practice, remains intact despite attempts to unsettle that language. The debate is settled by the IUCN in suggesting that 'wilderness' should be written in inverted commas (Thomas and Middleton 2003, 4).

It is not until the 'bottom' of the hierarchy (Categories V and VI) that there is evidence of people and their activities, other than a distant scientific interest. Here we find 'recreation' and 'sustainable use' of resources, as the kinds of interventions constructed as appropriate in 'natural' places. Places where

> the interaction of people and nature over time has produced an area of distinct character with significant ecological, biological, cultural and scenic value: and where safeguarding the integrity of this interaction is vital to protecting and sustaining the area and its associated nature conservation and other values. (Dudley 2008, 20)

can be classified as Category V Protected Landscapes.

Of a different value again (and here we see the entrance of resource extraction value), Category VI areas

> conserve ecosystems and habitats, together with associated cultural values and traditional natural resource management systems. They are generally large, with most of the area in a natural condition, where a proportion is under sustainable natural resource management and where low–level non–industrial use of natural resources compatible with nature conservation is seen as one of the main aims of the area. (Dudley 2008, 22)

Cultures, present in different ways in this classificatory system depending on the 'position' on the continuum, are constructed as one aspect that requires management attention: 'Managers have to ensure that these spiritual values are protected alongside natural heritage' (Dudley 2008, 64), 'managers' of course being rendered acultural.

In addition to providing this classificatory system, the IUCN also establishes benchmarks for the knowledge base of protected area planning and management. An 'initial dataset' of 'quantifiable facts' (Thomas and Middleton 2003, 30) should be established, used to 'determine management objectives (e.g. protect rare habitat and species)' (ibid, 26). Producing knowledge is presented as a linear formation of stages in understanding: background information is gathered; a 'field inventory' is undertaken and this is all collated in a document or report that describes the protected area (ibid, 26–7). Certain types of discrete knowledge sets become the objects of scientific knowledge production, through a 'checklist' of essential types of information. These include such aspects as 'ecological resources'; 'cultural resources'; 'aesthetic aspect'; 'physical facilities'; 'visitor characteristics'; and 'predictions of the future condition of each of the above factors' (ibid, 27).

Local knowledge (including Indigenous knowledge) is recognized as important to the process of knowledge production, as another discrete subset of interest. The IUCN's guidelines state that 'the traditional knowledge of indigenous peoples regarding plants and animals and how they should be looked after should be drawn on where available' (ibid, 30).

Producing Gariwerd as a National Park

Gariwerd, as set out in Chapter 1, is a place in western Victoria, Australia, that was declared a national park in 1984. In its recommendation for reservation as a national park, Victoria's Land Conservation Council[1] (LCC) noted that Gariwerd was important because of its 'large area of forested land, the combination of unusual geological features, rugged topography, and scenic grandeur, and the rich variety of native flora and wildlife habitat' (Land Conservation Council 1982, 12).

---

1   The government body, now known as the Environment Conservation Council, established by statute to advise the Victorian State Government on the use of public lands.

Gariwerd, then, is valued as a 'natural' place. As a Category II protected area under the IUCN guidelines, Gariwerd is:

> set aside to protect large–scale ecological processes, along with the complement of species and ecosystems characteristic of the area, which also provide a foundation for environmentally and culturally compatible spiritual, scientific, educational, recreational and visitor opportunities. (Dudley 2008, 16)

Management of, and planning for, Gariwerd, like all national parks in Victoria, is the responsibility of Parks Victoria. A review of the original plan of management was commenced in 1998, and released in its final form in March 2003. Primary management objectives for Gariwerd are set out in the vision statement in the plan of management:

> A future visitor to Grampians National Park finds an outstanding park renowned for its spectacular natural scenery and wildflowers, diversity of flora and fauna, range of highly significant cultural sites, and opportunities to enjoy these features in a variety of settings…The park's natural environment is well protected and conserved by management based on a sound and increasing understanding of the park's natural values, ecological processes, and the specific requirements of significant plants and animals. (Parks Victoria 2003, 8)

This statement shows the three key objectives underpinning national park management discourse, originally emanating from the IUCN guidelines. These include nature conservation ('the park's natural environment is well protected…'); scientific study ('management based on a sound and increasing understanding…'); and tourism and recreation ('a future visitor…'). Gariwerd is constructed as an object of knowledge and spatial practice through its designation as a national park, and its consequent emplacement in an international system of protected areas. That designation arises from a particular spatial culture operating in planning's relations to Gariwerd, that ascribes value to a set of identifiable, discrete elements. Gariwerd is visible to planning because it can scientifically measure, or make legible, those elements in the following ways:

> spectacular landforms,…seven broad vegetation types…high flora and fauna diversity…148 threatened species…massive fissured sandstone cliffs contrasting with surrounding plains, and…nationally renowned and striking wildflower displays. (Parks Victoria 2003, 3–4)

Those natural features, and their legibility to science and management (see Table 4.1), are what places Gariwerd within the protected area system. That emplacement, as a classification for a particular style of management, then situates Gariwerd within a specific set of governmental techniques: international guidelines, institutional arrangements, statute and knowledge production.

Table 4.1   **Western scientific knowledge base in Gariwerd**

Discipline	Scientific knowledge base
Ecology and Biology	'high flora diversity (975 vascular species), and high fauna diversity (312 vertebrate species)' (3)
Cartography	'EVC and FC maps for the Greater Grampians Study…are used in detailed environmental planning and management for the park' (15)
Ornithology	'Five of the 30 Victorian rare or threatened bird species that occur in the park are covered under international agreement' (17)
Hydrology	'Ensure that consents for the operation and maintenance of water supply facilities in the park avoid or minimise deleterious impacts on stream ecology…' (14)
Zoology	'The park is considered to have high macropod diversity…there have been unconfirmed sightings of the Spot–tailed Quoll…' (17)

Source: Parks Victoria 2003.

Such forms of knowledge are widely inscribed in park management in Victoria. In 2000, Parks Victoria released the first edition of its State of the Parks report, an ongoing reporting and monitoring arrangement for park management, following the IUCN guidelines, designed to help determine whether park management is effective. The Report (Parks Victoria 2000) was released in two volumes, the first focusing on the overall 'park system' in Victoria, and the second reporting on each park within the State via a system of indicators. Each indicator is monitored by quantitative measurement of certain characteristics: park size, length of boundary, time since reservation, park land use, density of vegetation, visitor numbers, pest plants and animals, and frequency of fire. The data sources include research reports, management plans, resource inventories of public land in Victoria, and the Department of Sustainability and Environment's Corporate Geospatial Data Library.

Yet even in state–based planning terms, Gariwerd has not always been known in this way. Prior to its declaration as national park in 1984, it was a State Forest. In its 1977 plan of management, the Victorian Forests Commission noted how multiple uses of Gariwerd were balanced through prescriptive zoning, including natural zones to protect environmental values, special feature zones which mentioned 'aboriginal paintings' as a particular kind of feature, and timber production zones (Forest Commission 1977). From the early colonial period, different parts of the ranges and valleys of Gariwerd have been utilized for a range of productive activities: timber harvesting, beekeeping, grazing, water harvesting, and gold and sandstone mining. At one time, it was this view of the utilitarian functionality of space that performed the construction of Gariwerd as a place.

Gariwerd's classification as a national park, however, is produced directly by how it is known as an overwhelmingly natural place under threat from these degrading developments and uses. Reservation of these features into a higher level of the protected area hierarchy is the primary means of protecting those features from perceived destructive influences of Western society. The preservation of Gariwerd as a national park, then, was predicated upon its identification as a place that could be venerated as overwhelmingly and romantically natural (and thereby unsullied by Western cultural forces) and yet in need of protection from those same forces, many of which had been operating for many years. By virtue of its new position in the protected area hierarchy, Gariwerd became, in 1984, a different kind of place – one valued for its natural beauty, pristine environment, and rugged remoteness – to the extent that it is now these values that override all other ways of knowing Gariwerd. Such is the power of planning's production of place through the technique of classification in a management hierarchy.

Gariwerd is brought to the protected area system as a particular modality of 'nature', but the classification of nature also requires the classification of culture that works as an Othering of the natural. Cultures are made visible by being different from nature. The plan of management is divided into a set of five strategies, the first two of which are strategies for natural values and cultural values respectively. Under natural values, strategies include minimizing erosion, conserving water catchments and protecting habitat.

Strategies for cultural values are broken into three areas: 'Indigenous cultural heritage', 'Brambuk: The National Park and Cultural Centre', and 'Post–settlement cultural heritage'. Indigenous interests clearly feature prominently in this plan of management – identified as both 'heritage' and also as 'contemporary' in the context of the Brambuk cultural centre. Indigenous presences in Gariwerd, then, are constructed temporally: as pre–historic with implications for modern management (cultural heritage – a theme discussed in greater detail in Chapter 5), and as post–contact. This temporal placement of Indigeneity in Gariwerd is complicated by two modes of constructing Indigenous culture: as an extension of nature, and as cultures that 'know Nature differently' (Jacobs 1996, 136).

An Indigenous presence in Gariwerd has long been acknowledged, but as a pre–historic extension of the natural realm. A further point of justification the LCC saw as relevant for recommending Gariwerd be classified as a national park was the existence of Indigenous rock art sites within the ranges. Rock art in Gariwerd has been sketched, analysed and tested over many years (Coutts and Lorblanchet 1982; Gunn 1983a, 1983b and 1984). Specialist archaeologists have focused on their unique characteristics in comparison with other rock art in Victoria, use of colour and motif, size, placement, and antiquity. Much of the day to day work of park rangers and management staff in Gariwerd is concerned with the protection of rock art paintings from vandalism, fire and other natural processes of degradation, whilst also keeping them available to the public for visitation, much like any other natural feature (see Figure 4.1). Park management structures include a Rock Art Sites Committee, made up of representatives from Indigenous communities, the regional Indigenous cultural heritage programme, Parks Victoria, locally–based archaeologists and AAV, to advise park managers on rock art site protection and management.

Figure 4.1 Gariwerd rock art

Rock art paintings feature prominently on Gariwerd's tourist maps and information brochures as a key visitor attraction, one amongst many visitor attractions including wildflower displays and spectacular vistas across the ranges and valleys. Rock art sites become a feature listed along with other natural features to perform the spectacle of Gariwerd.

Indigenous interests in Gariwerd are positioned in the planning framework as a type of cultural approach to nature. There is now an explicit recognition of Indigenous knowledge as applied to particular 'natural resource' management issues. The current plan of management sets out to consult and engage with Indigenous peoples on a range of management issues such as cultural heritage, commercial tourism, flora and fauna conservation, and controlled burning (see also Chapter 6). Indigenous cultures, then, are positioned as knowing nature differently and this key planning instrument constructs a method of drawing that knowledge into its own domain, to enhance already existing management efforts toward nature conservation. Non–Indigenous presences in the Park are also made visible through an emphasis on 'post–settlement heritage sites'. These are particular monuments or locations where a specifically European culture can be identified, since Major Mitchell's 'opening up' of the western plains of Victoria through his 1836 survey.

In these ways, Gariwerd's key planning instrument practices spatial culture by dividing natures and cultures. Then it scales cultured bodies by placing cultures and natures in formation with each other, so that Indigenous cultures come to be visible as differently oriented to nature and nature knowledge, and contemporary non–Indigenous cultures become invisible. Indigenous claims for a greater role in the management of protected areas has given rise to a body of literature documenting the nature and usefulness of what has become known as 'traditional ecological knowledge' (see Inglis 1993; Daniels and Vencatesan 1995; Langton 1998; Fourmile 1999; Laird 2000). This knowledge arises from the cultural practices and lifeways of distinct Indigenous groups, and is increasingly being incorporated alongside scientific knowledge to enhance the management of protected areas. It is positioned as absolutely different from scientific knowledge in its origins, practices and sometimes outcomes (see Lewis 1989). Yet this incorporation is also deeply problematic, because it reduces the act to a technical problem of combining two 'datasets' in a framework that remains unchanged (Nadasdy 1999). The act of incorporation is a facsimile of power, a method of drawing into the domain of scientific experts a realm of knowledge positioned as radically different from, but nevertheless useful to, ecological science. Once 'incorporation' has occurred, scientists become 'qualified' to 'use' traditional ecological knowledge because of their new-found expertise in its practices (ibid). Traditional ecological knowledge is contained in western scientific discourse as one more (neutral) layer of information to be pressed into the service of environmental management ends.

The production and emplacement of Gariwerd within a system of spatial hierarchy renders it legible in certain kinds of ways for planning knowledge and action. This is not innocent and can result in a foreclosure on what can legitimately be construed as natural or cultural in park management terms, and how planning decisions with regard to natural and cultural values are enacted. Here, the park can be produced either as beautiful wilderness, or as cultural artefact made available through the presence of material evidence of 'past Indigenous occupation'. Separating natures and cultures was evident within the institutional structure of the Halls Gap regional office of Parks Victoria. A 'Cultural and Historical Team' was responsible for managing Indigenous and European heritage, an 'Environment Team' was responsible for managing the natural values of Gariwerd, and an 'Assets Team' managed key facilities and utilities. There were also teams responsible for visitor services (the largest number of staff are allocated in this area), capital works and education.

Identifying and knowing 'culture' in Gariwerd's planning frameworks is about those things identifiably Indigenous, as well as places significant to European history in the region. It is the Indigenous 'heritage' of Gariwerd that proves, however, the more important story in the performance of culture in the planning framework. As part of its recommendations for Gariwerd to be declared a national park, the LCC pointed to the existence of the large number of Indigenous rock art sites occurring within the ranges. Here, 'culture' becomes part of the nature/culture equation: but it is culture performed as a particular kind of nature. This is where the Gariwerd story is interesting in its own peculiar nature/culture split. As I will show in the following sections, planning and management talk in Gariwerd produces the nature/culture split in a way that allows a certain level of interaction between the two poles when culture is either Indigenous or the heritage of European occupation. In other words, planning and management talk in Gariwerd produces a particular kind of culture in the nature/culture equation.

Two stories highlight where this nature/culture split is performed by state-based environmental planning. Firstly, enfolding the identification of culture (always Indigenous) within the consumption of visitor and tourist services in Gariwerd, and the associated naming of the park and places within it. Secondly, in (post)colonial politics about appropriate use of those resources designated natural within the state–based planning framework: a highly contested domain with Indigenous people, who assert rights to utilize those resources as part of their traditional owner status. The next two sections look specifically at these exemplifications.

Tourism and the Commodification of Culture

Gariwerd is the third most visited National Park in Victoria after Mornington Peninsula and Port Campbell, and attracts over 800,000 visitors each year, mostly from within Victoria and South Australia, and especially from Melbourne. Tourism in the region has been estimated to generate approximately $AUD100 million per annum to the state's economy (Parks Victoria 2003, 4). Given this, the park is considered to be 'high profile' in the Victorian context, and is often described as the 'Kakadu of the South' (pers. comm. Parks Victoria Project Officer), giving further weight to its iconic status in the Victorian tourism industry. A consultancy report commissioned by Parks Victoria to look at interpretation of the park noted that Gariwerd receives higher visitation rates than Uluru and Kakadu, generating a value of national and international significance because of its role 'in encouraging appreciation, enjoyment and appropriate use of national parks and appreciation of natural and cultural values in Australia generally' (Pizzey 1994, iii).

If you visited Gariwerd, you might pick up a brochure from the National Parks Visitors Centre, which would describe Gariwerd to you in the following way: 'Renowned for rugged mountain ranges and spectacular wildflower displays, this national park is one of Victoria's finest. The park is home to a rich and diverse range of plants and animals, and has important cultural heritage' (Parks Victoria 2001, 1). Thus, one of the key tourist drawcards for Gariwerd is Indigenous heritage. In the early 1990s, the Victorian Tourism Commission specifically targeted the Grampians for interstate and international cultural tourism promotion. The 1994 interpretation plan stated 'With the sites themselves and the Brambuk Cultural Centre in Halls Gap, the Park provides one of the best opportunities in the State to increase awareness and understanding of Aboriginal heritage' (ibid, 64).

The cultural heritage values for which Gariwerd is so highly regarded are predominantly produced within state–based tourism and planning frameworks in the context of Indigenous rock art sites. Gariwerd is marketed as housing the largest concentration – over 60 per cent – of Indigenous rock art sites in Victoria (Parks Victoria 2003).

Proof of Indigenous heritage in Gariwerd is usually provided by antiquity (dating of occupation) as well as the prevalence of material evidence of occupation. Parks Victoria's current plan of management for Gariwerd states:

> The use of one site in the Victoria Range (Billawin Range) has been dated from 22,000 years ago. Recent archaeological investigations have demonstrated that there was intensive Aboriginal occupation of Grampians–Gariwerd. The draining of Lake Wartook in 1997 for maintenance works exposed 32 sites around the margin of what was once a swampy basin…These sites included: Thirteen grind stones; two grinding patches; eleven piles of hearth stones; anvils for flaking quartz pebbles; and dense scatters of waste flakes. The park also contains a range of other known places and archaeological sites of particular significance to the Indigenous community. These include sites associated with rock shelters, quarries, mounds, surface scatters and scarred trees. (Parks Victoria 2003, 22)

Tourist and visitor services are provided for in park planning and management through three strategies: interpretation, education and information. Parks Victoria defines its management of parks as including a primary role of interpreting park landscapes for the visitor in order to communicate 'ideas, feelings and values to help people enrich their understanding of natural and cultural values, to foster positive attitudes towards the conservation of natural areas (particularly parks) and to increase awareness of the relationship between people and the natural environment' (Parks Victoria 2003). Thus, park 'interpretation' is about telling particular kinds of stories about the unique features of a place. Stories about both 'nature' and 'culture' feature as key tourism and interpretation themes, and both natural and cultural values of the park are the subject of interpretive material in different parts of Gariwerd. The current plan of management, for example, nominates designated 'interpretation sites' in Gariwerd, where there is some form of service, signage or guidance provided to the visitor (Parks Victoria 2003). These are listed in the plan in terms of their dominant features and use, for example:

- Zumsteins (kangaroo–viewing);
- MacKenzie Falls (spectacular waterfalls);
- Gulgurn Manja, Ngamadjidj and Billimina rock art shelters (Aboriginal rock art);
- Victoria Valley and the Wonderland precinct (mountains, valleys, diverse flora and fauna).

(Parks Victoria 2003)

Each of these moments in the production of Gariwerd as a place for tourists to visit powerfully constructs the designation of what is natural and what is cultural. It thereby powerfully constructs the legitimate *location* of Indigenous interests in state–based planning and tourist management actions. Gariwerd is produced as a cultural landscape by quantifying the number and antiquity of its 'rich concentration' of Indigenous rock art sites, which themselves become listed as a peculiar version of the spectacular natural features for which Gariwerd is revered. Thus, rock art sites are listed as one of many other 'natural' features, but are designated as a peculiar cultural turn on those natural features. They are presented as static artifacts representing a prehistoric occupation of Gariwerd in the time before colonial contact, and are managed to preserve the authenticity of their antiquity and the availability of that authenticity to the visitor.

Naming Gariwerd: (Post)colonial Contest I

(Post)colonial politics surrounding tourism services in Gariwerd also circulate around the naming of the park and its features. In 1989, then Victorian Minister for Tourism, Steve Crabb, proposed to 'restore' Indigenous place names in the park and especially the name of the park itself: from The Grampians (the name Mitchell had given the ranges) to Gariwerd, its accepted Indigenous name. Research was commissioned to determine traditional names and how they should be applied, finding that there were 31 Indigenous place names currently in use that should be retained (though some required changes to spelling); that nine rock art sites, a further 11 then 'un–named' features, and a further 44 other features have Indigenous names adopted (Clark and Harradine 1990, 7). Crabb was resoundingly criticised by local Indigenous people for his lack of consultation with them before announcing the proposal. Indigenous historian Tony Birch, in an article outlining the controversy, points out that an Indigenous tourism survey was conducted in 1988, in addition to reports from a well–known archaeologist on the importance of the rock art sites in the park, had 'alerted the tourism commission to the possibility of exploiting the region's Koori culture and history'. Crabb wanted to market Gariwerd as 'Victoria's Kakadu' (Birch 1997, 13–15).

The proposal also created a furore within the non–Indigenous community. The Victorian Place Names Committee received many protests from local government, concerned residents, and tourist operators, and even a petition with 60,000 signatures. Some of the names proposed for change were those now considered to be highly inappropriate and derogatory toward Indigenous people: 'Mt Lubra', 'The Picanninny' and so on. There was strong sentiment expressed from local (non–Indigenous) people that such names were not in fact offensive, and some even attributed their use to Indigenous people (Birch 1997, 16–17).

In the end, it was decided to 'restore' a total of 49 Indigenous place names by placing them in parentheses after the English name for the feature. The park remains officially gazetted as The Grampians, but increasingly the hyphenated name Grampians–Gariwerd is adopted. Birch argues that this thoroughly undermined Indigenous languages because they became 'linguistically subordinated, "handcuffed" in parentheses' (ibid, 27). Further, he discusses the idea of 'restoration' of names, as a means of 'returning' to some kind of 'former' past designated by 'former' names for places. Such an approach relegates Indigenous peoples to pre–history, the Aborigines were before, but not now. Thus, to acknowledge a place to be Indigenous land is to 'return' to a former time, or a former understanding, rather than understanding how that concept is now constructed in (post)colonial Australia (Birch 1997).

At a meeting in May 2002 of Parks Victoria management staff with Indigenous native title claimants and community representatives regarding the development of the new plan of management for Gariwerd, Indigenous participants expressed a strong desire to encourage use of the name 'Gariwerd' instead of 'the Grampians'. On this issue, however, Parks Victoria staff were reluctant to budge outside the legal definition of the park in the *National Parks Act 1975 (Vic)*. For state–based planners, the park is gazzetted as the Grampians National Park, and therefore this is how it must be identified. But further, the park is known in wider, tourist circles as 'the Grampians'. This becomes the marketing 'hook' for the place itself, drawing visitor numbers. The achievements of colonization are realized when places are settled through their naming and mapping, becoming recognizable on the grid of cartographic relations (Carter 1987). Gariwerd is an unknown place in the public mind, a place that does not invite visitation by virtue of its name. But 'the Grampians' is known, safe, settled, and available to the public for exploration and experience. The new plan of management for the park was thus given its official title as the *Grampians National Park Management Plan*.

However, within the text of the plan itself, and within both Indigenous and non–Indigenous talk about the place, are buried myriad slippages about naming in Gariwerd. These raise a series of questions about how Gariwerd continues to be constructed in the non–Indigenous planning mind as a place once Indigenous, but now natural with some cultural features of interest to tourists. One of the cultural officers at Brambuk joyfully informed me during an interview that 'when they [Parks Victoria] do a sign and things like that well its got to be Gariwerd–Grampians now, not the Grampians–Gariwerd…its Gariwerd–Grampians now.'

Yet the Project Officer responsible for the integration of Brambuk and the National Park Visitors Centre clarified Parks Victoria's perspective on the name of the park:

> [its still called] Grampians National Park…On this [integration] project, on this site [the NPVC], our aim is to use Indigenous words, alongside European ones. And that's something we need to resolve, but from Parks Victoria's perspective this is still the Grampians National Park. But from Brambuk's perspective, it's Gariwerd.

This 'split identity' – knowing the place literally in two ways – forms a productive tension between Indigenous communities and park planners, which has created enough space to allow park planners to grant some concessions on this point, and sometimes use the name Gariwerd within the management plan text, but to do so in ways that discursively reproduce the designation of natural and cultural values, and thus powerfully inscribe where Indigenous interests might be legitimately inserted into the planning canon.

Any reference to an environmental management European heritage issue in the plan of management utilizes the park's officially gazzetted name 'the Grampians'. When issues of an 'Indigenous' nature are discussed in the plan, including around cultural heritage management or about Brambuk, the park is identified as 'Grampians–Gariwerd'. For example, the Introductory chapter to the plan sets out past land use, beginning with: 'The Indigenous Nations associated with the Grampians–Gariwerd inhabited a rich and diverse land. Gariwerd provided rock shelters, stone quarries for tool making, ample timber for cooking and warmth, and extensive forests...'. Further into the text, different kinds of 'European' uses of the park are described: 'Livestock grazing in the park dates back to the mid 1800s. After 1938 grazing was not permitted in the central area of the Grampians...' (Parks Victoria 2003, 5–6). Table 4.2 shows how the split identity of the park as Gariwerd/the Grampians is performed through the two sections of the plan of management designating natural values and cultural values management in the park. I have emphasized the nomenclature used.

Table 4.2   Naming in Gariwerd: A case of split identity?

Strategies for Natural Values Conservation	Strategies for Cultural Values Conservation
The sediments which make up *the Grampians* were deposited about 400 million years ago and are approximately 3,700 m deep (13)	Recent archaeological investigations have demonstrated that there was intensive Aboriginal occupation of *Grampians–Gariwerd*... (22)
The high–quality water harvested from *the Grampians* is of fundamental importance to the economy of western Victoria (13)	Develop a *Gariwerd/Grampians* Aboriginal Cultural Heritage Strategy for protecting, conserving and promoting an understanding of Aboriginal tradition... (23)
Several species are at the limits of their range in *the Grampians*. The Mountain Grey Gum and Victorian Christmas–bush are at their westernmost limit... (15)	
The Grampians wetlands, particularly those in the south of the park, support a diverse community of waterbirds... (16)	

Source: Parks Victoria 2003.

It is entirely appropriate, of course, that when speaking about Indigenous associations and interests in the park, the name Gariwerd is used. I am interested, however, in why this is not applied elsewhere in the document, and argue that this discursive practice powerfully produces the nature/culture split that has underpinned dominant environmental management discourse in Australia. It seems that the place can be literally named differently depending on whether the subject is deemed 'natural' or 'cultural'.

This particular tactic performs a split between the 'real' park and its other identity: the one still partly lying in the shadows of dominant environmental management discourses. Amongst this criticism, however, is a sense of the possibilities that the politics of naming in Gariwerd is now able to highlight. The battles about naming fought in the late 1980s and early 1990s have ultimately brought some hard–won gains, despite trenchant (and continuing) opposition. Naming is opening up 'new territories' for dialogue between state–based planners and Indigenous communities in Gariwerd, that are just now beginning to translate into a more optimistic (post)colonial politics (Jacobs 1996).

Using Gariwerd: (Post)colonial Contest II

Indigenous peoples in Gariwerd use 'park resources' regularly through hunting, gathering and fishing practices. Under the provisions of the *National Parks Act 1975 (Vic)*, however, it is a criminal offence to take any kind of natural resource from a park. Destruction or killing of wildlife is expressly forbidden under this Act, because, as the then DNRE's Senior Policy Officer for national parks explained:

> the major objective of [the *National Parks Act*] is the protection of indigenous flora and fauna and it doesn't have any ability for the Secretary or the Minister to [allow anyone to] hunt and destroy wildlife unless it's required for the management and care and protection of that park such as they might be dangerous or [because of] population explosion or various other management reasons. (pers. comm. 12 March 2003)

Further, the provisions of the *Wildlife Act 1975 (Vic)* also make it an offence to kill or destroy wildlife on public lands, without a permit. This Act was amended in the early 1990s to enable permits to be issued free of charge for the taking of wildlife for cultural purposes, on Crown lands outside National Parks (pers. comm. Senior Policy Officer, DNRE, 12 March 2003). Victoria remains the only state in Australia where Indigenous people still require a fishing licence to fish in their traditional waters (pers. comm. Manager Indigenous Programmes, Parks Victoria, 12 September 2002).

Indigenous peoples with interests in Gariwerd, both traditional and historical, have continually used Gariwerd's resources since colonization. A Wotjobaluk native title holder for the region adjacent to Gariwerd describes Wotjobaluk aspirations for having those practices properly recognized, and how Parks Victoria has historically responded to this:

> One of the things that we've been talking about is that we would like…to be able to go into the park area and sustain some of our culture. And that is in the way of camping, fishing, hunting, and gathering. So, that has been a new concept to [Parks Victoria] and they would probably have to change legislation. And we're saying, well hang on our people have been doing this for x amount of

years...they've been sneaking into these areas...we don't want to sneak in there anymore. (pers. comm. 15 July 2002)

That Indigenous practices currently constitute a criminal offence under modern Australian planning statute means that Indigenous custodians are forced to practice their customs furtively, always hoping they are not caught by Parks Victoria rangers, who have the power to prosecute. Indigenous people with interests in Gariwerd regularly represent their aspirations to undertake these practices based on a recognition of their right to openly do so as traditional owners, to park management staff. One Parks Victoria senior executive describes his feeling about the 'awkward position' he sees this puts Parks Victoria staff in:

> Some communities that we go to are adamant that they'll do it [hunt] anyway, and that puts [Parks Victoria] officers in an awkward position...[because we have] to say that's the law, we can't just flaunt it, so if you're out there then we're going to have to do the right thing [and prosecute]. (pers. comm. 12 September 2002)

By way of response to this predicament, he comes up with the following solution to get around the problem of legislative compliance:

> What we've got to do is say well at the moment under the Act, it's not allowable, not a permissible thing. We've heard what you've said, we'll take that on board, but we can't guarantee anything will change. But in the meantime we'll look at your aspiration [that you] want to be able to take kangaroos four times a year [for example] for ceremonies. Alright, well under the Wildlife Act, the Chief Executive can provide a permit for that, but it has to be out in State Forest, or some other Crown Land. Or [it] could be part of a permit on private land because they've got a problem with the [kanga]roos overgrazing or something like that.

Ridiculous, according to the Wotjobaluk people:

> I laugh at Parks Victoria [when] I say [to them] 'I'd like to go out and shoot a [kanga]roo'. But [they say] 'you can't do it on Parks ground'. Oh, okay, so if I get a road kill then I can take it into [the] Park? 'Yeah you can'. So, [we have] this joke that we herd all these roos out [of the park] and then we shoot one and take it back in! They're really, really skeptical about those sorts of things. (pers. comm. 15 July 2002)

Hunting practices and their sustainability are the subject of considerable debate. There are now many cases where Indigenous traditional owners have developed management plans for the sustainable use of particular natural resources (for example, the Hope Vale community in far north Queensland's Turtle and Dugong Hunting Management Plan). In the wider non–Indigenous community, however, there exist strong objections to traditional hunting practices. One survey in northern Queensland found that visitors to national parks overwhelmingly opposed Indigenous hunting practices in those parks because this contravened principles of equity and justice (why should one group be allowed to hunt and not others), and that Indigenous peoples were no longer traditional and therefore should not be allowed to undertake such practices (see Marsh 2003).

Indigenous rights, especially those asserted as native title rights, to hunt and destroy fauna were tested in the Australian court system in the case of *Yanner v Eaton [1999] HCA 53 (7 October 1999)*. Here, an Indigenous man was prosecuted under Queensland law for killing two estuarine crocodiles. His defence was that he was exercising his native title rights and that the licence provisions of the relevant Queensland statute did not apply to him. His defence was upheld by the High Court after a series of appeals through the court system, who found in the majority that the meaning of the Queensland statute vesting all fauna on public lands in Queensland as property of the Crown could only be interpreted as the 'aggregate of the various rights of control', rather than the ordinary meaning of property as absolute ownership (see Hiley 2001). Thus, the High Court had found, in this case, in favour of traditional hunting rights for Indigenous traditional owners. The recognition of native title may mean that governments might be unwilling to take action against Indigenous people undertaking particular hunting practices that are in contravention of Australian statutes. Courts have in the past found in favour of Indigenous people and set precedents that may not necessarily be perceived to be in the individual State Government's interests.

Environmental planning and management knowledge assumes a linear connection between the observable elements of nature and our actions upon those elements: action x will lead to 'natural' outcome y. Conservation action is founded on the belief that the activities of park managers are distant from the nature they are acting upon. Indeed, conservation action is positioned as necessary for allowing and enhancing natural processes. There is little recognition that conservation action is a cultural activity. Indigenous cultural practices, by contrast, are seen as intrinsically 'cultural' yet don't have the scientific standing of western management action, and so cannot be sufficiently distanced from nature. Instead, they exemplify ways of 'being close' to nature or as cultures that 'know Nature differently' (Jacobs 1996, 136). This is clearly illustrated through contests about the use of 'nature' within protected areas between Indigenous peoples and park managers. Indigenous use of what are seen as 'park resources' by environmental planners and protected area managers, is a contested issue in many places.

In settler states, Indigenous use of 'natural' resources in protected areas remains 'uncommon ground' (Cronon 1995). The dominant view of protected areas as essentially pristine natural places, and human intervention as essentially destructive in its intent and outcome, is powerfully inscribed into the protected area management legislative framework in ways that foreclose on Indigenous rights to use park resources. The dominant discourse of environmental planning, and the power of its scientific knowledge base remains intact.

The Making of Nyah as a Forest

At another position on the protected area classificatory system, is a classification for those places that are the focus of natural resource extractive activities (Category VI), or what is termed 'sustainable use of natural ecosystems' (International Union for the Conservation of Nature 1994). Called different things in different places, in Victoria, Australia, this classification is known as State Forests. They are managed to achieve the objectives of natural conservation; protection of water catchments; provision of timber and other forest products on a sustainable basis; protection of landscape, archaeological and historic values; and provision of recreational and educational opportunities (Department of Sustainability and Environment 2003b).

Nyah, as discussed in Chapter 1, is a small state forest in northwestern Victoria. It was classified as a State Forest, or S2 zone, after recommendation by the LCC in 1989. Those recommendations pertained to a large area, known as the Mildura Forest Management Area, and nominated Nyah Forest as an important reserve for timber harvesting amongst a wider recommendation to classify lands elsewhere along the Murray River in a 'higher conservation status' known as the River Murray Reserve (Land Conservation Council 1989). The key strategic planning document governing Nyah's management is the Department of Sustainability and Environment's 2004 *Management Strategy for the Floodplain State Forest of the Mildura Forest Management Area*. The Strategy focuses on productive forest uses – predominantly timber harvesting – in the planning area. Under the heading 'scope and purpose', the Strategy notes that 'forests of this area provide a diverse range of natural and cultural values, and make an important contribution to the local economies and social wellbeing through forest production, recreation and tourism' (Department of Sustainability and Environment 2004, 1).

State Forests in Victoria are directly managed by the Department of Sustainability and Environment and primarily governed by the *Conservation, Forests and Lands Act 1987 (Vic)*, which establishes a framework for management of public lands in Victoria. Like national parks, however, State forests are equally constructed for management action within a hierarchical web of national and international guidelines and policy. The National Forest Policy Statement (NFPS), released in 1992, was a joint intergovernmental response (by all State, Territory and Federal governments in Australia) to concerns about sustainable forest use. It binds all governments to achieve balance between the competing interests of commercial forestry production and nature conservation objectives.

What is a 'forest' in this sense, and how do particular places, such as Nyah, become classified in this way? The Commonwealth Government's policy defines a forest as

> an area, incorporating all living and non–living components, that is dominated by trees having usually a single stem and a mature or potentially mature stand height exceeding 2 metres and with existing or potential crown cover of overstorey strata about equal to or greater than 20%. (Commonwealth of Australia 1992)

In other words, a forest is defined by the characteristics of its trees. The NFPS takes this definitional uniformity one step further and differentiates between 'wood' and 'non-wood' values of forests. This contrasts with definitions of other types of protected areas, national parks for example, which tend to be defined in terms of the integrity of the network between all of the ecological component parts of those systems.

The discursive move in defining forests as forests is one implicated within the commercial imperative of timber production, a primary use of State Forests in Australia. In Victoria alone, timber harvesting is worth $AUD18 billion annually and provides around 19,500 jobs (Victorian Association of Forest Industries no date). Timber harvesting from public lands in Victoria is only permissible in State Forests (a considerable percentage of timber produced in Victoria comes from privately owned forests). Of the 8.8 million hectares of public land in Victoria, approximately 0.12 per cent of the public forest estate is available for timber harvesting (ibid). The proportion is higher if privately owned forests are included.

For places designated 'forests' the balance equation between competing public interests is already weighted towards the 'appropriate and desirable' use of forests for commercial resource harvesting (Commonwealth of Australia 1992, 7), qualified by sustainability directives. My interest here is not in the sustainability of logging in Australian forests, or anywhere else. What is important to my analysis is, instead, the discursive production of 'forest'. Reading this alongside the designation of Gariwerd, we will begin to see similar modalities of planning's spatial culture at work in bringing knowledge and action to bear on forests.

Approximately 5,300 hectares of the Mildura FMA is zoned available for redgum timber production, around 13 per cent of the total floodplain State Forest estate in the FMA (Department of Sustainability and Environment 2004, 33). In Nyah Forest itself, approximately 600 hectares is available for timber production. In the overall timber production context, then, Nyah is quite important, constituting almost a quarter of the available redgum in the State Forests of the FMA. The impact of timber harvesting within Nyah itself, however, is positioned by forest managers as limited to only two per cent of the total land area in the Forest, thus not constituting a threat to biodiversity or natural values. Consequently, Nyah is known in planning terms predominantly for its hardwood timber production value: a 'public interest' use of a natural feature and thus is constructed as nature with a value. Or rather trees with a value, as nature in the case of Nyah is defined by the physical characteristics of its trees.

This 'filling' of nature with trees also produces a discursive production of its 'other': culture. Indigenous interests concerning Nyah are visible at two junctures: as a management issue (cultural heritage site protection), and as a legal issue (native title). An overwhelming focus is on 'site protection', or the management of Indigenous cultural heritage. The existence of Indigenous cultural heritage values was the only mention of Nyah Forest in the LCC's recommendations for zoning of the land:

Sites of significance associated with Aboriginal culture of occupation throughout State Forest need to be identified and protected (their management should involve the local Aboriginal community). Among these are the sites associated with the spring line along the northern fringe of the Big Desert and the mounds and scarred trees along the riverine plain, in particular Nyah Forest. (Land Conservation Council 1989, 133)

In the context of timber harvesting, cultural heritage protection is the only acknowledged intersecting point between that extractive activity and Indigenous interests (that relationship is explored in more detail in Chapter 5). A legal disclaimer to native title in the Strategy acknowledges the existence of claims and adopts a 'minimum legislative compliance' approach. It states that the Strategy will 'ensure all future acts undertaken within State forests are done so in accordance with the provisions of the *Native Title Act 1993 (Cth)*' (Department of Sustainability and Environment 2004, 60).

It is the exchange value of Nyah's nature (its trees) that makes it visible to the state, and amenable to management action. The partial visibility of Nyah's nature is intertwined with its arbitrary emplacement within the protected area system as a space of differently valued nature. The achievement of that exchange value requires the inscription of culture within the same framework, in order to manage and settle the potential for disruption from Indigenous claims. Natures and cultures are seen separately, yet they stubbornly refuse to remain in this separated state as Indigenous claims for knowing Nyah differently continue to unsettle the realization of the exchange value of Nyah's trees. I will return to this particular (post)colonial contest in Chapter 5.

Forests are also the subject of a science being pressed into the service of exchange value. The NFPS explicitly states that 'management and use of forests must be based on a sound understanding of forest ecosystems and their associated values' (ibid, 14). It establishes the National Forest Inventory – a database of forest values and ecosystem characteristics – to achieve this. Victoria has also developed its own local form of this inventory, the Statewide Forest Resource Inventory (SFRI), defined as a 'process of keeping stock of what you own' (Department of Sustainability and Environment 2003b). Implied within this is an assessment of the value of that stock. To stocktake forests, scientists use aerial photographs and remote sensing to measure 'where forests are' in the Victorian landscape, that is to produce the forest estate in Victoria by naming it as such. This is known as 'stand mapping', described by DNRE as 'the art and science of examining...similarities and grouping the trees together in a logical and consistent manner' (Department of Sustainability and Environment 2003b).

Prescribing what counts as natural or cultural, and what constitutes a legitimate knowledge base about nature and culture in Nyah Forest is neither innocent nor without material effects. Where nature can be 'seen' is intimately bound up with who is legitimately able to recognize 'nature' and measure its import. In planning terms, things natural or cultural can be recognized, and knowledge about them legitimized, by a series of Western scientific discourses as shown in Table 4.3.

Table 4.3   Western scientific knowledge base in Nyah

Discipline	Nyah
Ecology and Biology	'806 vascular plant species in the floodplain of the MFMA and…401 mammal species, 282 birds…' (University of Ballarat 1997, 16)
Cartography	'complete pre–1750 mapping of ecological vegetation classes for the FMA' (Department of Sustainability and Environment 2004, 11)
Ornithology	'Identify Regent Parrot nesting colonies and individual nest trees' (Department of Sustainability and Environment 2004, 21)
Hydrology	'Appropriate watering regimes for all floodplain communities are addressed for forest areas through the preparation and implementation of water management strategies' (Department of Sustainability and Environment 2004, 29)
Zoology	'The Inland Carpet Python is a slow–moving, nocturnal snake that has an average adult length of 170 to 190cm…' (Department of Sustainability and Environment 2003a)

In the next section, I recount how the carpet python became a momentary symbol of the struggle over identity and the legitimacy of knowledge and action in Nyah Forest.

Who Can See a Carpet Python?

Carpet Pythons are a non–poisonous snake that prefers a habitat of woody debris on forest floors, particularly in the redgum forests of northwestern Victoria. They are listed as 'threatened taxa' under the *Flora and Fauna Guarantee Act 1988 (Vic)* (Department of Sustainability and Environment 2003c) and have been spotted from time to time in Nyah Forest. Many local people have campaigned for some years for greater protection of the carpet python, particularly in Nyah Forest, as a primary threat to their habitat is logging. At the 2000 Swan Hill Red Gum Festival, the FONVF group marched a huge imitation carpet python through the streets of the regional city of Swan Hill to raise awareness about the creature and its endangered status.

The planning and management Strategy for the region lists the Inland Carpet Python as one of a number of threatened or rare species that is known to occur in the Mildura Forest Management Area (Department of Sustainability and Environment 2004). It determined that five areas within the State Forests of the Mildura FMA would be designated as 'State Forest Special Protection Zones', once an Action Statement for the carpet python was released, under the *Flora and Fauna Guarantee Act 1988 (Vic)*. These zones would preclude commercial firewood collection and timber harvesting, in order to 'protect quality habitat for a regional population of at least 200 adult pythons' (Department of Sustainability and Environment 2004, 18). However, the Strategy qualified the selection of those Special Protection Zones: 'the timber resource implications of the additional reserves will be considered in selecting areas for reservation. Subject to the provision of adequate habitat for the Carpet Python, *options that minimise timber resource costs will be preferred* (ibid, 19, my emphasis).

The DNRE has prepared an Action Statement for the Inland Carpet Python. The Statement identifies a key threat to the survival of those remaining python as the removal of large hollow–bearing trees, logs and other coarse forest–floor litter, which provides important shelter and breeding habitat for pythons. Timber harvesting is cited in the Action Statement as one activity that directly produces this threat to carpet pythons (Department of Sustainability and Environment 2003c).

As a result of the power of Nyah Forest's designation as 'available for timber harvesting', and its location nearby to the major township of Swan Hill, DNRE has not included Nyah Forest in its Special Protection Zone for the carpet python, declaring that no carpet pythons are located in Nyah Forest. This is despite evidence from the Wadi Wadi traditional owner group about the significant sighting of a carpet python. In early 2002, the Wadi Wadi people hosted a 'Spiritual Unity Gathering' in Nyah Forest where Indigenous Elders from across the world met in Nyah Forest. During this event, a carpet python was sighted near the ceremonial fire site. The sacred fire was the centrepiece of the Gathering, where people met to talk and learn, and ceremonial business was conducted (both for the Gathering 'public' and the privately conducted business of Indigenous Elders). Further, the sacred fire site remains of importance both to Wadi Wadi traditional owners and others in the regional Indigenous community. The sacred fire is constantly cared for with great reverence as people pass through the Forest. The site is kept clean of rubbish, is regularly relit and thus the area smoked according to cultural protocol, and simply visited by people to reaffirm their presence at this place. That the carpet python was sighted at this particular place is of great significance to both Wadi Wadi and other people. It was considered to be a sign of approval for both the Gathering and wider land management activities undertaken in the Forest by ancestral spirits. DNRE's conceptualization of which spaces are suitable for protection of the carpet python precludes discussion of the importance of carpet python to Wadi Wadi people, and in particularly the contemporary cultural significance of its sighting near the sacred fire.

Man and the Biosphere at Clayoquot Sound

Clayoquot Sound is an archipelago of islands on the west coast of Canada. It was designated a UNESCO Biosphere Reserve in 2000 after a long struggle involving First Nations peoples, environmentalists and logging companies in the region. UNESCO's Man and the Biosphere Programme is a research and capacity building effort toward improving the relationship between people and their environments. Established in 1970, it has developed a global network of biosphere reserves. The programme has a much more explicit integration of human and non–human elements than the protected area estate system. Yet underpinning the criteria for designation as a biosphere reserve is a requirement that an area 'encompass a mosaic of ecological systems representative of major biogeographic regions, including a gradation of human intervention' (Clayoquot Sound Biosphere Nomination 1999, 3). Some areas, then, can be identified as more natural than others by virtue of the extent to which human activities have intervened.

The reserve is described, for the purposes of nomination for designation, in a series of ways that both perform and unsettle the nature/culture split. The human population is measured through a census count. The significance of the Indigenous population in numerical terms is noted. Then 'biological characteristics' of the reserve are provided, supported by a biogeoclimatic and habitat map. Different natural things are recorded: western hemlock trees, verterbrate species, proportions of dead biomass providing habitat, numbers of gray whales. The report discusses, in turn, a series of natural processes in each type of habitat zone, and a series of human impacts on these natural things: clear cut logging, over–fishing, marine transportation and oil spills.

The designation of Clayoquot Sound as a biosphere reserve rests on *both* its distinctive natural and cultural features with a distinct hierarchy within the reserve operating between those places least interrupted by human activity, such as those that remain 'untouched by logging' (Clayoquot Sound Biosphere Nomination 1999, 3) and those places most transformed, for example human settlements. This in part reflects the requirements of the nomination criteria set by UNESCO to be considered under the 'Man and the Biosphere' programme.

Seeing Clayoquot Sound in this diverse way has been the outcome of a long struggle. Much of the area was previously public forest and open, through licencing by the provincial government, to logging and other resource extraction activities. In the postwar period, the provincial government of British Columbia granted long–term timber licenses that assured private timber companies of virtually perpetual clear–fell logging in public forests of the province (Carrick 1999, 181). It was in 1984 that a major dispute arose when MacMillan Bloedel, the province's biggest forestry company, sought to commercially log Meares Island in Clayoquot Sound. In response, the Clayoquot Band Council declared the island a tribal park and claimed title to the island (see Chapter 1), forcing a stay in the company's logging plans. What ensued was a series of events, ongoing disputes, negotiations and coalitions culminating in the BC government ending clear–fell logging in Clayoquot Sound in 1995. A significant moment in that decision–making process was a report of the Clayoquot Sound Scientific Panel acknowledging Indigenous interests as integral to the region, and noting the inadequacy of existing arrangements in recognizing First Nations values (see Carrick 1999, 195).

This dispute was hugely significant for the global environmental movement, and for movements in Indigenous sovereignty and land rights (Magnusson 2003; Carrick 1999; Willems–Braun 1997). Initiatives to nominate the area as a Biosphere Reserve arose from the dispute, and included representatives of all the First Nations on working groups to develop the proposal. Half of the Board of Directors of the Clayoquot Biosphere Trust are First Nations representatives and the rights and knowledge of First Nations groups are very prominent within the Trust itself and the wider set of activities that circulate around the Reserve.

The governance arrangements for the Clayoquot Biosphere Reserve are complex and multi–scalar. The Clayoquot Biosphere Trust is funded by the Canadian Federal Government and facilitates and funds research education and training in relation to biosphere themes. It serves as a central administrative body, but has no planning or resource management responsibilities. In terms of management planning, the Reserve is constituted by a number of parks and reserves, each with their own individual management plans and guidelines, and a number of other negotiations and planning activities impact upon the Reserve including various First Nations management plan activities, and the Nuu–chah–nulth Treaty Framework Agreement. The Trust itself is governed by its Board, and a series of Committees which act in an advisory capacity to the Board. A range of committees have been established with terms of reference. One of these is the Culture Committee, which has defined 'culture' in a broad sense. It encapsulates arts and heritage, significant sites and places, sports and festivals. Yet it also incorporates 'natural history' with the ability to coordinate projects that cover a selection of nominated scientific disciplines including 'geology', 'botany' and 'zoology' (Clayoquot Biosphere Trust Cultural Advisory Committee, no date, 2). In a sense, it is a re–culturing of nature, a re–incorporation of characteristics of nature within a cultural frame.

Planning and land management within what is now the Clayoquot Sound Biosphere, however, remains within the existing protected area management system of Canada, BC specifically. This means that planning and management functions are retained within the various BC provincial government departments responsible for park management, forestry and land use planning. Each individual protected area within the Biosphere is managed through those existing structures and frameworks. One such protected area is the Strathcona Provincial Park. This is British Columbia's oldest declared park, and is considered significant because of its 'Wilderness Conservation Zone', which accounts for 75 per cent of the park area (BC Parks 2001, 2):

> Strathcona Park is the wilderness heart of Vancouver Island. It is part of a system of connected natural areas that conserves the biodiversity of the island and protects ecosystems which are representative of the natural environment of British Columbia. (BC Parks 2001, 4)

This classification and systematization of land as 'wilderness' makes invisible Indigenous agency in that very same place. As the Clayoquot Band Tribal Council declared in 1984 in their declaration of sovereignty over nearby Meares Island (see Chapter 1), those lands and waters remain the economic and social territorial base of the Nuu–chah–nulth regional tribes. In no way are they 'wilderness' in the sense of untouched, pristine nature.

Aoraki/Mt Cook and the Tōpuni of Ngāi Tahu

When Ngāi Tahu chiefs were party to the signing of the Treaty of Waitangi in Aoteoroa–New Zealand with the British Crown in 1840, some had suspicions about whether the British could be held to their promises (Te Runanga o Ngāi Tahu 2009). By 1849, those suspicions were confirmed as correct, as the Crown began defaulting on the Treaty itself and the specific terms of a series of major land sales that failed to include agreed provision for, and respect of, Ngāi Tahu peoples ownership of those lands (ibid). It was not until 1998, after a series of legal battles that began in 1849, that Ngāi Tahu have been formally recognized as the Maori owners of land, with appropriate mechanisms for partnership in land management, and compensation for economic loss since 1849. One of the significant elements of the settlement was the return of the sacred mountain Aoraki (known since colonization as Mt Cook) to the peoples of the Ngāi Tahu *iwi*,[2] who then 'gifted back' the mountain to the nation while retaining rights in management of the area. Aoraki sits within the Aoraki/Mt Cook National Park, a World Heritage listed area on Aoteoroa–New Zealand's South Island.

Prior to the Ngāi Tahu settlement, this place was known in planning terms as 'Mt Cook National Park' and was managed as one of Aoteoroa–New Zealand's pre–eminent tourist and climbing destinations (Aoraki is the country's tallest mountain) as well as a key ecosystem asset. The park was established in 1953 and together with other national parks in the region, declared a World Heritage area in 1986 (DOC 2004). Even with the passage of the *Conservation Act (1987)*, which gave a legislative commitment to co–management with *iwi*, the Park was still known and managed under European names and terms until well into the 1990s (Carr 2004). The current management plan, gazetted in 2004, declares the significance of the park as due to the

> cross–section of landforms and vegetation that extends from the South Island high country's braided riverbeds to the highest peaks of the Southern Alps/Ka Tiritiri o te Moana. It also includes New Zealand's highest mountain Aoraki/ Mount Cook, which is also highly significant to Ngāi Tahu as their most sacred mountain. (DOC 2004, 11)

The planning and management approach at Aoraki/Mt Cook has undergone a significant change since the Ngāi Tahu settlement. Previous plans, such as the 1989 management plan had mentioned 'Maori traditions' in the area and that Aoraki was significant to Maori people (Carr 2004), but there was little recognition beyond this and minimal attention paid to the history of dispossession in the area. A significant factor in the shift in management principles toward a much greater emphasis on the rights and values of the Ngāi Tahu *iwi* was the adoption of Ngāi Tahu law into mainstream Aoteoroa–New Zealand law through the recognition of Tōpuni. This concept,

---

2   Maori tribes.

derives from the traditional Ngāi Tahu tikanga (custom) of persons of rangatira (chiefly) status extending their mana and protection over a person or area by placing their cloak over them or it. In its new application, a Tōpuni confirms and places...an 'overlay' of Ngāi Tahu values on specific pieces of land managed by [the Department of Conservation]. A Tōpuni does not override or alter the existing status of the land (for example, National Park status), but ensures that Ngāi Tahu values are also recognised, acknowledged and provided for. (Te Runanga o Ngāi Tahu 2009, no pagination)

Aoraki is one of 14 significant places over which Tōpuni has been recognized, and this is formalized within the Aoraki/Mt Cook Management Plan of 2004 as one of a series of regulations with which the Department and the management plan must comply.

Formalizing Tōpuni allows the recognition of 'Taonga Species', which are those Indigenous plant and animal species that are listed in the Ngāi Tahu Deed of Settlement and exist within the Park boundaries. Taonga species are managed in consultation with Ngāi Tahu peoples and their special status is particularly acknowledged within the plan of management. In this case, then, the formal recognition of Maori ownership of lands has led to a substantial shift in management practices. The recognition of Taonga species and the formal inclusion of Tōpuni as a type of 'material consideration' in planning and management in the park, has led to a shift in the way natures and cultures are classified in the Aoraki/Mt Cook National Park. The document continues to construct 'pristine' nature for management purposes, yet this is consistently unsettled, within the text, by the presence of Ngāi Tahu values. This is best shown in the following extract, section 4.1.3 of the plan of management, which relates to the management of waterways in the Park:

4.1.3(b) [Objective]:
To manage the Park's waters and, in particular, the Aoraki Tōpuni area and the waters flowing from the area, so that as far as possible, the mauri of the waters for Ngāi Tahu is protected.

Explanation
4.1.3(a) – The attraction of Aoraki/Mount Cook National Park is in part dependent on the *pristine nature* of its snowfields, glaciers, rivers and streams. Every effort needs to be made to preserve that condition. Particular attention needs to be paid to Glencoe Stream and Black Birch Stream above the Village, as these streams provide the water supply for the Village...Maintaining the *natural state* cannot be absolute, as this would prevent a range of recreational activities and protection works for facilities, which are of benefit to public use and enjoyment of the Park...

4.1.3(b) – For Ngāi Tahu, the snow and ice on Aoraki and the surrounding tīpuna mountain and the waters that flow from them, have special significance, a mauri (see 1.3.2). Activities such as bathing or washing in the waters, waste water disposal, or defecating on the mountain, adversely affect Ngāi Tahu values. (DOC 2004, 50, my emphasis)

In this extract, rivers, snowfields, glaciers and streams are no longer only 'pristine nature', no longer only something to be preserved and marveled at, but also the social, economic, and cultural resources of a people.

Conclusion

A colonial order of space persists in the contemporary formulation of land regulation and management in settler states. In (post)colonial spatial cultures, space can be deemed either natural or cultural, named and measured through the canons of western science, and made legible to certain classificatory and regulatory structures. Nature and culture are separately (though always relationally) produced in certain places, and can be recognized in certain ways in modern environmental planning. The production of 'natural' and 'cultural' space shapes and limits where Indigenous interests can be recognized. The production of an externalized nature and an Othered (more natural) Indigene actively constructs those locations in state–based planning frameworks within which Indigenous 'inclusion' is deemed justifiable. These locations are themselves informed by the (post)colonial imagination of Indigenous subject selves as traditional and in their traditionality, closer to nature. Indigenous interests are rendered legible in state terms so that traditional knowledge, cultural heritage, and joint management are reified as appropriate subjects with which to engage Indigenous people. The colonial cultural roots of contemporary state–based planning frameworks and actions are hidden from view and the veneer of instrumental decision–making, of rationality acting in the service of the public, of policy informed by proper science, remains intact. That powerful performative work of planning – of deciding what counts as nature and what counts as culture – both constrains and produces possibilities for Indigenous presence and power.

Chapter 5
Managing the Sacred

...a claim for a sacred site...these days is nothing less than a modern phenomenon; the relationship between Aboriginal sacredness and modernity may be more intimate than first might be imagined.

(Gelder and Jacobs 1998, 1)

Indigenous claims about the presence of the sacred in settler, secular states 'shake the nation' (Gelder and Jacobs 1998, 21). Places that were once known, ordered, settled suddenly look different, have different qualities, ones that are unknown (sometimes secret) and unquantifiable. But they are desired. The international images of places like Canada, Aoteoroa–New Zealand and Australia are built on the tourist drawcard of ancientness and authenticity. The Indigenous sacred is re–invented as a form of national identity, even while it is shunned and denigrated.

Indigenous claims for the presence of sacredness in particular places, usually because those places have become threatened in some way, brings to the fore differently constructed (Indigenous) spatial rationalities and practices. The appearance of the Waugul spirit, for example, at a site (known as the Swan Brewery site) marked for redevelopment in the Western Australian city of Perth challenged planning's way of knowing that same site. A plot of property, with a certain proximity to a river and Perth's city centre, with a certain land value (making it especially ripe for redevelopment) all of a sudden became something unfamiliar – the resting place of a spirit, knowledge about which was conveyed through intergenerational narrative (see Jacobs 1996).

It is this unsettling power of the Indigenous sacred, its unpredictable ability to make once–settled places and knowledges suddenly unfamiliar to dominant non–Indigenous cultures, which gives rise to the governmentality of cultural heritage management. Sacredness and its management manifestation as 'cultural heritage' has a peculiarly (post)colonial politics, because its existence arises out of the (post)colonial experience. Cultural heritage is constituted by a series of colonial essentialisms: primitiveness, authenticity, and cultural loss. The contested politics around these tropes both limits and shifts the recognition of Indigenous interests particularly in land management frameworks, as I will explore in this chapter. This is because cultural heritage becomes a dominant location within land management and planning frameworks where Indigenous interests in land are recognized. As I set out in Chapter 4, spaces and 'things' are deemed either cultural or natural in plans, and it is those that have a 'cultural' classification that are seen as open for legitimate Indigenous scrutiny and claim. Indigenous interests become literally visible to planning in relation to cultural artifacts and places of significance. Simultaneously, 'cultural heritage' becomes a planning issue, a 'thing' that planning must manage. Management of cultural heritage is one of the technologies by which the state attempts to redress those conflicts, and settle the sacred.

Yet cultural heritage also potentially represents a struggle about spatial ontologies: about how place exists and how it is known and given meaning through different spatial cultures. Cultural heritage plays a vital role in the strategic politics of Indigenous communities. In fact it is *because* of its reification as an appropriately Indigenous space in land management that Indigenous people find greater scope for the expression of rights, and sources of material change. In this sense, we might see cultural heritage, the management manifestation of the sacred, not only as a type of tactic of government (Smith 2001 and 2004) as I will discuss shortly, but also as a hybrid space of contested identities, memories and spatial rationalities. This chapter looks at the construction of cultural heritage as a particular site of governmental techniques, and at the politics of cultural heritage as a hybrid moment of contested spatial rationalities. In doing so, the chapter crosses many different places and contexts, but draws these together in a more detailed examination of the politics of cultural heritage and its governmentalities operating in Nyah Forest, Australia (published previously in Porter 2006b).

Cultural Heritage as Governmentality

Like roads, zones, trees, water and fauna, cultural heritage is an item on the management inventory for consideration, analysis, consultation and practice: it is an 'object of regulation' (Smith 2001, 97). This heritage might be Indigenous or non–Indigenous cultural heritage, my focus here will be on the particular manifestations of planning and spatial management techniques that relate to Indigenous cultural heritage.

Cultural heritage, seen through planning's construction of it as a land management issue, has an identifiable set of tangible, material characteristics. Similarly to a 'natural' feature, it can be identified by a set of characteristics, a series of 'things' around which knowledge and power coalesce. This is the type of state power that Foucault has termed governmentality (see Foucault 1991), which is constituted through a complex series of governmental apparatuses, forms of knowledge, and techniques of management and control 'which has as its target population, as its principal form of knowledge political economy, and as its essential technical means apparatuses of security' (Foucault 1991, 102). Such apparatuses, Foucault posits, are all of the procedures, tools, forms of calculation and analysis that generate and allow a governmentalized state to emerge and act. As Smith (2004; 2001) has shown, cultural heritage is one form of this kind of governmentality in modern settler states. Through cultural heritage management, 'culture' becomes imbued with the same kinds of governable possibilities as 'nature'. It occupies a specific place and time, is knowable through scientific method, can be categorized and classified according to certain kinds of features (and valued according to that classification), and can be managed through the application of standardized tools and techniques, the 'tactics of government' that Foucault observes. These particular tactics in cultural heritage management are constituted through the discipline of archaeology, as Smith (2004) has theorized. The combination of archaeology and the tactics of government around territory and people produce what we see as the field of cultural heritage management. In this way, cultural heritage becomes the object of regulation, archaeology the scientific foundation of knowing and making legible that object of regulation (see also King 1998), and a variety of mechanisms and tools to manage, protect and conserve that object of regulation become the daily practice of state agencies, groups and organizations in settler states.

In the US, cultural heritage protection is regulated principally through the *National Historic Preservation Act (1966)*, based on the principle that the 'historical and cultural foundations of the Nation should be preserved as a living part of our community life and development in order to give a sense of orientation to the American people' (*National Historic Preservation Act 1966* S1.b.2). Under this legislation, it is a function of the Secretary of the Interior to expand and maintain a National Register of Historic Places composed of districts, sites, buildings, structures, and objects significant in American history, architecture, archaeology, engineering, and culture (*National Historic Preservation Act 1966* s101.a.1.A).

Cultural heritage protection and management in Canada is the jurisdiction of the provinces, each of which have their own legislative and regulatory regimes for recognizing, classifying and protecting cultural heritage. In British Columbia, for example, this is achieved through the *Heritage Conservation Act (1996)*. The purpose of this legislation is to 'encourage and facilitate the protection and conservation of heritage property in British Columbia' (S2), and this is primarily through the identification and categorization of different cultural heritage objects, sites, buildings and structures on a provincial register (S3.1).

In Aoteoroa–New Zealand, cultural heritage protection has been governed since 1954 by the New Zealand Historic Places Trust Pouhere Taonga, with its functions prescribed by the *Historic Places Act (1993)*. This includes the maintenance of a register of historic places and object, although in Aoteoroa–New Zealand this register does not automatically bestow regulatory consequences or protection upon those objects or sites listed. Like Canada, the US and Australia, this legislation and government agency manages both Indigenous and non–Indigenous cultural heritage. The NZHPT has a specific Maori Heritage Council and Maori advisers based in its regions, to advise on the protection and management of Maori cultural heritage and also the tools and mechanisms for use in particular places. This especially relates to the protection and use of Maori marae.[1]

---

1   Marae are the sacred meeting places of Maori people, the basis of all community life, and the location of ceremonies, meetings and community life.

Cultural heritage management in Australia is in the jurisdiction of the States, each of which has its own legislative and regulatory structures, though they each take a similar kind of approach. Most states utilize a register system that lists cultural heritage properties (widely interpreted depending on the state jurisdiction) and then affords protection to those properties listed through a series of regulations and permit mechanisms.

This construction of cultural heritage is also powerfully shaped by colonial spatial cultures, and the separation of natures and cultures, as explored in Chapter 4. Decisions about what can be managed as an item of cultural heritage presupposes identifying things that can be classified as cultural differently from things that are deemed natural. 'Compartmentalising culture' (Jackson 2006) in this way is an act of power, because it enables authority over what can and cannot be considered valuable in environments and for whom. In relation to land and water management in the Daly River region of northern Australia, Jackson (2006) shows how culture and cultural heritage management in particular is used to obscure Indigenous interests in 'other' categories like economic, social or environmental. In this case, a community–based reference group (that included significant Indigenous representation) was established to prepare a strategic plan for the Daly river catchment area. Four value 'types' were defined by the reference group – economic, social, cultural and environmental. Cultural values were defined as 'Indigenous', whereas social values were those (cultural) attributes that belonged to non–Indigenous communities. An Indigenous Values Subcommittee was established to look specifically at cultural values and report back to the reference group. Culture was compartmentalized in the material practices of the reference group, in the planning process itself. As Jackson (2006) reports, there was a total failure to recognize the implications of the plan for Indigenous economies, and an absolute reliance only on Western scientific knowledge to prepare the 'environmental' part of the plan. Indigenous interests were entirely limited to 'culture', itself defined as those characteristic tangible moments where an authentically Indigenous use could be seen in the landscape, complete with its archaeological and anthropological record.

This works as a strategic limitation on Indigenous rights, a peculiarly (post)colonial form of re–settling the same place over again, because it legitimates where Indigenous interests can be recognized. Contests between sacred sites and modern development proposals or use in settler states around the world are always predicated on wider Indigenous rights claims than 'merely' cultural heritage. They are fundamentally contests about the recognition of sovereignty and Indigenous law, recognition of land ownership, and the effective functioning of customary economies and societies. Many of these conflicts have been high–profile and came to occupy the central focus of national governments in their resolution of what might at first glance appear to be localized issues.

A good example of this is the eruption of controversy around mining at Guratba (Coronation Hill) in northern Australia. The hill itself is part of a wider complex of places situated on the upper South Alligator River in the province now known a

Australia's Northern Territory. It is the traditional lands of the Jawoyn people, and is known as Guratba in Jawoyn language (Gelder and Jacobs 1998, 66). An area of around 250 square kilometres was registered by the Aboriginal Sacred Sites Protection Authority, because of identification of the area 'as one which contains a number of powerful sites linked to an apocalypse–causing figure called Bulardemo' or Bula (Merlan 1991, 342). At around the same time, the area had been identified as a prospective mining area, was also gazetted as Stage III of Kakadu National Park, after which a land claim was lodged by the Northern Land Council on behalf of Indigenous custodians. The area then, is the site of a very complex set of claims, regulations, possible land uses and actors (for more detailed accounts see Merlan 1991; Gelder and Jacobs 1998).

What became famously contested in relation to the presence of Bula in the area, was the 'traditionality' and authenticity of Indigenous claims and beliefs. A significant body of anthropological evidence already existed and was further added to in the early 1990s through the activities of the Resource Assessment Commission (Keen and Merlan 1990). Contestation over this evidence came from a variety of pro–mining and right–wing quarters and related to the perceived inauthenticity of the claims of senior Jawoyn men about the presence of Bula and the catastrophic effects mining would have for the people around this 'Sickness Dreaming Place' (Gelder and Jacobs 1998, 67). Indigenous claims were undermined as 'too recent' to be traditional enough to be considered authentic. The claims were also presented as a kind of reverse 'land grab' by Jawoyn people, whom one commentator (Davis 1989) claimed had never been the traditional owners of this country and were using the story for their own territorial expansion (see analysis of this extraordinary claim in Gelder and Jacobs 1998 and Merlan 1991). This is the 'struggle for control over territory' that Said (1995, 332) posits is central to colonially constituted relations.

This construction of cultural heritage as a land management problem is discursively entangled in a (post)colonial web of dispossession, loss, authenticity, and cultural essentialism. Colonial perceptions of Indigenous peoples as primitive and lacking in sovereignty or land title, yet simultaneously noble in their savageness, persist in these (post)colonial relations surrounding culture and identity. In many settler states, contemporary cultural heritage management is powerfully shaped by the discursive production of Indigenous cultures in the region as tainted, corrupted or even lost. Authentic sites are those that bear the characteristics of pre–contact kinds of uses and activities, and are places to be revered for their connection to past times, othered ways of life, a lost humanity. Sites and places that are more recently produced, or hold contemporary significance, or bear characteristics not recognized within the anthropological or archaeological scientific classifications, are not so easily recognizable to cultural heritage regimes steeped in an essentialized view of identity and structured through the knowledge truth claims of the archaeological discipline. The spatiality of the sacred is also a key issue, especially for the relationship between cultural heritage and planning. *Where* is the sacred, in settler states? Can it be contained, so that 'certainty' returns to capitalist land markets and use rights of territory? It is to these questions of the spatial sacred that I now turn.

The Discursive Production of Sites

Management of Indigenous cultural heritage in settler states is everywhere bound up in a discourse that limits the sacred to particular places, 'spots' on a map. This 'sites discourse' (following Smith 2001 and I have also explored it in Porter 2006b) operates along two axes. First, it discursively settles Indigenous claims by reducing them to particular geographic locations in a landscape and erasing them of anything but 'cultural' value. 'Sites' are tangible relics in discrete locations, disconnected from each other but ordered on a hierarchical inventory according to their 'significance' in archaeological terms (Jones 2007, 100). Such a reduction of 'culture' to material objects is a widely critiqued feature of cultural heritage management regimes (see King 1998; Smith 2004).

According to state–based planning, a cultural heritage 'site' is that point on a landscape at which material evidence is visible and archaeologically classifiable concerning the prior occupation of lands by Indigenous groups. These might be burial grounds, sacred trees, meeting places (each has its own archaeological classification), and they are deemed 'sites' when they are seen, known and can be made visible on the various planning instruments that govern their management. Sites have specific scientifically defined archaeological characteristics, classifiable through size, age, and possible (past) use, which influences 'the meanings given to the site and subsequently the assessment of its significance' (Smith 2004, 106). In settler states such as the US, Canada, Australia and Aoteoroa–New Zealand, sites are listed on a register managed and owned by a government department, usually with some kind of consultation mechanism with nominated Indigenous groups. Places of significance to Indigenous people, sacred spaces, are given a registration number and then a location on a cadastral map. They have significance in archaeological and land management terms by virtue of their status as 'known' sites and the archaeological recording (by an archaeologist, trained in the discipline) of the characteristics that support such a status. The sites 'fit' with the agreed technical definition of what constitutes cultural heritage and render those newly constructed things ready for control. Indigenous cultural heritage is performatively and materially produced as an object of management.

Second, the sites discourse paves the way for 'unblocking' development proposals when they are contested by claims for sacredness. The emergence of the sacred within modern settler states is itself a peculiarly modern, (post)colonial phenomonon because the sacred is 'quite often realized as a topic or a claim only at the moment at which it is about to be desecrated' (Gelder and Jacobs 1998, 69). This can be seen in many different contemporary contests about meaning and value inhering in places in settler states. It is also a peculiarly modern, postcolonial phenomenon because of its imbrication in modern methods of land management, in the continuous business of government and private interests.

It is not only the discursive production of 'culture' and 'sites' that has serious material implications for Indigenous peoples, but also the material practice of cultural heritage management. Sites are able to be made known through scientific observation. Archaeological practices (digging, measuring, recording features) classify a site according to those features and list that site on a register maintained by the state and used for a variety of management purposes, and in particular the protection of those sites. This protection requires removing them from modern uses. Boundaries, fences and zones become critical tools to demarcate the precise spatiality of sacredness (even when it is recognized to be in more than one place) and 'work around it'. Natural resource use remains possible through this hierarchy by spatially differentiating sacred spaces. Once sites are known and mapped, they become manageable and contained. This is a governmentality especially important in places where natural resource extraction depends upon the containment of the sacred.

Boundaries, fencing, zoning and other forms of cultural heritage management are often seen as inappropriate to Indigenous peoples because of the interconnectedness of places with each other, and with material practices. A decision to fence off midden sites in the Arthur–Pieman Conservation Area of Tasmania, for example, helped protect them from damage, but interrupted the landscape and denied access to Indigenous people for other activities (Jones 2007). Zoning sacred sites to protect them from forestry activities on Navajo country in the Chuska mountains is considered rather pointless as the 'power of the place' is gone anyway if everything around the sacred place is destroyed (Rudner 1994).

The discursive production of sites is entwined with a preservation regime of regulation. The state's classification of sites or cultural heritage artifacts is deemed critical for preservation, which in non–Indigenous management terms means, with a similar operating rationality to nature conservation, 'non–use'. In conservation terms, the 'proper care' of cultural heritage is to be 'seen and studied, but not used or handled' (Ogden 2007, 277). For Indigenous peoples, and here Ogden is referring specifically to Native Americans, the object is the material manifestation, the functional item, of the sociocultural practices that make use of it. Value, then, resides in objects differently: in their *use*, which maintains rather than preserves social, cultural and economic practices. In relation to sites and places, this point is also pertinent. Fencing 'sites' off restricts accessibility for their ongoing use by Indigenous peoples to maintain everyday practices, and fails to recognize cultural practices that transcend space, such as the connection with sacred places through prayer (Welch and Ferguson 2007). Let's turn now to how this mode of governmentality operates in one specific (post)colonial space, that of Nyah Forest in Victoria, Australia.

Nyah and its 'Sites'

Cultural heritage management and the discourse of sites has long been a focus of (post)colonial politics and contestation in Nyah Forest. The story is complex, and involved. While I cannot give the whole story here (see Porter 2004, 2006 and 2007 for more detail), it is important to understand some basic elements of that story. Many Indigenous and non–Indigneous people in the district, and particularly the Wadi Wadi people, had been attempting to ensure the protection of a number of significant Indigenous places in the Nyah Forest (and its neighbouring Vinifera Reserve) over many years. Timber harvesting, and other forestry uses such as grazing and tourism, have oftened threatened the integrity of particular places. In 1997, for example, bulldozers re-grading the roads through Nyah Forest to allow access for logging trucks destroyed a burial mound, an event that sparked a contest over logging in the Forest that remains unresolved at the time of writing. Cultural heritage protection legislation at that time in Victoria allowed certain registered people under the Act to place injunctions and stop orders on activities that threatened cultural heritage. One such registered officer at the time was a Wadi Wadi representative. He placed an injunction on further logging in the Forest until management plans could be established. In the ensuing years, as the injunction remained in force and the contest grew, the government departments responsible for forest management and forestry activities continually sought, through a variety of means, to enable timber harvesting in Nyah Forest. One of those efforts was a proposal, announced in 2002, to spend $AUD65,000 in an operation known as 'thinning' (clearing smaller trees and debris) and selling the timber product as firewood. The 'sweetener' was to employ Indigenous people to do that work, thereby from the DNRE's point of view, generating local employment for Indigenous peoples. In addition, the DNRE was offering the potential to undertake further archaeological surveys of Indigenous cultural sites, long an aspiration of many local people including the Wadi Wadi.

This proposal divided the local Indigenous community. Many Indigenous people not belonging to the Wadi Wadi claimant group were keen to see the proposal go ahead. It had the potential to create employment, achieve further cultural heritage surveying, and reduce the fire risk (by managing the fuel load) in the Forest. For others, and particularly the Wadi Wadi people, the proposal was seen as an attempt to buy off their resistance to logging by the sweetener of jobs and archaeological survey. Those divisions were actually manipulated and used by the DNRE in their round of consultation about the proposal. A meeting was called by the Department in August 2002 to discuss the proposal amongst all the relevant stakeholders. At that time, this had to include the nominated cultural heritage officers responsible for the region who worked through the registered cultural heritage body. This was at the time the Swan Hill and District Aboriginal Cooperative. It also had to include the interests of native title claimants, but this could be achieved, according to the legal requirements at the time, by consulting the representative body for native title in Victoria, then Mirimbiak Nations Aboriginal Corporation (MNAC). Others were also invited to the meeting: Indigenous peoples from neighbouring native title claim areas and the umbrella claim group (the North West Nations), and the Indigenous Facilitators recently employed by the DNRE in the region. I discuss how this meeting was arranged and manipulated in much more detail in Chapter 6. For the purposes of this chapter, it is important to know that Wadi Wadi people were not themselves directly invited to the meeting. Representation of their interests was 'assumed' through invitations to MNAC and the Cooperative, both bodies which were technically representing Wadi Wadi interests, although officers of the DNRE were well aware that relations between Wadi Wadi people and both those organizations were significantly strained at the time.

At this meeting, and the events and relations surrounding it, cultural heritage became a source of control and management by the state, as well as the site of struggle and resistance by the Wadi Wadi people. What is interesting (but by no means unique to this case) in Nyah Forest is the multiple and hybrid ways that the regime of cultural heritage management could be used for different agendas. The original injunction on logging can also be seen as part of the potential that cultural heritage protection, and the state in general, offers Indigenous people to give material effect to their rights claims. Yet that same cultural heritage management regime can also be read as a strategic and quite profound limitation on Indigenous rights. In that sense, cultural heritage management is the site of both 'freedoms and unfreedoms', to borrow a term from Scott (1998).

Cultural heritage as a govenrmentality, a controlling technology of the state, is to be located in the way that 'culture' is established as the only legitimate place for Indigenous claims, knowledge and action in relation to Nyah Forest. Each of the documents that frames planning actions in Nyah Forest recognize Indigenous interests, virtually exclusively, in terms of cultural heritage sites (see Chapter 4). The LCC's report for the district in which Nyah is located discussed Indigenous interests in planning recommendations only in the context of site protection. The management strategy for the Mildura FMA in which Nyah is located also produces the intersection between land use management activities and Indigenous interests within the 'protection of sites' discourse. Indigenous interests are represented only in one chapter of the strategy, with the aim to:

> Protect places with significant cultural and historical values...Encourage the sensitive use of selected sites and places for the education and enjoyment of the public...[and] maintain regular and effective dialogue with Aboriginal agencies and communities. (Department of Sustainability and Environment 2004, 56)

The management strategy for the FMA notes the existence of 170 sites as listed on the AAV register, as well as others that are as yet 'unknown' in archaeological terms (not yet classified). The background study to the strategy categorizes these various sites into types: '14 burial sites, four surface scatters, six isolated hearths, 12 shell middens, 24 scarred trees and 124 mounds' (University of Ballarat 1997, 19). That study further notes that 52 per cent of the sites occur in the Nyah Forest, these being recorded in the late 1970s during an intensive archaeological survey conducted by the Victorian Archaeological Survey (VAS) – a project whose activities included the removal of Indigenous remains from burial sites within the Forest, finally to be returned to Wadi Wadi people in a ceremony in 2000. Those sites recorded in the Nyah Forest mainly occur in an area that is classified as the 'Nyah Forest Mounds Area', a geographic location listed on the Register of the National Estate as a 'significant Aboriginal area' (see Figure 5.1).

Figure 5.1 Nyah's cultural heritage 'sites'

Despite a recognition within the Victorian legislative regime, through the *Aboriginal Heritage Act 2006 (Vic)*, of the non–material aspects of Indigenous culture, the practices of archaeology in Victoria have been slow to move beyond this sites discourse. A senior AAV field officer describes how this is practiced in Victoria:

> The perception of cultural heritage in the more remote areas [of Australia] is places like sacred sites and places of spiritual significance. While in Victoria and the rest of southeast Australia, there's a history of dispossession, and it's more focused on archaeological heritage, so physical, tangible material evidence, rather than spiritual or sacred. We operate under the concept of place, which could include an archaeological site, it could include a place of historical or contemporary significance, but most of the records we hold and the way most people perceive cultural heritage as a result of the history of administration in Victoria is archaeological sites. (pers. comm. 30 January 2003)

Cultural heritage is practiced as a relic of prehistory. Through this temporal fixing, authenticity operates only 'within an imagined pre–colonial moment, viewing all forms that diverge from this, and the people with whom those forms are associated, as diminished culture' (Hinkson 2003, 296). Cultural heritage is discursively and administratively produced in Nyah's planning framework as the primary means by which state–based planners will engage with Indigenous people. This is in a sense a 'recovery' of at least some forum for the expression of Indigenous rights. Yet the very recovery, as shown by Jacobs in relation to the Swan Brewery site in Perth, is 'contained by the limits imposed by a combination of planning pragmatism and "representative categorization"' (1996, 114). Indigenous interests therefore remain invisible within the rest of the planning framework for Nyah Forest. For example, the Strategy nowhere mentions Indigenous interests in its proposed management actions for water catchments, timber harvesting, or endangered species and biodiversity protection. There are two primary 'things' being constructed for governing here: cultural heritage in its various material forms, and the Indigenous population itself, including its historical relations and contemporary rights claims. Territory and population, and specific classifiable elements of territory, intersect to produce its own site of governmentality, and its own techniques of power. Planning's production of Indigenous cultural heritage through the sites discourse operates to settle claims of an Indigenous sacred and to create a certain set of institutional moments where Indigenous rights and interests are rendered legitimate.

Managing the Sacred: The Technology of Buffer Zones

Sites are managed within the contemporary planning and management framework in Victoria (especially regarding timber harvesting) in order to provide planning decisions and actions with certainty. The technique employed by the state to manage the Indigenous sacred is buffer zones – an environmental and cultural heritage management extension of that most important planning tool of zoning. Buffer zones are a physical space demarcated around a site within which certain kinds of activities, such as logging or grazing, are excluded. In the case of Nyah Forest, this especially means the exclusion of logging activities. Generally, the minimum buffer zone requirement for logging in Victorian forests for a midden (burial site) or oven site is 50 metres and 20 metres for a scarred tree. Where additional protection is deemed necessary, this is negotiated between nominated Indigenous cultural heritage officers and Forestry Victoria staff. Once the zones are determined, field staff mark the trees on the outer edge of the buffer zone with blue spray paint to indicate where logging is prohibited (pers. comm., Senior Forester, Forestry Victoria, 13 February 2003). Buffer zones are also used for natural conservation values – such as protection of waterways, billabongs or habitat trees – and are widely used in Victoria to protect cultural heritage sites during timber production activities. They are considered by Forestry Victoria, DNRE and AAV to be an efficient method of site protection because of the 'scattered' nature of sites throughout the landscape. Buffer zones contain the potential for sites to spill into each other and in doing so allow natural resource extraction activities in the presence of the sacred.

Buffer zones do not, however, feature as part of the legislated prescriptions for timber harvesting operations. A brief mention of 'cultural values' amongst a list of other environmental values is the only mention that Indigenous cultural heritage receives in DNRE's *Code of Forest Practices for Timber Harvesting*. Further, DNRE's *Management Prescriptions for Timber Harvesting in Mildura*

FMA is silent on cultural heritage issues or broader Indigenous interests in timber harvesting operations. Given that this latter document is the primary means of operationalizing the Code and ensuring that its standards are appropriately varied to reflect the particular circumstances of a specific forest (such as responding to knowledge that a place like Nyah Forest has a high number of sensitive cultural sites), this silence is remarkable. There are no other guidelines published for planners and land managers (or timber harvesters) regarding the use of buffer zones, despite their widespread use across the State.

Buffer zones are a technology developed in part by archaeological requirements for sensitive areas, and as such are a standard recommendation in archaeological or cultural heritage studies. The archaeological study of the three proposed forestry coupes in Nyah Forest, for example, recommended the use of buffer zones to protect the sites identified in the study (Cusack 2000). Buffer zones, however, are not considered to necessarily be the 'ideal way of doing business' within AAV. Indeed, the Director of AAVs Heritage Services Branch considered that:

> they're a compromise situation that has been negotiated over the years. The thing about the buffer zones is that it's about identifying known sites, in forests that are to be logged, but that process doesn't necessarily lead to identification of other heritage values which might be affected...it's not the ideal way. (pers. comm. 30 January 2003)

Cultural Heritage as Bargaining Tool

A key aspiration expressed by Wadi Wadi people and others in the Indigenous community (including the regional cultural heritage staff and DNRE's Indigenous Facilitators) is to undertake comprehensive archaeological surveying of Nyah Forest and nearby Vinifera Reserve so that adequate protection and management can ensue. In their 2002 thinning proposal, DNRE proposed to Indigenous communities that such studies would be undertaken, and they could achieve their goal of proper cultural heritage protection, if logging were to proceed. Many in the local Indigenous community (non–traditional owners) supported the logging proposals for Nyah Forest because of the bargaining power that they would have with regard to cultural heritage protection. One of DNRE's regional Indigenous Facilitators described how this would occur:

> This [proposal] offers us the potential to be able to provide training to the Indigenous community, it provides us with the opportunity to do more on cultural heritage preservation. And this is the bit that I can't get my head past either in that [Wadi Wadi people] want a full–on cultural heritage study done of the area and that's never going to happen. I mean AAV are never going to fund a three month program where you've got 10, 15 people out there full–on for three months...three or four hundred thousand dollars, potentially, to go over every inch of the ground. Whereas you might get something out of, say, a selective

logging program, by building that in and saying well okay before an area is logged, we then want it surveyed, we want the skilling up on that. So, there's no reason why AAV couldn't come in and do the skilling up of people. And then they can go in and if they find that there's too many sites, things of significance, then okay that's taken off the area that's to be logged and you move away from it. And that to me would be a win–win situation, so that Wadi Wadi start to get their site surveying done, it might happen over a longer period of time, but it happens. Whereas at the moment [they say] we want it now, and we want it in the next three months, and we want it to happen over that period of time. Well, it ain't going to happen! (pers. comm. 19 September 2002)

Site protection is also positioned within discourses about the fire risk that Nyah Forest currently constitutes because of its high fuel load, ostensibly due to lack of 'thinning':

> Whether we like it or not, at some point we will get someone, whether it be a redneck or whether it be just through carelessness…a fire will start down there at some stage…And potentially we lose all of our cultural heritage. (pers. comm. 19 September 2002)

Sites themselves have thus became a bargaining tool in the logging debate, both within the Indigenous community, and between Indigenous interests and state–based planners. Indigenous people use sites to bargain more successfully for recognition of rights and interests, or at the very minimum for inclusion of cultural heritage protection in planning and management activities. In this case, sites are used in two different ways: firstly as a means of subverting the planning agenda for Nyah Forest (which is to realize its designation as 'available for timber harvesting'), and secondly as a bargaining chip for those who support timber harvesting activity because of the other benefits it may provide. The state, however, powerfully circumscribes Indigenous interests in Nyah Forest within the discursive structure of site protection, thus foreclosing on a range of other moments whereby positive and productive (post)colonial relations might result.

An example of this foreclosure arose when I visited Nyah Forest with members of the native title claimant group and a senior elder after the August meeting about the thinning proposal. During this visit, I was shown areas of the Forest that were considered to need urgent management intervention, because of changes to the flooding regime of the Murray River. The Murray River should flood at least every couple of years, but massive irrigation schemes coupled with drought all along the River have sapped it of its normal water levels. In principle, when the river floods, new trees seed in the creek–beds and floodplains, and the new growth of redgum takes root. When the next flood comes around, the waters clear out very small growth ('suckers') that have taken hold. The last flood occurred in 1996, resulting in a huge overgrowth of new suckers in the Parne Milloo creek–bed, an anabranch of the Murray river that runs through Nyah Forest, that took root in that flood but have not been subsequently washed out. They are now small, sturdy trees, and constitute a great risk to the forest on two fronts, according to Wadi Wadi people. Firstly, they add considerably to the fire fuel load in the forest, a matter which is also of concern to both DNRE management and other Indigenous community representatives, as discussed earlier. Secondly, because they are now so established as small trees, when the next flood does come, they may change the flow of the creek and cause damage to the mounds and burial places sited on the banks.

Wadi Wadi people consider that it would be a far better use of the $65,000 offered by DNRE to employ Indigenous people to clear out all the suckers from the creek bed before the next flood instead of logging for firewood. I am not aware of an occasion when Wadi Wadi people expressed this knowledge and concern about the new growth in the Parne Milloo creek–bed to DNRE forest managers. Certainly at no time during the controversy about the thinning proposal was any consideration given by DNRE to assign the monies to such a project. This small example highlights the power of Nyah's designation as available for timber harvesting and how the desire by forest managers to realize that planning objective has foreclosed on possible negotiations with Wadi Wadi traditional owners about alternative methods of forest management. I argue here, then, that the tension within the Indigenous community regarding site protection and its intersection with timber harvesting in Nyah is made unproductive by the actions of state–based planners in this case. Certain micropractices of state–based planning power have been invoked in this case to manipulate already deeply felt divisions within the Indigenous community (in particular between Wadi Wadi traditional owners and others) about aspirations for site protection and management of Nyah Forest, as I will explore in more detail in Chapter 6.

Indigenous Challenges: Hybrid Spaces?

Wadi Wadi people practice different spatial rationalities in relation to sacredness in Nyah Forest. While the term 'sites' is often used, particularly when lobbying for their interests in planning forums, Wadi Wadi traditional owners prefer to construct 'places' of significance, structured by their ancestral law and spatial philosophy:

> They are not sites, they are places of importance to us. They are landscapes, not just a site here and a site there and a site over there. We've got very important places where you go in under our rules and jurisdictions, when it comes to our heritage…And we're still out there. They're not old sites! They're living… we're descendants of the people who made them, we're still making them. (pers. comm. 1 September 1999)

In Wadi Wadi terms, sacredness cannot be reduced to dots on a map. Instead, places are intimately connected through spatial practices and manifestations, connected by the 'stretching of the being of conscious–place' (Swain 1993, 33). They exist within a sovereign Wadi Wadi domain of law and are continuously rearticulated, indeed recreated, by social practice.

Wadi Wadi people see buffer zones as a disruption and denial of the meaning of sacred places in Nyah Forest because they interrupt this interconnectedness, and the cultural practices which operate within these places. Sites cannot be contained by fences, boundaries or blue spray paint because they 'radiate out' (Jacobs 1996, 114). They need to be rethought through Wadi Wadi spatial ontologies, as this Wadi Wadi representative argues:

> Now we want to [get] out and show them where the buffer zones are going to exist by the cultural landscape, not by what they said back in the 70s![2] (pers. comm. 21 August 2002)

Here, buffer zones are reconstituted as a part of Wadi Wadi social practice. How buffer zones are defined (their size, shape, location) would be constructed through Wadi Wadi law (according to the 'cultural landscape'), not by the designation of AAV consultant archaeologists. This strategy recognizes the discursive power of buffer zones and sites especially in the context of this contested planning event in Nyah, but extends and shifts this understanding by reading buffer zones through Wadi Wadi law structures.

Indigenous people across settler states have long mounted arguments that the forms of legal protection for Indigenous cultural heritage (diverse, yet based in the same fundamental principles) are a poor fit with Indigenous cultural perspectives. Key areas that have come under sustained critique are: the location of decision–making power and even the vesting of legal ownership of cultural heritage in the hands of non–Indigenous bureaucrats; the constraining nature of a narrow focus on tangible heritage, on sites and artifacts; and the inappropriate public registration of sacred places (O'Faircheallaigh 2008, 31–2). Yet a widely used strategy is to incorporate the techniques of contemporary cultural heritage management within Indigenous practices and daily management routines. For the Wadi Wadi, this means thinking buffer zones through Wadi Wadi law and spatial epistemologies, and being the active agents of cultural heritage protection on a daily basis in the Nyah Forest. This includes regular visits to the Forest to check on particular sites, clear weeds and debris, re–erect fences, maintain signage and develop new infrastructure such as paths and bridges to facilitate protection and visitor management. Similarly, the Chinook Nation have been actively involved as leading partners and consultees with US federal agencies on the archaeological excavation and protection of the Cathlapotle site near the mouth of the Columbia River in Washington state (Daehnke 2007). Far from rejecting modern, western

---

2 This is a reference to the archaeological study of Nyah forest conducted by Coutts et al. (1979) through the Victorian Archaeological Survey, where Wadi Wadi human remains were excavated and stolen from a large burial mound.

tools of archaeology and cultural heritage management, Indigenous peoples are actively using those tools through cultural and economic practices.

Perhaps the greatest power of the Indigenous sacred in settler states lies in its emergent possibility, its potential for eruption (Gelder and Jacobs 1998). Settling the sacred through legislative regimes can never be completely achieved. There is always the potential for more sacredness to emerge, more sacred sites or places of Indigenous significance to be revealed. Sacredness has its own immanence for Indigenous peoples, and a significance in religious and social terms that while I cannot comment on in this context, I want to respectfully acknowledge.

It also has the potential, though my comments here are not intended to suggest a reduction to this potential, as a strategic tool for struggle. Sacredness works for Indigenous rights claims in a number of ways. It can strategically buttress a land claim, especially as the invocation of sacredness seeks to affirm legitimacy and authenticity: as the rightful people to speak for particular country and to be seen as 'traditional enough' to have that land claim recognized. Equally, it can strategically buttress other types of claims, such as for legal recognition of Indigenous identity. For example, the Chinook Nation's work, in partnership with US federal agencies, to archaeologically excavate the Cathlapotle site on the Columbia River was important in assisting their fight for status as a federally recognized tribe under US law (Daehnke 2007, 254). The reification of lifestyle and cultural difference in this instance is a form of strategic essentialism (Spivak 1994), of how difference operates as a distinctive claim (and a claim for distinctiveness) in the pursuit of rights. The reification of difference, through sacredness and the imbrication of sacredness within modern land management frameworks, is critical to Indigenous claims for meaning, identity and sovereignty.

In the case of Nyah forest, it operated as a strategic tool of dominance, but also as a site of resistance, a mode of regulation which could be turned back on itself and used to attempt to reorient the management agenda in Nyah Forest away from logging (see Porter 2006b for a full account). Similar potentialities exist in other settler states. In British Columbia, for example, contemporary forest policy frameworks require that Indigenous cultural and spiritual values 'must not be unjustifiably infringed upon by the resource development activities of the Crown' (British Columbia Ministry of Forests 1995, Section 5). In the US, listing of a sacred site on the National Register of Historic Places requires the state to consult with Indigenous peoples prior to any plans or developments being confirmed. Such moments of potential recognition are small and fragile, particularly in this context as the consultation results are not binding (Rudner 1994) and the legitimacy of different Indigenous groups is itself regulated through western systems of 'recognizing' who is authentically Indigenous and who is not (for examples of the power this form of recognition see Daehnke 2007; Dodson 1996; Choo and O'Connell 1999; Atkinson 2002; Muir 1998; Strelein 2003).

Changing practices in cultural heritage management are evident as a result of these Indigenous challenges. One particular manifestation of those shifts is the now relatively common practice of including Indigenous peoples in decision-making processes that concern registered places of significance or sacred sites as indicated above. In some places, partnership–based mechanisms for cultural heritage management have been developed. In Tasmania's Arthur–Pieman Conservation Area, for example, cultural heritage is managed in cooperation with the Indigenous community with significant representation on boards of management, and established methods for consultation about options for cultural heritage protection (Jones 2007).

Others argue that these are indicative of a broader shift in the kinds of attention being paid to Indigenous cultural heritage. In a study of Indigenous presences within metropolitan Sydney, Hinkson (2003) observes a shift from the protection and marketing of a highly stylized, essentialized version of 'real' (meaning pre–contact) Indigenous cultural heritage toward a more (post)colonial acknowledgement of contemporary Indigenous identity and meaning, as well as political contestation. Reinterpretation of places such as Old Government House in Parramatta Park in Sydney's west to incorporate some (limited) aspects of Indigenous history; Parramatta Riverside Walk which engages with the specifics of local important events such as massacres, sites of Indigenous resistance and the local impacts of the stolen generations (Hinkson 2003, 299) indicate small but important shifts in the construction of what constitutes culture. Perhaps, then, Indigenous cultural heritage as a modern manifestation of the sacred, might be conceptualized as a hybridized form of heritage that is constituted within the (post)coloniality of social relations in settler states. A 'between' state as Long observes, but also a becoming–space that opens something by highlighting 'the hybrid nature of cultural interactions and production between exotic and familiar elements' (2000, 319).

Conclusion

The presence of the sacred in settler states interrupts the dominant reading and utilization of once–familiar places. Moreover, the presence of the Indigenous sacred always has the potential to unsettle planning's claims to authority over space and its management. One form of resettling space is through the operation of cultural heritage management: a form of spatial governmentality to manage the Indigenous sacred. Culture, similarly to nature as I showed in Chapter 4, becomes a 'thing' made available for management, and simultaneously becomes the location within planning frameworks where Indigenous interests can most easily be recognized.

Yet if we are interested here in the unsettling of dominant spatial cultures, we need to question whether these are methods of inclusion, or methods of incorporation. Our questions must concern two different but interlocking aspects. First, whether those shifts constitute a re–articulation of spatial cultures that privilege Indigenous ontologies and epistemologies and how much it matters the extent to which they are uttered through the 'language of the master' (Tully 1995, 34). Second, whether those shifts work to reduce rights claims to spatially and temporally bounded notions of 'culture', and seek to settle those claims. As cultural heritage inscribes Indigenous rights into planning and land management frameworks it simultaneously erases those rights and interests from other parts of those same frameworks. At the very same time as it constitutes a key enabling mechanism for Indigenous communities, it radically circumscribes the legitimacy of Indigenous claims beyond the designated 'cultural'. I will return to these questions in Chapter 6 and explore the possibilities for a transformative re–articulation of spatial cultures in Chapter 7.

Chapter 6

Modes of Governance: The Difference Indigeneity Makes to Progressive Planning

...First Peoples have distinctive rights and a special status based on prior and continuing occupation of land, and authority and autonomy as distinct polities.

(Dodson and Strelein 2001, 838)

...enabling all stakeholders to have a voice.

(Healey 1997, 5)

New approaches to the inclusion of Indigenous peoples in land planning and management are proliferating all over settler states. In the environmental planning field, the model of joint management (sometimes called co–management) of protected areas has been widely adopted, albeit in slightly different forms. Examples include Uluru–Kata Tjuta in Australia, Kluane National Park Reserve in Canada, and Te Waihora Lake and surrounds in Aoteoroa–New Zealand to name just a few. The different models are diverse, but the underlying principle is that Indigenous people co–manage an area of land in partnership with government through different forms of agreement and representation on boards of management. There is an apparent evidence base here, then, of a shift in approaches to planning and land management, and it is quite widely seen as a shift to more collaborative forms of planning, influenced by theories of deliberative democracy and communicative ethics. 'Community–based' planning in these kinds of settings is widely pronounced, in practice as well as in their analysis, as more inclusive and able to accommodate Indigenous perspectives in new and innovative ways: an advance on top–down, technocratic decision–making in planning.

This is, of course, the case. Community–oriented modes of planning, especially as they are currently being tried and formulated in the natural resource management field, have been generally successful in empowering Indigenous peoples within new governance arrangements. This is especially the case where it is Indigenous peoples themselves who have been instrumental in developing and establishing these arrangements and methodologies.

In this chapter, I will take a critical look at the application of collaborative and deliberative approaches to planning (both within and outside the natural resource management domain), at the approaches that as Healey (1997) notes in the opening quote to the chapter are about 'enabling stakeholders to have a voice'. This should not be read as a criticism of initiatives that have widened the scope of participation for Indigenous peoples. My critical attention, instead, is focused on what happens within collaborative and deliberative 'moments' in planning when they fail to include an actively deconstructive stance, one that recognizes the challenging claim made by Dodson and Strelein (see the opening quote to the chapter) that Indigenous peoples constitute something other than 'another stakeholder'. The peculiar and specific challenges that Indigeneity, or Indigenous identity rights claims, make to planning expose how the assumptions of the collaborative/ deliberative models are insubstantial on their own. Indigeneity makes such a difference, I will argue in this chapter, that collaborative or deliberative planning models become highly suspect in (post)colonial contexts when they do not include a sufficiently deconstructive stance towards historical relations of dispossession and racism. I will draw a detailed analysis of two planning processes situated in the different contexts of Nyah and Gariwerd in western Victoria, Australia, to expose just how much difference Indigeneity makes, and explore whether in (post)colonial settings, the collaborative turn in planning potentially constitutes new forms of governmentality and colonial domination.

New Planning Frameworks in Gariwerd

In March 2003, the Victorian Minister for Environment launched a new plan of management for the Grampians National Park in Victoria, Australia (see Chapters 1 and 4). Symbolically, this official public launch was held at the Brambuk Living Cultural Centre, a sign of some significant changes that had recently taken place in Gariwerd's management. The plan had taken five years to prepare and finalize, a longer than usual review period brought about largely by the expression of rights, interests and aspirations for Gariwerd by Indigenous traditional owner groups in the region. When Parks Victoria released its draft plan of management for the park in 1998, Indigenous groups were concerned at the lack of consultation and negotiation with them. Other than the standard references to Indigenous cultural heritage and its protection (required by the power vested in Indigenous communities under cultural heritage legislation), the draft plan made only one reference to Indigenous interests. This was a one paragraph disclaimer in the introduction which stated: 'An application for a native title determination was lodged with the Native Title Tribunal in 1997 covering, among other areas, Grampians National Park' (Parks Victoria 1998, 1).

Standard management planning consultation procedures were to develop the plan and then provide the public, and key stakeholders (including Brambuk), with an opportunity to comment. Indigenous interests were just one of the many stakeholders in this process, a situation objected to by Indigenous groups. Since the 1998 draft plan, Indigenous communities, first by virtue of their native title claimant status, and second by the growing importance of Brambuk Cultural Centre as a representative body for (some) community interests, were able to enter into extended negotiations with Parks Victoria staff about the plan of management and the representation and recognition of their interests within it. These negotiations resulted in a plan of management very different from the first draft. The 2003 plan contains multiple references to the Indigenous communities and their 'strong associations' with Gariwerd (Parks Victoria 2003). A section, as discussed in Chapter 4, is dedicated to 'Strategies for Cultural Values Conservation'. It overwhelmingly relates to Indigenous cultural issues, and significantly expands on the definition of these issues from past interpretations, in which Indigenous culture was usually relegated to prehistory.

Elsewhere in the plan, even in those sections dealing with natural values conservation, Indigenous knowledge or aspirations also have a presence. For example, surveys and research into flora and plant communities is to be encouraged 'in consultation with Brambuk Incorporated and the Indigenous Nations' (ibid, 16). Most of the management strategies under each element of the natural values section (water, fire, vegetation, fauna, landscape and geology) include a strategy to 'develop and implement...programs...in consultation with Brambuk Incorporated and the Indigenous Nations' within an overall aim to 'respect, consider and as appropriate apply Indigenous Nations aspirations for the park, perspectives of environment and landscape, and tradition, to all aspects of park planning and management' (Parks Victoria 2003, 23). This is a substantial change in approach to park management in Gariwerd, although one that has its limits, as I argued in Chapter 4.

One of Parks Victoria's senior managers directly responsible for the organization's liaison with Indigenous communities, reflects on how the shift in the new plan of management for Gariwerd came about:

> the [draft] Grampian's plan probably had a column and a half, maybe two columns [on Indigenous issues]. And the structure of the plan is geology, flora and fauna, pest plants, pest animals, Indigenous culture...In the old plans [there are] probably three paragraphs about cultural heritage and it's just about artifacts and obligations under the Act...I said well that's not good enough. We've pulled it out and developed a cultural values conservation strategy...now it talks about consultation partnerships approach, developing MOUs [memoranda of understanding], protocols, working together like that. (pers. comm. 12 September 2002)

This senior manager points to the two locations where major shifts have occurred in management planning. First, he challenges *where* Indigenous interests have historically featured in the planning canon as 'artifacts' for cultural heritage management. Indigenous interests are now recognized as being more central to planning and management practices. Second, he challenges *how* Indigenous people and their interests have been 'managed' by Parks Victoria, historically as 'obligations under the Act', but now as partners in park management enterprises, with the legal backing of contractual agreements. These are significant shifts in terms of the level of inclusion of Indigenous interests in park management and planning in Gariwerd over the past ten years. In bureaucratic terms, they are tectonic shifts and are the result of very considerable efforts by some individuals, including the person cited above, within the bureaucracy to bring them about.

How to do this was the subject of many discussions amongst Parks staff. At a meeting of Parks Victoria staff with Indigenous native title claimant and community representatives in 2002, Parks staff expressed anxieties about how they might successfully 'sell back' to their own staff, as well as the wider public, the idea of referring to 'Indigenous Nations' in the new plan of management. To do so would substantially challenge preconceived notions of Indigeneity in Victoria, moving well beyond the safe confines of cultural heritage management and the provision of Indigenous employment and training programmes. Park managers involved in the preparation of the new management plan for Gariwerd talked frankly about real resistance from within the state bureaucracy:

> I mean some people have struggled [with the idea of partnership] when [we were doing] the drafting. [They said] 'you can't say we're going to have a partnership. Partnership means, if you look up the dictionary, a 50–50 equal say in the business'. And yet we've had documents for years that say we're in a partnership with local government, [or] we're in a partnership with the CMA [Catchment Management Authority], and no–one even thinks twice. Put 'Indigenous' in front of it, and it's paranoia. (pers. comm. 12 September 2002)

Achieving 'partnership', then with Indigenous peoples is a major shift, fragile in its bureaucratic and public acceptance. In the next section, I look at how this model of planning came about and what it signifies.

Integrating Brambuk and Parks Victoria: Genuine Partnership or Culture as Product?

For the past six years, Brambuk and Parks Victoria staff based in Gariwerd have been working together toward integrating the functions and operations of their two organizations. This integration programme has become a flagship project for the park, and for Parks Victoria's efforts in realizing Indigenous interests in protected area management in Victoria. Considerable resources have been poured into the project by both organizations, but particularly by Parks Victoria. A permanent full–time member of Parks Victoria staff was employed at the Gariwerd office to work on the integration programme, a series of consultants reports have been funded looking at the feasibility of the project and producing an interpretation and site plan, and a glossy prospectus was prepared setting out how the new arrangements – now known as 'Brambuk: The National Park and Cultural Centre' – will operate. The 'National Parks Act Annual Report for 2001–2002' declared the integration programme 'one of the best examples of providing Aboriginal interpretation to park visitors' (Department of Natural Resources and Environment 2002b, 13).

The idea was brought about by Brambuk management and Board, sparked by concerns about lack of tourist numbers visiting the Centre. Two buildings – Brambuk and the National Park Visitors Centre (NPVC) – are located on what has now become known in local parlance as 'the site'. This is an area of land just to the south of the Halls Gap township on the main road through the park. The NPVC is located at the 'top' of the site, closest to the car park and the main road. Brambuk is located further down towards Fyans Creek, a little 'tucked away' from the NPVC by a small lake, vegetation and landscaped areas. Currently, visitors have to make a conscious decision to visit Brambuk after they have been to the NPVC, it requires a few minutes walk along the path joining the two buildings.

Brambuk management wanted to realize greater tourist dollar benefits from the high visitation to the park. An Indigenous custodian of Gariwerd and the then Director of Brambuk explains:

> at the end of the day Brambuk was at a halt in terms of going any further forward in terms of enterprise development, in terms of tourism...So all our options run out in terms of where do we go from now. The next stage was basically we need to sit down with government, how we can better do business as partners. So we entered into a three year contract, which is basically an MOU [Memorandum of Understanding]...It included looking at the buildings, so you've got the National Park Visitor Centre, you've got the Brambuk building. Basically we will take over [the Visitors Centre], or part of the arrangement is to use the two centres as one in terms of delivering cultural tourism and environmental tourism, park management all in one. So, we didn't have any duplication on site, basically. (pers. comm. 21 March 2003)

According to the Parks Victoria Project Officer whose job was to make the integration programme a reality, 'Brambuk: The National Park and Cultural Centre' is about

> developing this site as the region's pre–eminent site for the appreciation of Aboriginal culture, heritage and the environment. We want to combine high quality visitor services and interpretive experience that embody the principles of recognition, respect and reconciliation. So, fundamentally...it is improving services and facilities on this site for visitors, and combining cultural and environmental interpretation. (pers. comm. 6 February 2003)

The integration programme is a business agreement, not a park management agreement, and is spoken about quite firmly as such by representatives of both organizations. Yet in all the talk about the integration, is the presence of a broader purpose of the proper recognition of Indigenous aspirations for Gariwerd, which are understood to include a possible future Indigenous or joint management arrangement. In this sense, then, while the programme specifically excludes any talk about park management, nevertheless those aspirations are always present within dialogue between the two organizations, and wider conversations between Parks and other Indigenous communities not necessarily represented through Brambuk.

Integrating the two organizations has been programatically split into three stages. Stages one and two sought to integrate the existing services and facilities on the site and expand the range of services available to visitors, including developing new educational activities and guided activities. Stage three planned to expand the physical infrastructure of the site by actually rebuilding the existing NPVC (Brambuk et al., no date). Parks Victoria and Brambuk together developed a common vision for the programme, and a collaborative management structure, which I have drawn as Figure 6.1 below.

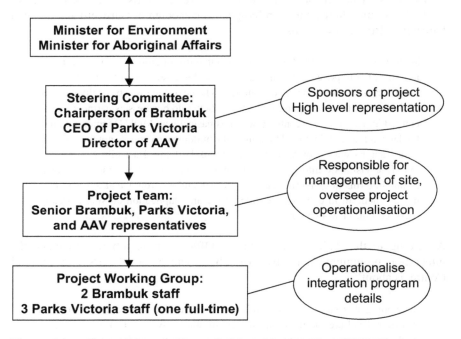

Figure 6.1 **Committee structure of planned integration of Brambuk and National Park Visitor Centre, Gariwerd**

A pilot joint Easter holiday programme was successfully run in 2002, and the staff responsible for education programmes in the two organizations have since worked jointly on their initiatives. Much of the signage around the NPVC has also changed to reflect the integration. Flags with Indigenous designs now adorn the car park, and there are new welcome signs at the front of the NPVC, saying '*Nga Keenatt*', which are words of welcome from the Tjapwurrung language (see Figure 6.2). There is a specific policy with the new interpretive plan for the site to use Indigenous language alongside English language words.

Figure 6.2 New signs of welcome in Tjapwurrung at the National Park Visitor Centre, Gariwerd

Sustaining the business of Brambuk is a key requirement for Brambuk Board and management, not least because of Brambuk's pivotal role as a training and employment centre for young Indigenous people, and its iconic status as a place to visit and 'experience' Indigenous culture. Brambuk, initially funded through a series of government grants, receives an annual grant from AAV to maintain the building. Over past years, Parks Victoria had increasingly been pushing Brambuk to be completely self–sufficient, a point that had generated (back in 1999, when I first interviewed him) considerable concern with the then Brambuk Director:

> they want us to stand alone, but [I] say well hang on…you're talking about our country here and [Parks Victoria] get sent a lot of money in grants for cultural heritage protection – stuff which we don't see…and they employ a lot of non-Aboriginal people as part of that works group…and the park attracts, what, a million tourists a year?…they incorporate camping fees, and…you know there's a big bookshop over the road… (pers. comm. 21 March 2003)

The issue here is the extent to which Parks Victoria *recognizes* Brambuk, and the communities it represents by virtue of its cooperative structure, as traditional owners with rights and interests in the park and its use. Recognition of rights, as shown in this statement should flow through to receipt of economic benefits generated by the park's use, the major contributor to which is tourism. Integrating the business operations of the NPVC and Brambuk is a direct response to the issues that Indigenous people at Brambuk had been raising. One of the key aspects of the integration programme is that Brambuk (or Gariwerd Enterprises, Brambuk's business entity) completely takes over the retail operations of the National Park Visitors Centre, combining its own shop and café with the NPVC shop. As such, Brambuk/Gariwerd Enterprises is the recipient of all the takings through the shop, café and other retail aspects (such as educational programmes, tours and talks etc.) of the new integrated centre (pers. comm. Project Officer, Parks Victoria).

This is a significant achievement for Gariwerd Enterprises, Brambuk, and the communities represented on its Board, because it properly recognizes through a financial arrangement the aspirations of those communities, and their interests in the interpretation of Gariwerd to visitors. In comparison with some other Indigenous tourist initiatives elsewhere in Australia it appears to represent a significant step beyond the mere appropriation of Indigenous culture as a performed product for tourist titillation. For example, development of an ecotourism centre in Brisbane attempted to include Indigenous interests, but that participation fell short of Indigenous economic control of the centre (Jacobs 1996, 135). Certainly at face value, the genuine integration of the two 'businesses' represents an optimistic moment for (post)colonial relations around Gariwerd, and important achievements by the Indigenous communities.

In addition to these important objectives, the integration programme is also positioned by many of those involved as a means of breaking down the distinction between 'cultural' and 'environmental' interpretations of Gariwerd. One Indigenous custodian, and Team Leader for Indigenous Cultural Heritage with Parks Victoria in the region, considers that this also means breaking down what he described as the 'Aboriginal slot' in park management. Culture, he says, is not limited to rock art sites or site monitoring, and should be allowed to cover the broad range of park planning aspects that are culturally important. Achieving this is proposed through two mechanisms: the integration of the two organizations under the one management structure (so that both Brambuk and Parks Victoria employees will report to the same manager, and the presentation of interpretive material about Gariwerd. Even now, Parks Victoria and Brambuk staff work under the one organizational name: 'Brambuk: the National Park and Cultural Centre', the name 'Brambuk' no longer referring only to the iconic cockatoo–shaped building. The presentation of interpretive material, according to Parks Victoria's Project Officer '[will not] separate the cultural and the environmental. So, in the past to receive cultural information you'd go down to Brambuk, to receive environmental information you'd come [to the NPVC]...which is kind of silly' (pers. comm. 6 February 2003).

This integration of the 'cultural' and the 'natural' has been driving the integration programme since its inception, particularly from the perspective of Parks Victoria, where there has been a sense that the relationship between environmental managers and Indigenous people has largely been ignored in the past. Similarly, there have been important changes to how those environmental managers provide visitor services, changes which also underpin the integration programme. In the past, the major purpose of the NPVC was to give visitors some basic 'orientation'. This purpose has changed, with a new focus on environmental interpretation such that this has become a key park management aim.

The glossy new prospectus developed to provide information to the public about the integration programme represents the integration of the natural and cultural in particular ways. Like the management plan (see Chapter 4), the term 'Gariwerd' tends to be used (sometimes italicized) when referring to Indigenous interest, whereas the term 'Grampians' (never italicized) is used to describe other aspects of the place: its recreational opportunities and wealth generation through tourism. Yet to say that there is a definite 'split' in this sense of nomenclature would be to misrepresent what is in fact a weaving together of these two 'identities' of place, as I discussed in Chapter 4. The sense about which there are dual ways of describing and relating to this place (as either Gariwerd or the Grampians National Park), strikes the reader of these documents deeply. These two identities are sometimes in tension but also allowed to co–exist. The place is both Gariwerd and the Grampians, sometimes one or the other, the name designating the kind of identification the speaker may have with the place, though not always. 'Gariwerd' as an identifier is prominently located as 'the indigenous name for the area' (Brambuk et al. no date).

Despite calls to weave together the 'natural' and the 'cultural' through the integration programme, both organizations nevertheless draw on levels of expertise in their own domain. Most of the resources for the project come from Parks Victoria who, according to the Project Officer

> bring a range of people with different skills to the project...we pull on our entire organization to deliver the services that we're after. Brambuk provides expertise in the cultural areas. So, they can bring in those people... (pers. comm. 6 February 2003)

It is entirely appropriate, of course, that Brambuk is designated the expert on cultural matters (presumably Indigenous cultural matters, though this is not specified as such). What is interesting is what else this statement says by virtue of omission. The expertise that Parks Victoria brings to the table, as the Project Officer is pointing out in the above quote, is expertise about environmental interpretation, capital works design and project management. Designating the boundaries once again around these two domains of 'Aboriginal culture' and 'everything else' (which includes most importantly land management) once again subtly draws on the power of Western scientific discourse to designate what is natural, and what is outside history and culture, namely environmental management practice and Western science itself. This powerful and 'subtle political mapping' is found elsewhere such as the Bowali Visitor Centre in Kakadu National Park where initiatives ultimately failed to genuinely represent Kakadu as an Indigenous place (Palmer 2001, 154).

Nevertheless, there is an attempt to interpret and re/present Gariwerd as a cultural landscape, not just from the Indigenous perspective but also to place non–Indigenous associations with Gariwerd in the cultural frame. An interpretive plan for the site was developed by consultants in 2002–2003. The overriding interpretive topic as developed through this plan is the different interpretations of Gariwerd as a cultural landscape, or more fully: 'Gariwerd has been seen differently by different people, different cultures and in different times' (Look Ear Pty Ltd, no date).

Lying between the two buildings is an old section of redgum tree that has been carted onto the site from a farm on the outskirts of the park as a symbol of this idea of Gariwerd as a cultural landscape (see Figure 6.3 below). The Project Officer describes its importance:

> it's a river red gum that's about 800 years old…it's down at the wetlands at the moment, and it tells three stories, just through the markings on it. It has a coolamon cut,[1] so an Aboriginal scar, which shows the way they utilize the landscape, so the tree was left living, the scar was left, that's the mark that was made on it. The next scar is a ring–barking scar[2] which is another time–zone, where different land management practices were put into place…and the third scar is a chainsaw cut, where the top part of the tree was started to be cut up into foot blocks. So, that's the next stage of that story. And…it's now starting to interpret the landscape. (pers. comm. 6 February 2003)

This description of the tree and its markings shows a genuine effort to include non–Indigenous associations with Gariwerd within the cultural frame, where historically those associations have been normalized. But it is also shows the persistence of the colonial endeavour to contain Indigenous associations to 'prehistory' and to the kinds of practices that can be recognized as authoritatively traditional. The bark canoe marking on the tree is cast as a 'traditional Indigenous marking', produced in times gone by through the living of a reified 'traditional lifestyle'. The other cuts (chainsaw and ringbarking) are apparently nothing to do with Indigenous people, who are not present in this part of the tree's story. This silencing of the Indigenous voice in the post–contact period, the tendency to position appropriate Indigenous association as traditional, or a reproduction for the tourist gaze, is embedded with powerful colonial tropes about how Indigenous people can be appropriately 'placed' in a landscape. Such assumptions can work to silence contemporary Indigenous associations with *country* in powerful ways so that the only space left for Indigenous voices is as some kind of reproduced traditional Indigeneity.

---

1   A scar, or coolamon tree refers to a removal of bark from a tree to make boats, coolamons and other items.

2   Ring–barking is when trees have a deep ring cut into the bark at their base in order to kill the tree prior to logging.

Figure 6.3 Scarred tree at Brambuk and Visitors Centre, Gariwerd

A former Cultural Officer at Brambuk and Tjapwurrung custodian of Gariwerd, also talked about the tree and how it is used in tourist interpretation guides:

> [on the path] from Parks [NPVC] down to Brambuk there's a scarred tree. So, we [tell visitors about] the site of the scarred tree itself and then we go over to the European side, like as in [talk about] the ringbark of the tree, then what the tree's actually used for, for the wood; why they cut it down, because it'd take the moisture out of the air. So, we're telling them both things at once, that's a good thing that's happened. We learn a little bit off them, they're learning off us. But then I had a bit of a word with [Parks Victoria], I said any cultural issues, anything on those talks or anything, that's got to come to us instead of you talking about it. (pers. comm. 15 July 2002)

This Indigenous custodian's words similarly designate something that is European (the ringbark markings) as opposed to what are (unstated) Indigenous associations with the tree, that it is a 'scarred tree', an archaeological designation which gives the tree power in terms of its cultural heritage value. But in the final part of the statement, serious questions are raised about how integrated education and interpretation programmes might actually be delivered when the issue of who can speak for country and culture remains contested. This custodian's statement reveals the import of anxieties that many Indigenous custodians of Gariwerd express about the rights of non–Indigenous Parks Victoria staff to interpret Indigenous culture, practices or stories.

This raises some interesting practical conundrums for managing interpretation programmes in Gariwerd. There are limited numbers of Indigenous staff at either Brambuk or Parks Victoria, and some educational tours are inevitably going to be run by non–Indigenous Parks staff, leading to moments where those staff might perhaps find themselves 'talking for country' as the person quoted above fears. Indeed, it is a common occurrence now, and something that Brambuk staff and other people in the Indigenous community are constantly on guard against and have very strong feelings about. It is an always present and difficult tension, because it further raises the problem of how to avoid determining what is an appropriate place for Indigenous voices in the interpretation of Gariwerd. Indigenous communities in Gariwerd voice a central aspiration for recognition, as well as Indigenous control over cultural information and interpretation. How this call is responded to within the daily practicalities of delivering tourist services in Gariwerd is a critical question. A response that reduces the place for Indigenous voices to filling in a simplified cultural 'gap' within a normalized interpretive story will miss the opportunity present here to build more optimistic (post)colonial relations. Alternatively, creative ways could be found to ensure that Indigenous voices are at the heart of those stories, and given the space to raise the complex and difficult questions inherent in interpreting Gariwerd as an Indigenous place in (post)colonial Victoria.

Corresponding to this tree as an 'interpretive prop', the interpretation plan for the new integrated site recommends utilizing three 'eras' to communicate the general theme of 'Gariwerd – a cultural landscape'. Accordingly, the site would be divided into three spatial zones each designated a particular era: traditional (pre–contact), contact (100 to 200 years ago) and contemporary (now and the future). Eras are positioned within the plan as useful because they provide a framework within which 'the stories of conflict, dispossession and reconciliation can be presented' (Look Ear Pty Ltd, no date, 16). Further, the plan considers that these eras can 'help defuse the common perception in the non–Indigenous community that Indigenous culture is somehow frozen–in–time, and that anything that is not "traditional" is somehow not "authentic"' (ibid).

At face value, the idea of eras could have easily elided important themes of conflict and dispossession, such 'negative' stories kept hidden from the tourist view. Instead, those stories receive open recognition through one of the interpretive themes for the site: 'great changes to Gariwerd/Grampians occurred in the last 200 years'. Consultants developing the interpretation plan for the site recommend that under this theme a series of 'cultural storylines' should be told, amongst which would include:

- that Jardwadjali and Djab wurrung people 'struggled to survive the wave of new settlers and their new ways of living on the land';
- that 'the contact period was largely the waging of an undeclared war with the victors taking all...and the defeated being expelled to the reserves'; and
- stories about 'expulsion from traditional land and the relocation to the reserves at Framlingham, Lake Condah and Ebenezer'.

(Look Ear Pty Ltd, no date, 14)

One interpretation of this storyline would regard it as an overly negative portrayal, with Indigenous people cast as passive victims of a devastating, but inevitable, colonial process. The fact, however, that such a storyline is even being discussed at this level does indicate a large enough shift in thinking to potentially herald a more respectful recognition of history in Gariwerd. Recognition of the violent colonial history in Gariwerd and the surrounding region has never before been so central a storyline in park interpretation.

However, a deeper examination of the integration programme, in particular the site interpretation plan, reveals some more critical issues. As discussed earlier, one of the driving purposes behind this programme (especially from Parks Victoria's perspective) is the integration of culture and environment in park interpretation. In a sense, the integration of the two organizations (one supposedly cultural, one supposedly environmental) has become a symbol of that objective. The interpretation plan establishes a series of interpretive sub–themes to become the subject of the interpretive material on display in the new centre. Each of these sub–themes has a suggested set of storylines to represent it: these are divided into 'cultural storylines' and 'environmental storylines'. Apart from the sub–theme I discussed above (where post–contact dispossession is noted amongst some of the early European uses of Gariwerd), virtually all of the 'cultural storylines' relate to Indigenous culture, and all of the 'environmental storylines' display scientific 'facts' about Gariwerd. Within this splitting of storylines is also further evidence of the splitting of nomenclature similar to that discussed earlier in Chapter 4 about the new plan of management. The park is called 'Gariwerd' under Indigenous/cultural storylines, but 'the Grampians' under environmental storylines as Table 6.1 demonstrates.

The power of Western scientific discourse to separate the natural and cultural, and to reify the cultural as Other, is not easily undone. Indeed, the separation of natural and cultural is a distinctly western orientation to space, a feature of the spatial cultures that I have been trying to understand throughout the book. The question that lingers amid the talk and glossy brochures about the integration programme is whether this will achieve a radically different approach to the interpretation of Gariwerd as an Indigenous place (and perhaps ultimately filter through into genuinely new approaches to park management), or whether it will reduce Indigenous associations with Gariwerd to a reified 'cultural' tourist product. Is this a real shift, or is it just a new form of packaging for delivering tourist services in Gariwerd, tapping into the known potential for Indigenous cultural tourism ventures?

One recommendation in the interpretation plan for the site is to use it as 'an integral part of the interpretative and educational functions of the precinct' (Look Ear Pty Ltd, no date). In the 'traditional era zone' that would form part of this outdoor interpretive display, a range of ideas are suggested for displaying 'relatively "natural" bushland with a variety of plants (and attracted wildlife) that can be used to show various aspects of the environment, and the relationship that Indigenous people have with it' (ibid, 32). The area would include such things as

Table 6.1 Interpretive themes planned for Gariwerd

Theme: Gariwerd/Grampians National Park is a unique place	
Cultural Storylines	**Environmental Storylines**
The region's landforms are a rich and varied range of habitats and environments, and plants and wildlife	Grampians National Park is home to many rare and endangered species of plants and animals
Gariwerd contains a priceless record of a rich Aboriginal culture that encompassed a wide range of artistic expression	The Grampians National Park is recognized as the single most important botanical reserve in Victoria…
Aboriginal culture is tied to all aspects of the landscape	The Grampians National Park has 7 broad vegetation types. A total of 39 Ecological Vegetation Classes have been identified and 27 endemic species…
Native plants and animals are a rich resource (food and medicines)	
Gariwerd was visited in certain seasons… to hunt, to conduct ceremonies, to meet and exchange	Fauna: over 230 bird species, 40 mammal species, 30 reptiles, 6 fish species and 11 amphibian and butterfly species have been recorded in the Grampians National Park

Source: Look Ear Pty Ltd, no date.

bush foods and medicine plants, traditional bark huts or shelters, a 'simulated rock shelter', and fish traps in the nearby creek. These features, according to the Parks Victoria Project Officer, would provide the 'props' which Parks and Brambuk staff could use to conduct interpretive tours, pointing out to visitors things in the landscape along the way.

That these features are merely 'props' is highlighted by this former cultural officer with Brambuk:

> the only thing they won't let me do is put a fish trap in the water. It's a big issue here…see I want to make a fish trap, like how they used to do it. I went to the Water Board and all that, [they said] no you can't do it. Oh well, who needs your permission anyway! I feel like doing it anyway, but I thought I'd better try and do it the right way first…didn't work. (pers. comm. 15 July 2002)

Building a fish trap in the creek, then, is appropriate if it falls within the tourist gaze as a 'prop' for interpreting Gariwerd as a cultural landscape, and yet inappropriate if sought by an Indigenous custodian for non–tourism purposes. A vignette such as this story does not, of course, undermine the integrity of the entire integration programme, but it does raise important questions about whether the programme shifts power relations in Gariwerd, or merely re–packages the tourist experience in the park under a new banner that differently, but nevertheless powerfully, reproduces the nature/culture equation of scientific environmental discourse.

Collaborative modes of planning are generating new questions and possibilities in Gariwerd, as in other places in settler states. Yet, the persistent power of colonial, racist assumptions about Indigeneity are present here, and cannot be ignored. We need to turn, then, to settings where that racism is overtly present and observable and engage our analysis with its pernicious effects to look in different ways at the collaborative turn in planning in (post)colonial settings.

Colonial Presences in Nyah Forest

In Nyah Forest, in the northwest of the state, the then Department for Natural Resources and Environment (DNRE) had, through the late 1990s, been busily developing a new Wood Utilisation Plan for Nyah Forest. These plans would define the coupes, or logging areas, within the Forest. As part of the consultation process for that plan, statutory processes had been followed for consultation with the Indigenous community. This included wide advertisement of the Plan, and the direct invitation to Mirimbiak Nations Aboriginal Corporation (then the Native Title Representative Body for Victoria) and the Swan Hill and District Aboriginal Cooperative (the auspicing body for the North West Aboriginal Cultural Heritage Programme) for submissions on the proposal and the location of coupes.

As I discussed in Chapter 5, the question of logging in Nyah Forest had been at a stalemate since a stop order had been invoked in 1997. In 2002 DNRE sought to discuss a proposal to use the revenue from a more limited timber harvesting programme in Nyah Forest (mostly wood that would be sold locally as firewood) to fund a cultural heritage survey of the Forest and employ Indigenous people on short–term contracts to do the work. A meeting was arranged to discuss the proposal, and the invitees to that meeting included the statutory consultees (Mirimbiak, and the Cooperative), plus a number of Indigenous people many of whom worked for the DNRE at the time. The Wadi Wadi people, traditional owners and currently native title claimants of Nyah Forest and surrounds, were not invited.

Both Mirimbiak and the Cooperative constituted organizational representation, at least in name, of Wadi Wadi people. Mirimbiak, as Victoria's representative body for native title at the time, had a legal mandate to protect the interests, in general and their specifics, of all native title claimants in Victoria, and that included the Wadi Wadi people. However, Mirimbiak as an organization had been the site of controversial politics within the Victorian Indigenous community with concerns about effective representation and allegations of corruption. A consequence of those local politics was a complete cessation of contact, and abrogation of trust, between Mirimbiak and the Wadi Wadi native title claimants.

The Cooperative was, at that time, the designated cultural heritage management body in the region, and as such had a legally defined mandate to protect Indigenous cultural heritage and arrange negotiations with the owners of cultural heritage for that protection. The Cooperative was also embroiled in its own problems of internal organizational disputes, including a shift in the locus of power in the organization between Indigenous groups in the region. Again, the consequence was a substantial lack of contact between key members of staff within the Cooperative and the Wadi Wadi people as the owners of cultural heritage in the area. According to the Wadi Wadi people, neither Mirimbiak nor the Cooperative had communicated with them about the Wood Utilisation Plan or their approval of the coupe locations. A Senior Forester pointed out that this was not the Department's concern, and that standard procedure had been followed by contacting those organizations with legislative responsibility for site protection, and asking for their input. During an interview with me, the Senior Forester claimed he knew nothing about the *Native Title Act 1993 (Cth)*, nor the procedural rights of registered native title claimants, the push to consult with Mirimbiak came from elsewhere in the Department.

As I showed in Chapter 5, cultural heritage management as a field of governmentality is constituted by the existence of a colonial experience and history. The tropes around which the politics and social relations of cultural heritage management circulate are starkly present in Nyah forest around the issue of cultural heritage, land rights and logging. The extent to which Wadi Wadi aspirations, claims and challenges are taken seriously within planning was enframed in a discourse about Wadi Wadi competency to speak that pivoted on a series of perniciously racialized stereotypes: alcohol, cultural decay and inauthenticity.

A number of times during field observations with senior land managers within the Department, the following view was put forward: Indigenous people, and especially Wadi Wadi people, 'let themselves down by hitting the hooch' (getting drunk) (pers. comm. 6 June 2002). It was suggested that Wadi Wadi people would continually 'change their minds' about agreed approaches or solutions, and that these changes of mind always occurred after certain individuals had been drinking. Alcohol was consistently raised, an 'anxious repetition' (Bhabha 1994, 66), as an explanation for Wadi Wadi statements or actions, particularly when the native title claimants became angry about the logging proposals.

The effects of alcohol were also very powerfully utilized as a means of dismissing Indigenous practices. As a DNRE works crew undertook some routine site protection work, a senior Indigenous Elder who worked with the crew expressed concern that the female Indigenous member of the crew should not be present and working in one particular area of the Forest, due to it being a sacred men's area. In response, the Forest Manager wrote to the North West Region Indigenous Cultural Heritage Programme to say that such 'myths' restricting an employee's work commitments was unacceptable. Upon showing me the letter, it was expressed that the claims about men's business and places had only arisen because the Elder 'had actually just had too much to drink that day' (pers. comm. 19 August 2002).

The image of the 'drunken Aborigine' is a most pervasive colonial trope that has operated even before alcohol was readily available to Indigenous people. Alcohol was widely used in the frontier period by colonists to seduce Indigenous people to enter settlements, become reliant on rations, or as payment for labour and sexual favours (Langton 1993). It serves to 'tame' the 'dangerous native into the pathetic mendicant "Abo'" (ibid, 197) as well as explain the high imprisonment rates of Indigenous people and their structural exclusion from the productive economy. In Nyah, the stereotype of the 'drunken Aborigine' is used to 'project inauthenticity' upon the Wadi Wadi people, perpetuating notions of degeneration, loss and social pathology (ibid, 205). As a colonial trope, it operates as the Other of the romanticized, noble savage of primitivist discourse. Those who fall 'victim' to the vices of western society notionally lose identity as the romantic savage, to be replaced by the drunken 'Aborigine identity'. A 'drunk black can be an object of hatred in a way that a drunk white cannot, because the former is degenerate in the specific sense of being untrue to his or her racial and cultural nature' (Thomas 1994, 30). These two stereotypes circulate around the polar features of non–Indigenous subconscious feelings about Indigenous people: temptation (the desire to return to the Rousseauian dream of the noble savage) and fear (of the violent, drunken, wild, untamed Aborigine) (Goldie 1989; Lattas 1997).

Wadi Wadi people are also presented as 'incompetent' to speak or assert claims because they have developed alliances and coalitions with non–Indigenous anti-logging groups. Of crucial importance is the founding role that Wadi Wadi people, in coalition with other non–Indigenous local people, played in setting up the Friends of the Nyah–Vinifera Forest group. The FONVF is explicitly anti–logging in its stance and the coalition of the Friends and the Wadi Wadi people is used by Departmental staff to de–authenticate Indigenous claims in the forest on the basis that they have been 'hijacked' by the anti–logging campaign.

Relationships between the environmental movement and Indigenous people, both in Australia and elsewhere, have been the subject of much debate (Anderson 1989; Jacobs 1996; Langton 1996, 1998; Palmer 2004; Willems–Braun 1997). It is often assumed by environmentalists that Indigenous people will (and should) have aspirations and values commensurate with their own. The non–Indigenous West's sense of a looming ecological crisis has pricked a keen interest in Indigenous traditional ecological knowledge as a possible source of knowledge to avert that crisis. However, the very sense of crisis – how the crisis is defined and made meaningful – is embedded within its own set of cultural assumptions that have determined the categories of desirable or undesirable human impact. Biodiversity and conservation are fundamentally cultural constructs, presented as natural and universal truths by Western environmental science showing the peculiar persistence of a colonial heritage within environmental debates:

> environmental debate has become so deeply embedded in the rhetoric of persistance, continuity, and preservation of remnants that the vocabulary of change has been surrendered almost completely to the development lobby. As part of this process, Aboriginal people have become imprisoned by the same rhetoric; 'tradition' is seen as something static and unchanging. (Head 2000, 216)

In the case of Nyah, the relationship between the environmental lobby group and the Indigenous traditional owner group is somewhat less vexed (note there are significant tensions between the group and the wider Indigenous community). Anti–logging interests were substantially supported by Indigenous cultural heritage claims, and the structure of the lobby group has in turn provided broader community support, in addition to a public education role, to the Wadi Wadi traditional owner group. The state, however, as well as other sectors of the local Indigenous community, has challenged the legitimacy of Wadi Wadi aspirations and concerns, based on this alliance, in two ways. First, there is the view mentioned above that this particular environmental lobby group has hijacked and abused Wadi Wadi interests in order to support their anti–logging objectives. Second, that Wadi Wadi, in consenting to this relationship, have effectively voided the legitimacy of their cultural interests in Nyah Forest because of this first appropriation. These views profoundly shape the response of planners and land managers to Wadi Wadi expression of concerns and aspirations for Nyah Forest. It is assumed that when Wadi Wadi speak, they do so as a 'mouthpiece' of the Friends group. And simultaneously, the anti–logging protest is dismissed by this accusation of culturally inappropriate dealings. Ultimately, the result is the further marginalization and de–legitimation of Wadi Wadi jurisdiction for Nyah Forest.

As I discussed in Chapter 5, the other sweetener offered as part of DNRE's new 'thinning' project for Nyah Forest in 2002 was to employ Indigenous people to do the timber harvesting work. Secure and ongoing employment is a key aspiration for Indigenous communities in Swan Hill, Nyah and district, including Wadi Wadi traditional owners. Those communities currently suffer substantially higher unemployment rates than the wider population. In Swan Hill itself, the Indigenous community is burdened with a 26 per cent unemployment rate, compared with only 4.8 per cent for non–Indigenous people (Australian Bureau of Statistics 2001). Further, Indigenous people tend to become locked into seasonal, contract–based or casual work, with relatively low pay and very little job security. DNRE proposed to Indigenous communities and leaders that any thinning operations that took place in Nyah would employ Indigenous people from the then Community Development Employment Programme (CDEP). This was essentially a 'work for benefits' programme specifically for Indigenous peoples. That proposal, in the context of aspirations expressed by the Indigenous community, was attractive in its potential to realize this key aspiration.

One Elder in the community (not in the native title group), who was also employed by DNRE on rolling contracts from month to month, depending on the season and departmental funding arrangements, described his position:

> Well, I've been doing [forest and cultural heritage management] for fifteen years now and what I'm doing now is not enough. I mean its [a] casual job, I could finish up anytime and be redundant...I'd like to be in a permanent position like being a ranger or something, on a permanent basis. (pers. comm. 18 March 2003)

The Forest Manager for DNRE's North West Region is responsible for this Elder's employment status and the development of work programmes and funding arrangements to employ him. The contracts roll between the seasonal work available on the summer fire crew and a range of other programmes that may get funding throughout the rest of the year. One such programme was the employment of a works crew (that included this Elder and a young Indigenous woman on an apprenticeship training scheme) with DNRE to undertake some protective works around some of the mounds and burial places in Nyah Forest. All the crew (both Indigenous and non–Indigenous members) were employed on short–term contracts. Their brief was to build protective fencing and signage around those mounds and burial sites in Nyah Forest that were registered on the AAV sites register. This programme was important particularly to Wadi Wadi people and others, as it was recognition for ongoing work in Nyah Forest through the practice of cultural responsibilities for Nyah Forest (pers. comm. 22 August 2002).

These kinds of arrangements do not generate secure employment outcomes. This is a major concern for local Indigenous people, who are seeking long–term, satisfactory employment:

> over the years we've had contract employment here, bit of funding here and there, but six months is not good enough...The men get teed up to do their culture and heritage out there with the special feeling and the place that they need for survival in the social environment of our communities...and all they get is one–off funding all the time. We can't have any permanency. (pers. comm. Wadi Wadi representative, 1 September 1999)

One of DNRE's Indigenous Facilitators for the region expressed similar concerns about how DNRE and other government agencies approach Indigenous employment programmes:

> communities have been saying for so long that we have all of these initiatives but they've got a three year lifespan or a twelve month lifespan, and we're unstable. You know, it means shit to us in the sense that these things come and go and then you become a political pawn and you don't sort of get anywhere. How can you progress a project that's only a 12 month lifespan? (pers. comm. 19 September 2002)

DNRE's initiative to employ permanent, well–salaried Indigenous people into the Indigenous Facilitator positions in each of its administrative regions is a positive step in the context of these employment aspirations. Nevertheless, much remains to be achieved to address the level of social and employment inequity for Indigenous people in Victoria, as recognized in the Victorian Government's public service Indigenous Employment Programme, 'Wur–cum–burra' (Department of Natural Resources and Environment 2002a).

Insecurity of employment is the primary reason why this senior Elder quoted earlier is unwilling to talk to DNRE management about his perspective on the issue of logging in Nyah Forest. At the August 2002 meeting to discuss the thinning proposal he remained silent during the entire discussion, and declined an opportunity during brainstorming to list his view of the advantages and disadvantages of the thinning proposal. He felt that DNRE use his status as an employee of the organization (albeit only casual) to create further unrest in the community:

> DNRE seem to have a deaf ear [to Wadi Wadi concerns about logging]. They ask me a lot of questions about logging. [I say] no, don't talk to me because I'm working for you. You go and speak to [Wadi Wadi people]...Don't talk to me... just because I'm working here, doesn't mean it gives you the go ahead to go and cut down a couple of trees, does it. They try to get me in that predicament. [They say] 'you're alright if we cut down a few trees here and there, thin it out?' I say, 'no mate, I told you, go and see [Wadi Wadi people]'. That's the bottom line. (pers. comm. 18 March 2003)

DNRE's thinning proposal, then, was actively divisive. At the consultation meeting in August 2002, DNRE's Forest Manager described its purpose as attempting to achieve 'longevity in employment programs' and move away from the 'bandaid approach' to employment initiatives that is DNRE's normal practice. The Senior Forester for the region in charge of the proposed thinning programme also used the notion of employment generation as a key reason why the programme should be supported by Indigenous people. He argued that the thinning proposal constituted a 'pretty good offer' for Forestry Victoria to make to the local Indigenous community. Later he expressed disappointment that the $65,000 funding allocation was 'lost' back to the general Departmental budget because of lack of agreement. This 'loss' of funding means, according to the Senior Forester, that the possibility to create three to four locally–based jobs for Indigenous people has been foregone (pers. comm. Senior Forester, Forestry Victoria).

What is most interesting about this event is how the power of Forestry Victoria and the state's requirement to operationalize Nyah's designation as 'available for timber harvesting' ultimately rationalized all other commonsense (rational) planning options. When analysed in policy–evaluative terms, the decisions made in this case study do not appear to make sense. If the crux of the matter really was, as DNRE staff described it, the obligation to generate sustainable and long–term employment initiatives for Indigenous communities, then why wasn't the funding that had been made available switched to another programme after it became clear at this meeting that there was not broad support for the project? Far from providing 'longevity' of employment, the funds were limited to $65,000, only available for one financial year and would fund only casual, short–term positions.

Further, the crew would be employed through the CDEP programme. This was a national Indigenous employment programme, designed to assist Indigenous people move off unemployment benefits into jobs. It operated as a 'work for welfare' scheme, where communities design their own labour programmes for residents who, on the whole, then became ineligible for mainstream unemployment benefits. CDEP was roundly criticized especially by Indigenous leaders as the 'principal poverty trap for Indigenous individuals, families and communities' (Langton 2002a). Structural disincentives built into the scheme failed to encourage Aboriginal Community Councils (who operate local CDEP programmes) to redirect participants into the productive economy (ibid). Further, because the scheme operated as both a welfare and workforce programme simultaneously, it ultimately was powerfully shaped by local political interests (Rowse 1993). Thus, the extent to which the thinning project proposed by DNRE was really able to create 'real jobs' and provide 'longevity of employment to Aboriginal people' as claimed, is dubious due to the powerful operation of the entrenched interests in Nyah.

When Indigenous people (Wadi Wadi in particular) assert challenges to state–based planners and decision–makers, those challenges are often discarded as 'impure' or illegitimate by these powerful discursive practices. If a profound challenge is mounted to the state, it is put down as 'the grog speaking', or otherwise an Indigenous claim made 'impure' by contact with non–Indigenous affiliations. Despite operating under a banner of partnership, reconciliation and respect, the procedures of planning in Nyah work to engineer division and marginalization.

The (Post)colonial Limit of Collaborative Planning

There is a substantial effort within planning literature to approach an analysis of the kinds of planning stories I have been talking about in this chapter using the conceptual framework of deliberative democracy, or what has been identified (though not without qualifiers as to the diversity of the field) as the 'communicative turn' in planning. This is important, because a growing body of scholarship is turning its attention to whether 'community–based' environmental planning initiatives herald progressive approaches and new insights into the practices and operations of planning in settler states (Lane 1997; Lane and McDonald 2005; Lane and Corbett 2005; Chinhoyi 2004; Dale 1992; McCall and Minang 2005). In many cases these directly apply the Habermasian ideals of communicative rationality to (post)colonial planning conflicts.

We could, then, 'see' these two very different stories from Nyah and Gariwerd as different points on a continuum of better collaborative planning and 'not' communicative planning. Those conceptual ideas are also gaining some purchase, at least in their name, in policy environments. That many park management authorities, agencies and officers in settler states now talk freely about Indigenous 'partnership' and empowerment through collaborative approaches attests to both the relentless criticism Indigenous people have mounted to the environmental planning canon over the years, as well as this 'turn' in planning theory.

Yet, the (post)coloniality of relations in settler states unsettles the theoretical presumptions of the collaborative model. The two stories I have re–presented above (and equally the two I analysed in Porter 2006a), despite their apparent stark differences in process, attitude and potential outcome, are actually structured around the same problem: the production of a hierarchy of place and the spatialized scaling of bodies. We cannot, then, argue away the differences in procedure, outcome and approach as the vagaries of bureaucracy or individual bureaucrats. Instead, I want to show how these cases are intimately tied into colonial relations of power as I developed in Chapters 3 and 4. We cannot transcend, in these cases, the colonial specificity of the designation of land uses (parks, forests) and the scaling of bodies within that designation. What happens when we put together a critical understanding of (post)colonial relations of power with the search for deliberative democracy? This question is what I address in the remainder of this chapter, to look closely at the theoretical and practical difference Indigeneity makes to the search for deliberative democracy in planning.

If we take Brand and Gaffikin's (2007) exposition of the philosophical premises of the collaborative planning model we can begin to unpick the inherent contradictions of 'collaborative' planning in (post)colonial contexts. Brand and Gaffikin (2007) set out what they see to be the ontological, epistemological, ideological and methodological premises of collaborative planning. These include a philosophy of relational space with humans operating as political agents in organic systems; a de–privileging of knowledge to encompass multiple, emergent, co–constructed knowledges; a recognition of values, justice and difference; and a method that seeks to broaden participation to 'all stakeholders' within fully deliberative processes.

Shifts in the approach to park planning and management in Gariwerd may appear to be underpinned by these kinds of philosophies. There is certainly attention to cultural difference, the situatedness of Indigenous knowledge, and some attention to the question of land justice. The process of producing the revised park management plan sought to include a much wider range of people than previously, and has brought Indigenous interests to the fore in new ways. We might see, then, a collaborative validity in this process where the principles of decisions 'have been agreed by all affected by their consequences' (Mouffe 1999, 39). We might also see the presence of an orientation to questions of justice, especially where individual officers within the bureaucracy have taken on the responsibility (and it is a challenging and significant one) of pushing for reform in the face of entrenched racial stereotypes. In the case of Nyah, there is a much more limited attention to questions of justice, to the inclusion of different knowledges, to the construction of deliberative forums where all stakeholders can participate in decision–making. It is interesting to note that the story of Nyah has unfolded exactly at the same time as the same Department was developing its Indigenous Partnerships Strategy, an explicit statement of shifts to a more collaborative and inclusive approach that begins to recognize the particular position of Indigenous groups, and the difference that Indigeneity makes.

The process of place governance has to some extent changed, most obviously in Gariwerd, and there are signs of some shifts in the epistemological premises of planning, again most obviously in Gariwerd where Indigenous knowledges are given prominence. Yet the ontological philosophies of planning remain firmly intact, relatively untouched by the movement around them, and colonial relations of power are always present. Nyah represents more overtly the practice of persistent colonial relations of power, the domination of Indigenous peoples, the deliberate subversion of identity rights claims, and the ongoing practice of an epistemology of racial hatred. Gariwerd represents a quieter form of epistemic and ontic violence. An appearance that a subversion is taking place, an appearance of a shift to a colonial beyond, perhaps constitutes a 'front' for continuing forms of dominant power, masking the same persistent colonial spatial cultures.

The difference Indigeneity makes in these kinds of cases is, then, ontological and epistemological. It exposes that in some cases new kinds of process are being wrapped around plans and policies that are fully embedded in the rational–comprehensive models of 'traditional' land use planning. Such models are colonial spatial cultures, hegemonic in that they serve a mode of production. Even while this is always fractured and always partial, as Lefebvre (1991) shows, it is nonetheless an active reconstitution of colonial space production. They are also hegemonic in the sense that Mouffe posits, as the field itself (cultural heritage, environmental planning, co–management) is only consistent because of the presence of a master signifer (Mouffe 1999, 751). Procedure cannot fix the immanent difference Indigeneity makes. Indeed, procedure might be better conceptualized as a 'fix', as new forms of governmentality (Fischler 2000), and this has special relevance to the (post)colonial.

Collaborative planning or deliberative models of planning process, as has been explored and critiqued elsewhere (Hillier 2003; Huxley 2000; Huxley and Yiftachel 2000; Fischler 2000; Brand and Gaffikin 2007; Sandercock 2000; McGuirk 2007) creates an impossible positionality for planning. As a system, planning suddenly disappears from view, to be replaced by a 'therapist' (in the sense of the listening therapist that Forester 1989 suggests, and in the critical sense that Sandercock 2000 suggests for it) or even the 'critical friend' suggested by Pløger (2004, drawing from Mouffe's idea of the adversarial friend). These subjects then seem to float, apparently disconnected from the regulatory regime that enabled the position of 'planner' in the first place. Spatial cultures and systems of spatial rationalities, of planning objects and substantive interests, of regulatory interests and desires, dissolve. The planner, then, is left with no 'position', no situatedness, no context. In that move, planning and 'the planner' becomes an uncomplicated backdrop, culturally colourless, able to absorb and mediate the clamour of difference, interests, and divergent rationalities from 'outside'.

Yet as this book has shown, planning is neither empty nor colourless, but in fact replete with its ontological philosophies and its cultural assumptions, full of its own forms of problematization (Huxley 2000), its own methods and structures for defining solutions. Spatial cultures are fully present in planning as I have shown in relation to a number of places and especially Gariwerd and Nyah. 'Park' or 'forest' exist as particular kinds of entities, discursively produced and performed through the regulatory practices of western spatial cultures. Efforts for 'more inclusivity' of Indigenous people in decision–making concerning those places can only take place within those practices, constitutive of those already existing spatial cultures. The very relationship 'planner–Indigene' makes colonial pasts fully present. There can be, then, no uncomplicated position from which the planner can arbitrate, challenge and question those outside itself. It is already 'within' itself, within its own relations of power, its own rationalities, its own culture.

Related to this, is the assumption in the collaborative model that consensus based rationality is possible, and even desirable. Other critics (Huxley 2000; Huxley and Yiftachel 2000; Brand and Gaffikin 2007) clearly point out the fundamental problem here with the assumption that we have communicative competence and wish to use it. I want to focus on two particular points that have special relevance, and implications, in (post)colonial contexts: an assumed accessibility of cultural difference in 'others' and racialized assumptions within 'ourselves'; and the related suspension of history and context in the quest for ideal communicative processes. To do so, I will take a close look at one particular paper that seems to exemplify the problems within this approach.

In a paper exploring a participatory planning process with native Hawaiians, Umemoto (2001) explores the ways in which Indigenous cultural difference was rendered accessible to the planners involved. This was a community planning project with Papakolea, a Hawaiian homestead community in central Honolulu. Homestead communities arose in the 1920s to enable those Indigenous Hawaiians with sufficient Indigenous heritage, as defined by the law, to return to their lands. The project undertaken included in particular a community visioning process, collectively run by planning consultants and the Papakolea Community Association (Umemoto 2001, 20), to develop a community plan for the future of the lands.

Umemoto's notion of difference is as an individualized set of characteristics (I am different from you) that made itself present by exploring forms of 'culturally appropriate' practice and seeing difference as a 'resource' in deliberative decision–making (drawing from Young, I.M. 1995 and also 2000) rather than a fragmentation. Yet the only 'difference' that is ever posited here is that of the culturally–constituted Other: the native Hawaiian. The planners are never asked to bring their difference to the table. Instead it is the Indigenous participants who are asked to become self–aware and then expose their difference, their partiality, in the deliberative forum. Young (1995) herself explores the universalist tendencies within deliberative democracy theories and is looking to models that can 'recognize the cultural specificity of deliberative practices' and thus propose 'a more inclusive model of communication' (137). Her ensuing thoughts go some way to doing this. Yet the model itself is never centralized as the object of self–reflection, or deconstruction for cultural specificity, in an ontological sense. While the methods might shift (less emphasis on speaking, using storytelling and narrative), the prior existence of certain kinds of social 'facts' remains outside the mode of analysis.

Applied to planning in Umemoto's paper (2001), the result is a reification through 'honouring' of difference and Otherness, achieved in two related ways. First, practitioners' own cultural specificities are rendered invisible in the process, such that the problem becomes a methodological one (see Brand and Gaffikin 2007). Cultural translation, code switching and the like are the methodological forms Umemoto describes for making difference accessible and transcendable. Second, the presence of colonial pasts are naturalized and thus silenced. Umemoto makes a passing reference to the 'blood quantum requirement' in the regulations concerning Hawaiian homestead communities.

Her text naturalizes as a feature of 'cultural identity' this utterly racialized form of colonial power. The construction of 'race' as measured through blood, and spatialized through the regulation of bodies in place, and what that might mean for the very practice of spatial management, is the elephant in the room for collaborative planning in this particular (post)colonial context. Without attention to this history and context, its structural specificities, its strategic utterances, the modes of explanation it gives rise to (Fischler 2000), we cannot see that the problematization planning is creating and performing in this case should also be the subject of analysis (Huxley 2000).

The goodwill factor ever-present in the collaborative model assumes not only a full awareness, but indeed suspension of racialized assumptions. Yet as I have shown in this chapter, racism is pernicious fundamentally because of its tendency to be deeply embedded in our psyches, and to hide in the glue we use to render coherent our ways of being, social order, forms of governance, mores and values. A scaling of bodies (Young 1990) and a particular performance of spatial cultures helps keep that order intact. Both are written into the very structures of regulatory practice that enables planning to exist. As the story from Nyah demonstrates with some clarity, the move to rely on the suspension of racism and the goodwill of individuals is a very, very fragile way to proceed.

Conclusion

When planning seeks to 'negotiate', no matter how collaboratively and deliberatively, with Indigenous people in settler states it does so with colonial pasts fully present. The very act of the conversation, the possibility of the discussion, is constitutive within colonial relations. Spatial governance, planning, environmental management – these modern practices of the state exist in settler states because of their fully present colonial histories. That those conversations, then, are utterly framed and constrained by the existence of regulations, laws and procedures shows them to be already constituted within those master signifiers (Mouffe 1999; Hillier 2003). Consequently, we cannot transcend those present politics, histories and networks of power. More inclusive planning approaches in Gariwerd can only occur within the already existing parameters, language and institutionalized discourse of national park planning – framed by an Act of

Parliament, a suite of regulations, accepted procedures, institutions and actors that together perform systematic cultures of space that are by definition, by their very existence, constitutive of colonial relations of power. Power, then, or perhaps the products and productiveness of power, is ontological (Mouffe 1999) and in that sense impossible to transcend: 'it cannot be reasoned away' (McGuirk 2001, 213).

Indigenous claims, furthermore, radically unsettle the assumption within many progressive planning models that justice requires inclusivity. To assume that you get justice from inclusivity is troubled by Indigenous claims for 'special' status, and the ongoing practice in the lifeworlds of Indigenous people of a specifically Indigenous domain which may work against the grain of inclusivity. The model of procedural justice that the collaborative planning idea rests on, is the 'same sense of searching for the right decision–rules' (Huxley and Yiftachel 2000, 334) that underpin the model of planning the collaborative mode seeks to 'turn' away from. What do we do about the 'special status' claim of Indigenous sovereignty, if collaborative practice asks us to bracket off history? Where Indigenous rights claims have a newfound legal basis, how can any model that seeks to include 'all' stakeholders as equal participants ever achieve their normative ideals in (post)colonial settings? There is much more theoretical and practical work to be done here. If we accept, as Mouffe suggests, that power is 'constitutive of the social' then our focus should be 'not how to eliminate power but how to constitute forms of power that are compatible with democratic values' (1999, 753). We will need to explore 'what to do' about the presence of power, colonial context and the difference Indigeneity makes, questions that I turn to in the final chapter.

Chapter 7
Unlearning Privilege:
Towards the Decolonization of Planning

...Where is the hope of a clean tomorrow?
Hope only offers when justice is coming.
Now is the time to heal.

Where is the ground, the beloved country?
Women and men who have fallen silent?
Now is the time, now is the time,
Now is the time to heal.

(Midnight Oil 1996 'Time to Heal' from the album 'Breathe')

The endeavour of this book is to mark planning in settler states as a cultural form, and start to trace the specificities of that cultural form. I have written the book, and you have read it, because this really matters to our world and our times: especially for justice for Indigenous peoples. The domain of planning is one area of many where injustices against Indigenous peoples remain. In a sense, locating planning within a cultural frame has been a play on 'culture', because a significant orientation of my analysis has been toward unsettling the division of natures and cultures, or at least to expose, and in doing so make available for analysis, how planning produces that division. At least some of the work of recombination (Latour 1991) must be to historicize that which has set itself up as a universal norm: in this case, planning. A first effort, then, is to find ways of seeing planning as an active cultural agent in space: 'cultural' in the sense that it inhabits particular (rather than universal) explanatory schemas, structures of meaning. To invert Jacobs' critique of the reification of Indigenous cultures, my aim has been to see planning as a 'culture that knows nature differently' (1996, 136).

In doing so, I have endeavoured to look at how spatial cultures have operated within the emergence and practice of a cultural activity called 'planning', and how those rationalities have produced colonial space. Planning, as the ordering and management of space, was the early work of colonists 'on arrival'. Consequently, any kind of contemporary planning activity in settler states must be analytically cognisant of, and ethically oriented toward, that history–as–present. Moreover, we have seen that there are specific technologies to the work of producing abstract space in colonies (violence, dispossession, the scaling of bodies in space, racial hatred) as well as multiple forms of Indigenous resistance. These cast long shadows across planning in settler states.

Is it possible, or desirable, to generate a typology of this colonial spatial culture of planning? There is of course the potential to reify and essentialize a practice that is polyvalent, fractured, and multi-sited even as it performs its own myths of comprehensive coherency. Yet such a typology is available, particularly as a critical reading of the Cartesian cogito, and this book adds in a small way to that burgeoning analysis (Lefebvre 1991; Latour 1991; Whatmore 2002; Bennett and Chaloupka 1993; Castree and Braun 2001). A significant part of that spatial rationality we can now see in planning is a separation of natures and cultures, of the realms of material and mental, of the 'raw' to the 'cooked'.

Evidence of Lefebvre's three characteristics of abstract space – homogeneity, fragmentation and hierarchy (2003, 210), where exchange value dominates – is also apparent. Throughout the book I have explored how the planning canon collapses the specificities of places into a generalized set of spatial characteristics, producing a homogenisation of spaces. Certain combinations of vegetation and landform come to form an item within a general environmental planning category. Size and type of tree determines where 'forests' are, and they have a homogeneous composition within themselves, even as they are fragmented across time and space. Technologies of land parcelling, use and buffer zoning, recording discrete sites: all are signs of a homogeneity 'reduced to crumbs' (Lefebvre 2003, 210). The hierarchisation of places, according to their generalized spatial characteristics, is a coding of value in space. In this book, I have looked in detail at the particular hierarchy of spaces within protected area planning and management. A framework of how planning's (post)colonial spatial cultures operate would also have to include the production of knowledge, and the orientation of knowledge to particular kinds of (natural or cultural) things. I have discussed the dominance of scientific knowledge as an unquestioned evidence base, but also the incorporation (and it is not innocent) of Indigenous knowledges within that evidence base.

Inevitably, with such a framework or typology, we are back to those thorny questions of difference and essentialism. I want to return to those questions in some more detail in the closing sections of this chapter, so I will leave them hanging for a moment to readdress the wider significance of this work: attending to the politics of those variously operating (but generally consistent) spatial cultures. That project has especially been to orient our analysis toward the forms of domination they evoke, permit and extend, as well as the disjunctures that analysis can expose and offer as sites of resistance.

Why? Because there is something to care about here: a series of questions that must engage us ethically, intellectually and practically. All of this is worth writing about, and worthy of fuller investigations, because it seems to me unethical to permit a spatial practice to continue with such unjust outcomes for Indigenous peoples. It is not, then, a theoretical exercise, in the sense of that pursuit operating only at the mental level, or of not having application. Obviously it is a theoretical exercise in the sense of bringing all of our conceptual and analytical powers to bear on the questions that are arising. The point of this book is to begin the work of orienting planning towards its own oppression of Indigenous peoples, and towards a critical, deconstructed awareness of itself, of its spatial culture. I have tried to orient my analysis to an engagement with these questions, and of the necessity, ultimately, for transformative practice.

In the next sections, I explore some ideas for what that transformative practice might be, starting from the premise that a decolonization of planning is required. This is not a disavowal of already existing modes of planning (in its practice and theory), or of Western science. That would mislead us into imagining colonialism as a coherent project where the past, present and future are easily reconciled into a secure, progressive narrative. Further, it would advocate a 'return' to some essentialized form of original being and deny the very journey that I am trying to embark on in this book. The decolonization of planning must proceed as a complex renegotiation of values, knowledge, meaning, agency and power between planning and Indigenous peoples, and within planning itself. This work, as I will refer to it here, might occur along three conceptual and practical lines and I explore these in the remainder of this chapter: the question of recognition, justice and 'formal equality'; the continuing work of exposing and locating colonial spatial cultures in planning; and the necessity of a radical politics of love.

Recognition and Justice

The challenge of difference is everywhere, and this book is just one voice among a myriad that reiterates the point. More humbly, this book is merely a tiny report amongst the huge work of resistance, struggle, strategy and action being mounted by Indigenous people to fight injustice. The particular form of injustice that I have been concentrating my efforts on here has been cultural imperialism or domination (following a combined reading of both Fraser 1995 and Young 1990). Indigenous people are a group structured by many other forms of oppression as well: exploitation, marginalization, and violence (to use other aspects of Young's five faces of oppression). If that constant and persistent effort by Indigenous peoples cannot open non–Indigenous eyes to the difference that Indigeneity makes, the multiple forms of injustice that structure the lives of Indigenous peoples, the existence of 'multiple constitutions' as Tully (1995) would call it, and the importance of a right to difference, it is difficult to see what will. Liberal responses to the claims of difference (Indigenous or otherwise) has been structured along two lines: to see difference as a threat to unity, or to see difference and its protection as one item on a list of liberal 'goods' (Tully 1995). Both have been the subject of critique from the many angles offered by (post)colonial, poststructural, and feminist analyses. Modes and technologies of recognizing difference and institutionalizing forms of protection within this liberal frame (native title, treaty negotiations, cultural heritage legislation, forms of 'consultation' in planning processes) contain many ethical dangers. These stem partly from what Tully (2004) has theorized as the monological mode of settling identity claims and partly from what I have shown to be a fundamental fallacy in deliberative assumptions in (post)colonial contexts.

At some point, however, the work of fighting injustice requires a moment of 'rough social equality' (Fraser 1995, 90). Without that, if we work for a moment from inside the perspective of state–based planning, it is difficult to see how and where the first movement toward a more ethical (post)colonial practice can be located. A necessary precondition for that practice is a form of recognition of those multiple constitutions (Tully 1995), in our case of the continuing constitution that is the Indigenous domain, within existing institutions. In other words, the state must be one of the sites of struggle, because it is part of the 'extension of the field of democratic struggles' (Laclau and Mouffe 2001, 176) where recognition of Indigenous peoples, their rights and sovereign domains, must be waged and (contingently) won.

Difference is not a threat to liberal discourse. This is partly because that discourse has always had the capacity to recognize the multiple social organizations it has found itself in contact with (see Tully 1995; Gilbert 2007), and partly because 'the *meaning* of liberal discourse in individual rights is not definitively fixed' (Laclau and Mouffe 2001, 176 original italics). It should be possible, then, to find forms of action and knowledge production within planning that are oriented to the plurality of their every situated context. But more than 'hearing the clamour of difference', as the collaborative or deliberative modes of planning suggest, I argue that such recognition needs to advocate something closer to the 'transformative remedies' Fraser (1995, 70) offers: approaches that unsettle *all* fixity, that destabilize *all* identity positions and expose the frames of reference within which each situated action takes place. It is the form of 'democratic equivalence' that Laclau and Mouffe lead us toward (2001, 183), and the contemporary constitutionalism that Tully (1995) outlines. In a recent paper, Tully (2004) critiques the ways in which struggles over recognition have been analysed and addressed in modern political theory and practice. He argues that looking for definitive, final and substantive solutions to contests over identity recognition, has generated a series of ontological and practical problems. Two particularly problematic features he sees are firstly the top–down imposition of 'solutions' by elite theorists, courts and policy–makers; and secondly the assumption of a definitive finality to those solutions. An alternative is to instead see recognition as relational, mutual and multiple rather than fixed in substantive or rigid regimes of recognition. In other words the question of recognition is not 'for' recognition but instead *over* recognition as both Tully (2004) and Laclau and Mouffe (2001) show. Seen in this way, recognition becomes a transformative possibility, where there is a certain '*freedom* of those subject to a norm to have a say over it: to be agents as well as subjects' (Tully 2004, 89, original emphasis).

Plurality, situatedness, values, justice, the undoing of all fixity, the articulation of equivalences: all are forms of difference recognition already being discussed in the planning field (Healey 1997; Sandercock 2003; Watson 2006; Campbell 2006; Forester 1999; Holston 1998). Here I am adding my voice to the many in finding moments of recognition that will open the way for new conversations. In more concrete terms, I am advocating ways of recognizing the domain of the Indigenous polity within planning, either within or outside legal forms (both are possible), to enable different kinds of practices to become available. This does not necessarily have to be a formal, legal recognition of Indigenous rights. I say this, cognisant that such a statement may appear to be letting settler states 'off the hook' of the hard work of legal recognition. This is not my intent at all – that legal recognition is crucially important. Instead, I do not want to let settler states 'off the hook' of recognizing the Indigenous polity in everyday ways in state–based planning, in the *absence* of that legal recognition. Our 'recognition' of multiply constituted polities, Indigenous and others, can occur in a myriad of everyday ways. It can constitute some of the 'thousand tiny empowerments' Sandercock (1998b) suggests for locally based orientations to justice.

Yet this is only the start, or perhaps more accurately, only one part of what I see as a multiply–oriented work. It is only one part because of the immanent danger of continuing forms of colonial dominance, because of the long shadow that colonialism casts. (Post)coloniality requires a different order again of Fraser's transformative work. This leads us to a specific analytical task that forms one more line of action before us.

'Unlearning' Planning

In her attempts to find a way to *not* speak for the oppressed, *nor* to allow the oppressed to speak, Spivak calls for an 'unlearning' of our 'privilege' (Spivak 1994, 91). This is a method of working 'critically back through one's history, prejudices and learned...responses' (Landry and MacLean 1996, 4) in order to articulate, and make available for critique, the ideological formations and silences that lie within. This is the critical, analytical task I see before us for planning in settler states: a full excavation of planning's own complicity (not to mention strategic importance) with colonial processes, and an analytical cognisance of planning as having produced its own spatial ontologies and rationalities because it practices a spatial culture. A significant part of the work in this book has been to begin that work of 'unlearning' the privilege of planning, exposing that complicity, placing planning within the 'cultural' frame. This orientation in attitude is the beginning of a properly ethical relation with Indigenous people, by finding methods of 'speaking to' in a way that they can be answered (Spivak 1994).

Some points of clarification are necessary. The modality of 'speaking' that Spivak posits here crosses the entire transaction of listening and talking. Unlearning is a mode of practice rather than a reduction of practice to language. It is a practice that involves a necessary confluence, as most practice does, of acting and speaking (read also listening) together. We don't need to focus so much, then, on whether this is a privileging of language or not if we can also enrol Foucault's conceptualization of discourse and Said's methods of finding new combinations of textuality and practice in colonial domination. On the question of 'privilege', I read her meaning here as the ideological formations that have constructed particular subjects, and the relations between those subjects (see Spivak 1994, 92). We might think of that privilege in terms of its ability to make its power hegemonic, to dominate and oppress.

The work of 'unlearning privilege' in planning, then, is about historicising the ideological formations of planning, its silences and formative productions, its practices, expressions and rationalities. In other words, it is to persistently critique the structures we inhabit. Such analysis must be the programme of work for non–Indigenous peoples in settler states, it must be seen as a non–Indigenous 'problem'. In the context of planning, it must be a focus of work for those inhabiting the existing institutions of contemporary planning: governments, agencies, universities, and consultancies. In this book, I have tried to carve out new directions for how this work might be approached through what I hope can be seen as a generous critique of current practices and analytical stances. An overall attitude to employ is to bring the silences of planning under the frame of analysis. In doing so, the work is to expose those silences as forms of ideology: as spatial culture that are productive toward space. At least a part of the work is the acknowledgement, as I sought to more fully appreciate in Chapter 6, that because there is no view from nowhere, planning cannot claim for itself the status of 'backdrop'.

A range of analytical tools is available for this work. Methods I have found particularly helpful here are the genealogical approach offered by Foucault (1972 and 1984) and developed in specific contexts by Legg (2007b), Shaw (2007), Smith (2004), and Huxley (2006 and 2007). This automatically orients our analysis to historical contingencies, local manifestations, and discrete (neither disconnected nor comprehensive) practices. I have also found helpful Lefebvre's orientation to particular, contextualized 'space/times' as a mode of analysis. The tool that Spivak offers is deconstruction, following her reading of Derrida (see Spivak 1988), and closely relates to the kind of analytical attitude and effort I suggest we need for a thorough unlearning of planning's privilege.

This book is an effort in these kinds of directions: to create an historiographical account of planning in settler states and thereby to see planning as having its own ideological formations, ontologies and rationalities: spatial cultures that constitute one mode of producing space. This makes the epistemic violence of that productive mode fully present and visible, and presents a framework for investigating planning that invites power and domination to be made available for analysis. All of this requires an ethical stance of some kind, an attention to the living presence of power and domination, of injustice. In the final section, I discuss some aspects of what I see as that necessary ethical and practical orientation.

Love as Radical Practice[1]

I have no 'models' of practice to offer here. Insights into the plurality and indeterminacy of both the social, and therefore social struggle, the situatedness of knowledge, and the contingent structures that shape the conditions of our existence, suggest that models are not very helpful. Instead, I want to focus more on *orientations to practice* that are centred not on procedure but ethical attitudes. Radical practices can only be constituted in practice, and therefore are always situated (Young 2000; Campbell 2006; Watson 2006; Rangan 1999). How, then, do we find modes of 'doing' radical practice in these situated and contingent moments, particularly in (post)colonial contexts? How do we engage ethically and responsibly with those that we have Othered, and with operations of power that we are inextricably bound into?

Domination, oppression and injustice are the products of hatred and violence, not only of the maldistribution of rights and goods. This is often noticed in analyses that focus on oppression, domination and injustice. Yet equally often those analyses fail to connect with our most obvious and powerful spiritual wellspring of hope and transformation in the face of that hatred and violence: love. As hooks so powerfully observes:

> The absence of a sustained focus on love in progressive circles arises from a collective failure to acknowledge the needs of the spirit and an overdetermined emphasis on material concerns. Without love, our efforts to liberate ourselves and our world community from oppression and exploitation are doomed. (1994, 243)

This is not a romantic, sexual or intimate love, though hooks makes these kinds of links (see hooks 1994, 2000a and 2000b), nor is it a sentimental soppy affection. Instead, it is love as a deep practice of connection: of selflessness, humility and compassion. It is not a 'model' of being or a set of rules, but an ethic towards others, a daily practice.

Critical analysis, or a critical politics, is absolutely fundamental to a transformative (post)colonial politics. It is also absolutely fundamental to the decolonization of planning. It can highlight the moments of injustice, offer understandings of the structures and actions at work in particular historical circumstances. It can notice important detail and provide narratives to construct our knowledge about events and options for the future. Yet that is only some of the necessary work. Why would we bother, if we didn't actually care about these questions? What would motivate us to find transformative possibilities if not out of love? Why would we be moved to action if not from a deep ethical connection, beyond the realm of rational analysis, with others and their suffering (Nussbaum

---

[1] A rephrasing of bell hooks' 'love as the practice of freedom' (1994, 243).

1990)? To ignore the presence of love is surely to disavow our own humanity. Equally, to ignore the possibility, agency and power of love is to fail liberation.

One of the core themes of this book has been social relations, and in particular the relations constituted within and through colonial processes, and within and through planning. I have been discussing the positions of 'planners' and 'Indigenous peoples', of 'natures' and 'cultures', of struggle, dialectics, racism, and change. All these are the language and practice of social relations. We must, then, have a relational politics. Love is that relational politics. Love connects, rather than severs: it is only within relations that love can be identified, felt, mobilized. It gains its energy from that constitution as relations between peoples.

This relational nature of the practice of love has a number of important dimensions: service, compassion, and insight (hooks 1994; Nussbaum 1990). These three are important. Service to others recalls Spivak's 'speaking to' others and I suggest is an extension of that reading. An ethic of service can humble arrogance, and orient care and attention to where injustice exists. It would unsettle divisions by placing people in a different relation with each other: one of service, not of 'winning' the argument. An orientation to each other in service 'intervenes in our self–centred longing for change' (hooks 1994, 244) and instead places us differently in relation to each other and to the project of liberation from oppression. The stance of service acknowledges who we are, our position in the relationship Indigenous–non–Indigenous, but reminds us that we are always more than this, because we are in service to each other. Compassion invites connection with suffering and injustice at a level other than the analytical. It orients the energy of our care and attention, and is supple enough to operate anywhere, in any circumstances. Insight re–places the importance of understanding and analysis, and reminds us that any practice must be self–aware as well as world–aware. It must challenge us intellectually as well as move our hearts. The critical stance of analysis that is so necessary to the work of the decolonization of planning must take place within a spirit of love. That is where we will be moved.

This book constitutes a series of insights into particular moments of planning in a context of Indigenous claims for justice. Yet it highlights a set of dilemmas and significant problems that appear to be echoed in many different situational contexts for planning. The work ahead is challenging. Hope for transformative possibilities lies in these three modalities of practice, or orienting activities, I have outlined here. Acts of recognition and a critical analytical stance toward unlearning the privilege of planning provides us with intellectual modes of engagement to material questions. But it is love as a politics of service, compassion and insight that will move us to radical practice: toward a more transformative (post)colonial politics of planning.

Bibliography

Agar, M.H. (1996), *The Professional Stranger: An Informal Introduction to Ethnography* (San Diego: Academic Press).
Alden, J.R. (1944), *John Stuart and the Southern Colonial Frontier: A Study of Indian Relations, War, Trade, and Land Problems in the Southern Wilderness, 1754–1775* (Ann Arbor: University of Michigan Press).
Alexander, I. and Yiftachel, O. (1997), 'Sacred Site or Sacred Cow? The Frontier of Urban Racial Struggle in Australia', in Yiftachel, O. and Fenster, T. (eds.) *Frontier Development and Indigenous Peoples* (UK: Pergamon).
Anderson, C. (1989), 'Aborigines and Conservationism: The Daintree–Bloomfield Road', *Australian Journal of Social Issues* 24:3, 214–227.
Archer, W.H. (1861), *Catalogue of the Victorian Exhibition, 1861: With Prefatory Essays Indicating the Progress, Resources and Physical Characteristics of the Colony* (Melbourne: Clarson Shallard and Co).
Arndt, W. (1962), 'The Nargorkun–Narlinji Cult', *Oceania* 32, 298–320.
Arndt, W. (1966), 'Seventy year old records and new information on the Nargorkun–Narlinji Cult', *Oceania* 36, 231–38.
Atkinson, W. (2002), 'Mediating the Mindset of Opposition: The Yorta Yorta Case', *Indigenous Law Bulletin* 5:15, 8–11.
Australian Bureau of Statistics (2001), *Census of Population and Housing*. (Canberra, ABS).
Baker, R. Davies, J. and Young, E. (eds.) (2001), *Working on Country: Contemporary Indigenous Management of Australia's Lands and Coastal Regions* (Melbourne: Oxford University Press).
Bandler, F. (1989), *Turning the Tide* (Canberra: Aboriginal Studies Press).
Banner, S. (1999), 'Two Properties, One Land: Law and Space in Nineteenth-Century New Zealand', *Law and Social Inquiry* 24:4, 807–852.
Barsh, R.L. (1998), 'Prospects for International Action to Defend Sacred Land', in. Oakes. J, Riewe, R. and Kinew, R. (eds.) *Sacred Lands: Aboriginal World Views, Claims and Conflicts* (Edmonton: Canadian Circumpolar Institute).
Baxter, B., McCartney, D., Nicholls, D., Nicholson, S., O'Bree, L. and Pattenden, J. (1990), 'Matakupat: Aboriginal History of the Swan Hill Area', unpublished pamphlet.
BC Parks Strathcona District (2001), 'Strathcona Masterplan Amendment', <http://env.gov.bc.ca/bcparks/planning/mgmtplns/strathcona/strath-b_mp.pdf>, accessed 1 September 2009.
Beebeejaun, Y. (2004), 'What's in a Nation? Constructing Ethnicity in the British Planning System', *Planning, Theory and Practice* 5:4, 437–451.

Bell, K.N. and Morrell, W.P. (1928), *Select Documents on British Colonial Policy 1830–1860* (Oxford: Clarendon Press).
Beltran, J. (2000), *Indigenous and Traditional Peoples and Protected Areas: Principles, Guidelines and Case Studies* (Gland, Switzerland and Cambridge, UK: IUCN and WWF).
Bennett, J. and Chaloupka, W. (1993), 'Introduction: TV Dinners and the Organic Brunch', in Bennett, J. and Chaloupka, W. (eds.) *In the Nature of Things: Language, Politics, and the Environment* (Minneapolis: University of Minnesota Press).
Beverley, R. (1705), *The History and Present State Of Virginia, in Four Parts: By a Native and Inhabitant of the Place* (London: R. Parker).
Bhabha, H.K. (1990), 'Introduction: Narrating the Nation', in Bhabha, H.K. (ed.) *Nation and Narration* (London: Routledge).
Bhabha, H.K. (1994), *The Location of Culture* (London: Routledge).
Birch, T. (1997), '"Nothing has Changed": The Making and Unmaking of Koori Culture', in Cowlishaw, G. and Morris, B. (eds.) *Race Matters: Indigenous Australians and 'Our' Society* (Canberra: Aboriginal Studies Press).
Birckhead, J., de Lacy, T. and Smith, L. (eds.) (1992), *Aboriginal Involvement in Parks and Protected Areas* (Canberra: Aboriginal Studies Press).
Blue, G. (2002), 'Introduction', in Blue, G., Bunton, M. and Crozier, R. (eds.) *Colonialism and the Modern World: Selected Studies* (New York: M.E. Sharpe).
Bonyhady, T. (2000), *The Colonial Earth* (Melbourne: Melbourne University Press).
Booth, P. (2003), *Planning by Consent: The Origins and Nature of British Development Control* (London: Routledge).
Booth, P. (2005), 'The Nature of Difference: Traditions of Law and Government and their Effects on Planning in Britain and France', in Sanyal, B. (ed.) *Comparative Planning Cultures* (New York: Routledge).
Borrini–Feyeraband, G., Kothari, A. and Oviedo, G. (2004), *Indigenous and Local Communities and Protected Areas* (Gland: IUCN).
Borrows, J. (1997), 'Living between Water and Rocks: First Nations, Environmental Planning and Democracy', *University of Toronto Law Journal* 47:4, 417–468.
Bowen, Sir G.F. (1889), *Thirty Years of Colonial Government: A Selection from the Despatches and Letters of the Right Hon. Sir George Ferguson Bowen Vol I* (London: Longmans, Green and Co).
Boyer, M.C. (1994), *The City Of Collective Memory: Its Historical Imagery and Architectural Entertainments* (Cambridge Mass.: MIT Press).
Brambuk, Parks Victoria and AAV (no date), 'Brambuk: The National Park and Cultural Centre', (Melbourne: Parks Victoria).
Brand, R. and Gaffikin, F. (2007), 'Collaborative Planning in an Uncollaborative World', *Planning Theory* 6:3, 282–313.
Brandon, K., Redford, K. and Sanderson, S. (1998), *Parks in Peril: People, Politics and Protected Areas* (Washington DC: Island Press).
British Columbia Ministry of Forests (1995), 'Forest Development Plan Guidebook' (Victoria: Province of British Columbia, Ministry of Forests).

Broome, R. (1984), *The Victorians: Arriving* (McMahons Point, NSW: Fairfax, Syme and Weldon Associates).

Bunton, M. (2002), 'Progressive Civilizations and Deep–Rooted Traditions: Land Laws, Development and British Rule in Palestine in the 1920s', in Blue, G., Bunton, M. and Crozier, R. (ed.) *Colonialism and the Modern World: Selected Studies* (New York: ME Sharpe).

Burayidi, M. (2003), 'The Multicultural City as Planners' Enigma', *Planning Theory and Practice* 4:3, 259–273.

Bureau of Indian Affairs (2003), website <http://edocket.access.gpo.gov/cfr_2003/aprqtr/pdf/25cfr83.7.pdf>, accessed 4 August 2009.

Burroughs, P. (1967), *Britain and Australia 1831–1855: A Study in Imperial Relations and Crown Lands Administration* (Oxford: Clarendon Press).

Butt, P. and Eagleson, R. (1996), *Mabo: What the High Court Said and What the Government Did* (2nd edn) (Sydney: Federation Press).

Campbell, H. (2006), 'Just Planning: The Art of Situated Ethical Judgement', *Journal of Planning Education and Research* 26:92–106.

Cant, G. (1998), 'Ngati Pikiao and the Waitangi Tribunal: The Contributions of the Kaituna Claim to Bicultural Partnership in Aotearoa–New Zealand', in Oakes, J., Riewe, R. and Kinew, K. (eds.) *Sacred Lands: Aboriginal World Views, Claims, and Conflicts* (Edmonton: Canadian Circumpolar Institute Press).

Carr, A. (2004), 'Mountain Places, Cultural Spaces: The Interpretation of Culturally Significant Landscapes', *Journal of Sustainable Tourism* 12:5, 432–459.

Carrick, C. (1999), 'Indians, Planning, and Political Change: Environmental Conflict in British Columbia's Coastal Forests', *Plurimondi* I:1, 175–202.

Carter, P. (1987), *The Road to Botany Bay: An Essay in Spatial History* (Boston: Faber).

Castree, N. and Braun, B. (eds.) (2001), *Social Nature: Theory, Practice and Politics* (Massachusetts: Blackwell).

Cerutty, A.M. (1977), *Tyntynder: A Pioneering Homestead and its Families* (Kilmore: Lowden Publishing Company).

Chakrabarty, D. (2000), *Provincializing Europe: Postcolonial Thought and Historical Difference* (Woodstock: Princeton University Press).

Chatterjee, P. (1983), 'More on Modes of Power and the Peasantry', in Guha, R. (ed.) *Subaltern Studies II* (Delhi: Oxford University Press).

Chinhoyi, C. (2004), 'New Approaches for involving Communities in Wildlife Management including Community–Based Natural Resource Management and Conservancies in Southern Africa', *Game and Wildlife Science* 21:3, 197–216.

Choo, C. and O'Connell, M. (1999), *Historical Narrative and Proof of Native Title* (Canberra: AIATSIS, NTRU).

Churchill, W. (1992), 'The Earth Is Our Mother: Struggles for American Indian Land and Liberation in the Contemporary United States', in Jaimes, M.A. (ed.) *The State of Native America: Genocide, Colonization, and Resistance* (Boston, Mass.: South End Press).

Churchill, W. (1998), 'Yellow Thunder: Forging a Strategy to Win', in Oakes, J., Riewe, R. and Kinew, K. (eds.) *Sacred Lands: Aboriginal World Views, Claims and Conflicts* (Edmonton: Canadian Circumpolar Institute).

Churchill, W. (2002), *Struggle for the Land: Native North American Resistance to Genocide, Ecocide, and Colonization* (San Francisco: City Lights).

Clark, I.D. (1995), *Scars in the Landscape: A Register of Massacre Sites in Western Victoria 1803–1859* (Canberra: Aboriginal Studies Press).

Clark, I.D. (1998a), 'Rock Art Sites in Victoria, Australia: A Management History Framework', (Melbourne: Department of Management, Monash University).

Clark, I.D. (1998b), *'That's My Country Belonging to Me': Aboriginal Land Tenure and Dispossession in Nineteenth Century Western Victoria* (Beaconsfield: Heritage Matters).

Clark, I.D. and Harradine, L.L. (1990), 'The Restoration of Jardwadjali and Djab wurrung names for Rock Art Sites and Landscape Features in and around the Grampians National Park: A submission to the Victorian Place Names Committee' Unpublished report.

Clarke, B. and Chance, C. (2003), *Wisdom Man* (Penguin Books: Camberwell).

Clayoquot Biosphere Trust (1999), 'Clayoquot Sound Biosphere Nomination', <http://www.clayoquotbiosphere.org/documents/csubr/CSUBRNomination.pdf> accessed 12 September 2008.

Clayoquot Biosphere Trust Cultural Advisory Committee (no date), 'Terms of Reference', <http://www.clayoquotbiosphere.org/committees/Culture/Culture_TOR.doc>, accessed 4 September 2009.

Clayton, D. (2000), *Islands Of Truth: The Imperial Fashioning Of Vancouver Island* (Vancouver: UBC Press).

Clifford, J. (1988), *The Predicament of Culture* (Cambridge: Harvard University Press).

Clifford, J. and Marcus, G. (eds.) (1986), *Writing Culture: The Poetics and Politics of Ethnography* (Berkeley: University of California Press).

Commonwealth of Australia (1992), 'National Forest Policy Statement: A New Focus for Australian Forests', (Canberra: Commonwealth of Australia).

Coutts, P., Henderson, P. and Fullager, R. (1979) 'A Preliminary Investigation of Aboriginal Mounds in North–Western Victoria, VAS No. 9' (Melbourne: Ministry for Conservation).

Coutts, P. and Lorblanchet, M. (1982), 'Aboriginals and Rock Art in the Grampians, Victoria, Australia: *Records of the Victorian Archaeological Survey 12*', (Melbourne: Ministry of Conservation).

Craig, D. (1992), 'Environmental Law and Aboriginal Rights: Legal Frameworks for Aboriginal joint management of Australian National Parks', in Birckhead, J., de Lacy, T. and Smith, L. (eds.) *Aboriginal Involvement in Parks and Protected Areas* (Canberra: Aboriginal Studies Press).

Critchett, J. (1980), *Our Land Till We Die: A History of the Framlingham Aborigines* (Warrnambool: Warrnambool Institute Press).

Critchett, J. (1990), *A Distant Field of Murder: Western District Frontiers 1834–1848* (Melbourne: Melbourne University Press).

Cronon, W. (1995), 'The Trouble with Wilderness; or Getting Back to the Wrong Nature', in Cronon, W. (ed.) *Uncommon Ground: Toward Reinventing Nature* (New York: WW Norton and Co.).

Cusack, J. (2000), 'Nyah State Forest: An Aboriginal Heritage Assessment of Three Proposed Forestry Coupes', (Melbourne: Andrew Long and Associates)

Daehnke, J.D. (2007), 'A "Strange Multiplicity" of Voices: Heritage Stewardship, Contested Sites and Colonial Legacies on the Columbia River', *Journal of Social Archaeology* 7:250–275.

Daes, E.-I. (2001), 'Indigenous Peoples and their Relationship to Land: Final Working Paper Prepared by the Special Rapporteur', United Nations Commission on Human Rights, online source <http://www.unhchr.ch/Huridocda/Huridoca.nsf/(Symbol)/E.CN.4.Sub.2.2001.21.En?Opendocument>, accessed 15 March 2009.

Dale, A. (1992), 'Planning For Rural Development in Aboriginal Communities: A Community–based Planning Approach', in Moffatt, I. and Webb, A. (eds.) *Conservation and Development Issues in North Australia* (Darwin: North Australia Research Unit).

Daniels, R. and Vencatesan, J. (1995), 'Traditional Ecological Knowledge and Sustainable Use of Natural Resources', *Current Science* 69:7, 569–570.

Davies, J., Josif, P. and Williams, R. (2000), 'Indigenous Peoples and Protected Areas: Australian Approaches', paper presented to the Cultures and Biodiversity Congress, 21–30 July Yunnan Province, China.

De Lacy, T. and Lawson, B. (1997), 'The Uluru/Kakadu Model: Joint Management of Aboriginal–owned National Parks in Australia', in Stevens, S. (ed.) *Conservation through Cultural Survival: Indigenous Peoples and Protected Areas* (Washington: Island Press).

Dear, M. and Scott, A.J. (eds.) (1981), *Urbanization and Urban Planning in Capitalist Society* (London: Methuen).

Department of Conservation (2004), 'Aoraki/Mount Cook National Park Management Plan', http://www.doc.govt.nz/publications/about-doc/role/policies-and-plans/national-park-management-plans/aoraki-mount-cook-national-park-management-plan/, accessed 4 September 2009.

Department of Natural Resources and Environment (2002a), 'Wur–cum barra', (Melbourne: State of Victoria).

Department of Natural Resources and Environment (2002b), 'National Parks Act Annual Report 2001–2002', (Melbourne: DNRE).

Department of Sustainability and Environment (2003a), 'Flora and Fauna Guarantee Action Statement #175: Inland Carpet Python', (Melbourne: DSE).

Department of Sustainability and Environment (2003b), 'Forestry Services Homepage', <http://www.nre.vic.gov.au/web/root/domino/cm_da/nrenfor.nsf/frameset/NRE+Forestry?OpenDocument> accessed 5 June 2003.

Department of Sustainability and Environment (2004), 'Forest Management Plan for the Floodplain State Forests of the Mildura Forest Management Area', (Melbourne: Department of Sustainability and Environment).
Dirks, N.B. (1992), 'Introduction', in Dirks, N.B. (ed.) *Colonialism and Culture* (Ann Arbor: University of Michigan Press).
Dodson, M. (1994a), 'Towards the Existence of Indigenous Rights: Policy, Power and Self–Determination', *Race and Class* 35:4, 65–76.
Dodson, M. (1994b), 'The Wentworth Lecture. The End in the Beginning: Re(de)defining Aboriginality', in *Australian Aboriginal Studies* 1994:1, 2–13.
Dodson, M. and Strelein, L. (2001), 'Australia's Nation–building: Renegotiating the Relationship between Indigenous Peoples and the State', *University of New South Wales Law Journal* 24:3, 826–839.
Dudley, N. (2008), *Guidelines for Applying Protected Area Management Categories* (Gland: IUCN).
During, S. (1991), 'Waiting for the Post: Some Relations between Modernity, Colonization, and Writing', in Adam, I. and Tiffin, H. (ed.) *Past the Last Post: Theorizing Post–Colonialism and Post–Modernism* (Hemel Hempstead: Harvester Wheatsheaf).
Dustin, D.L., et al. (2002), 'Cross–Cultural Claims on Devils Tower National Monument: A Case Study', *Leisure Sciences* 24:79–88.
Dyck, N. (1985), 'Introduction', in Dyck, N. (ed.) *Indigenous Peoples and the Nation–State: 'Fourth World' Politics in Canada, Australia and Norway* (Newfoundland: Institute of Social and Economic Research, University of Newfoundland).
Edwards, J. (2006), *Writing, Geometry and Space in Seventeenth–Century England and America* (London: Routledge).
Evison, H. (1997), *The Long Dispute: Maori Land Rights And European Colonisation in Southern New Zealand* (Canterbury: Canterbury University Press).
Fanon, F. (1963), *The Wretched of the Earth* (Harmondsworth: Penguin).
Fanon, F. (1967), *Black Skin, White Masks* (UK: Paladin).
Fischler, R. (2000), 'Communicative Planning Theory: A Foucauldian Assessment', *Journal of Planning Education and Research* 19:358–368.
Fleras, A. and Elliot, J.L. (1992), *The 'Nations Within': Aboriginal–State Relations in Canada, the United States, and New Zealand* (Toronto: Oxford University Press).
Flyvbjerg, B. (2001), *Making Social Science Matter: Why Social Inquiry Fails and How it Can Succeed Again* (Cambridge: Cambridge University Press).
Foglesong, R.E. (1986), *Planning the Capitalist City: The Colonial Era to the 1920s* (Princeton: Princeton University Press).
Forest Commission (1977), 'Management Policies for the Grampians State Forest', (Melbourne: Forests Commission, Victoria).
Forester, J. (1989), *Planning in the Face of Power* (California: University of California Press).

Forester, J. (1999), *The Deliberative Practitioner: Encouraging Participatory Planning Processes* (Cambridge, Massachusetts: The MIT Press).
Foucault, M. (1970), *The Order of Things: An Archaeology of the Human Sciences* (London: Routledge).
Foucault, M. (1972), *The Archaeology of Knowledge* (London: Routledge).
Foucault, M. (1977), *Discipline and Punish: The Birth of the Prison* (London: Penguin Books).
Foucault, M. (1984), 'Nietzsche, Genealogy, History', in Rabinow, P. (ed.) *The Foucault Reader* (London: Penguin).
Foucault, M. (1991), 'Governmentality', in Burchell, G., Gordon, C. and Miller, P. (eds.) *The Foucault Effect: Studies in Governmentality* (Hemel Hempstead: Harvester Wheatsheaf).
Fourmile, H. (1999), 'Indigenous Peoples, the Conservation of Traditional Ecological Knowledge, And Global Governance', in Low, N. (ed.) *Global Ethics and Environment* (London: Routledge).
Frank, G., Frank, A. Sr, and Clayoquot Band Council (1984), Tribal Park Declaration, online source http://web.uvic.ca/clayoquot/files/volume1/IIA.1.pdf accessed 9 January 2009.
Fraser, N. (1995), 'From Redistribution to Recognition? Dilemmas of Justice in a "Post–Socialist" Age', *New Left Review* I:212, 68–93.
French, R. (1994), 'The role of the National Native Title Tribunal', in. Bartlett, R.H. and Meyers, G.D. (eds.) *Native Title Legislation in Australia* (Perth: Centre for Commercial and Resources Law).
Geertz, C. (1973), *The Interpretation of Cultures: Selected Essays* (New York: Basic Books).
Gelder, K. and Jacobs, J.M. (1998), *Uncanny Australia: Sacredness and Identity in a Postcolonial Nation* (Melbourne: Melbourne University Press).
Gibson, C. (1999), 'Cartographies of the Colonial/Capitalist State: A Geopolitics of Indigenous Self–Determination in Australia', *Antipode* 31:1, 45–79.
Gilbert, J. (2007), 'Historical Indigenous Peoples' Land Claims: A Comparative and International Approach to the Common Law Doctrine on Indigenous Title', *International and Comparative Law Quarterly* 56:583–612.
Goldie, T. (1989), *Fear and Temptation: The Image of the Indigene in Canadian, Australian and New Zealand Literatures* (Kingston: McGill–Queen University Press).
Gregory, D. (2001), 'Postcolonialism', in Johnston, R., Gregory, D., Pratt, G. and Watts, M. (eds.) *The Dictionary of Human Geography* (Oxford: Blackwell).
Gunn, R.G. (1983a), 'The Cave of Ghosts: Aboriginal Rock Art Site (Site 73242/016): Occasional Report Number 12 of the Victorian Archaeological Survey' (Melbourne: Ministry for Conservation).
Gunn, R.G. (1983b), 'Recommendations for the Protection of Aboriginal Art Sites in the Grampians, Victoria: A Report to the Victorian Archaeological Survey and the Forests Commission, Victoria' (Melbourne: Ministry for Conservation).

Gunn, R.G. (1984), 'Aboriginal Rock Art of the Grampians – The Drawing Phase', unpublished B.Ed thesis, Melbourne: CAE.
Hakluyt, R. (1599), *Principall Navigations, Voiages and Discoveries of the English Nation* (London: George Bishop, Ralph Newberie and Robert Barker).
Hall, C.M. (1992), *Wasteland to World Heritage: Preserving Australia's Heritage* (Melbourne: Melbourne University Press).
Hall, P. (1996), *Cities of Tomorrow: An Intellectual History of Urban Planning and Design in the Twentieth Century* (Oxford: Blackwell).
Harley, J.B. (2001), *The New Nature of Maps: Essays in the History of Cartography*, edited by Laxton, P. (Baltimore: John Hopkins University Press).
Harris, C. (2002), *Making Native Space: Colonialism, Resistance, and Reserves in British Columbia* (Vancouver: UBC Press).
Harris, C. (2004), 'How Did Colonialism Dispossess? Comments from an Edge of Empire', *Annals of the Association of American Geographers* 94:1, 165–182.
Harvey, D. (1985), *The Urbanization of Capital* (Oxford: Blackwell).
Harvey, D. (1989), *The Condition of Postmodernity: An Enquiry into the Origins of Cultural Change* (Oxford: Blackwell).
Harwood, S.A. (2005), 'Struggling to Embrace Difference in Land–use Decision Making in Multicultural Communities', *Planning Practice and Research* 20:4, 355–371.
Head, L. (2000), *Second Nature: The History and Implications of Australia as Aboriginal Landscape* (New York: Syracuse University Press).
Healey, P. (1997), *Collaborative Planning: Shaping Places in Fragmented Societies* (Hampshire: Macmillan Press).
Helms, G. (2008), *Towards Safe City Centres? Remaking the Spaces of an Old–Industrial City* (Aldershot: Ashgate).
Hibberd, M. (2006), 'Tribal Sovereignty, The White Problem, and Reservation Planning', *Journal of Planning History* 5:2, 87–105.
Hiley, G. (2001), 'Key Legal Developments in Native Title', paper presented to The Past and Future of Land Rights and Native Title: Representative Bodies Legal Conference, 28–30 August, Brisbane.
Hillier, J. (2003), 'Agonizing Over Consensus: Why Habermasian Ideals cannot be Real', *Planning Theory* 2:1, 37–59.
Hinkson, M. (2003), 'Encounters with Aboriginal Sites in Metropolitan Sydney: A Broadening Horizon for Cultural Tourism?', *Journal of Sustainable Tourism* 11:4, 295–306.
Holston, J. (1998), 'Spaces of Insurgent Citizenship', in Sandercock, L. (ed.) *Making the Invisible Visible: A Multicultural Planning History* (Berkeley: University of California Press).
Home, R. (1997), *Of Planting and Planning: The making of British Colonial Cities* (London: E and FN Spon).
hooks, b. (1992), *Black Looks: Race and Representation* (London: Turnaround).
hooks, b. (1994), *Outlaw Culture: Resisting Representations* (London: Routledge).

hooks, b. (2000a), *All About Love: New Visions* (New York: Harper Collins).
hooks, b. (2000b), *Feminism is for Everybody: Passionate Politics* (London: Pluto Press).
Howitt, R., Connell, J. and Hirsch, P. (eds.) (1996), *Resources, Nations and Indigenous Peoples: Case Studies from Australasia, Melanesia, and Southeast Asia* (Melbourne: Oxford University Press).
Huggan, G. (1989), 'Decolonizing the Map: Post–Colonialism, Post–structuralism and the Cartographic Connection', *Ariel* 20:4, 115–131.
Huxley, M. (2000), 'The Limits to Communicative Planning', *Journal of Planning Education and Research* 19:369–377.
Huxley, M. (2006), 'Spatial Rationalities: Order, Environment, Evolution and Government', *Social and Cultural Geography* 7:5, 771–787.
Huxley, M. (2007), 'Geographies Of Governmentality', in Crampton, J.W. and Elden, S. (eds.) *Space, Knowledge, and Power: Foucault and Geography* (Aldershot: Ashgate).
Huxley, M. and Yiftachel, O. (2000), 'New Paradigm or Old Myopia? Unsettling the Communicative Turn in Planning Theory', *Journal of Planning Education and Research* 19:333–342.
Inglis, J.T. (ed.) (1993), *Traditional Ecological Knowledge: Concepts and Cases* (Ottawa: International Program on Traditional Ecological Knowledge International Development Research Centre).
International Fund for Agricultural Development (no date), 'Indigenous peoples: fact sheet', <http://www.ifad.org/pub/factsheet/ip/e.pdf> accessed 26 January 2009.
International Union for the Conservation of Nature (1994), *Guidelines for Protected Areas Management Categories* (Gland, Switzerland and Cambridge, UK: IUCN and WWF).
Jackson, S. (1997), 'A Disturbing Story: The Fiction of Rationality in Land Use Planning in Aboriginal Australia', *Australian Planner* 34:4, 221–226.
Jackson, S. (1998), 'Geographies of Co–Existence: Native Title, Cultural Difference and the Decolonisation of Planning in North Australia', PhD Thesis (NSW: Macquarie University, School of Earth Sciences).
Jackson, S. (2006), 'Compartmentalising Culture: The Articulation and Consideration of Indigenous Values in Water Resource Management', *Australian Geographer* 37:1, 19–31.
Jacobs, J.M. (1996), *Edge of Empire: Postcolonialism and the City* (London: Routledge).
Jaireth, H. and Smyth, D. (eds.) (2003), *Innovative Governance: Indigenous Peoples, Local Communities and Protected Areas* (New Delhi: Ane Books).
JanMohamed, A.R. (1985), 'The Economy of the Manichean Allegory: The Function of Racial Difference in Colonialist Literature', *Critical Inquiry* 11:4, 59–87.
Jentoft, S., Minde, H. and Nilsen, R. (eds.) (2003), *Indigenous Peoples: Resource Management and Global Rights* (Delft: Eburon).

Johnson, T., Nagel, J. and Champagne, D. (eds.) (1997), *American Indian Activism: Alcatraz to the Longest Walk* (Chicago: University of Illinois Press).

Jones, E.R. (2007), 'Three Management Challenges for Protection of Aboriginal Cultural Heritage in a Tasmanian Multiple–Use Conservation Area', *Australian Geographer* 38:1, 93–112.

Keen, I. (1988), 'Introduction', in Keen, I. (ed.) *Being Black: Aboriginal Cultures in 'Settled Australia'* (Canberra: Aboriginal Studies Press).

Keen, I. and Merlan, F. (1990), 'The Significance of the Conservation Zone to Aboriginal People', Kakadu Conservation Zone Inquiry Consultancy Series (Canberra: Resource Assessment Commission).

Kiddle, M. (1961), *Men of Yesterday: A Social History of the Western District of Victoria, 1834–1890* (Melbourne: Melbourne University Press).

King, T.F. (1998), 'How the Archaeologists Stole Culture: A Gap in American Environmental Impact Assessment Practice and How to Fill it', *Environmental Impact Assessment Review* 18:117–133.

Kramer, M.H. (1997), *John Locke and the Origins of Private Property: Philosophical Explorations of Individualism, Community, and Equality* (Cambridge: Cambridge University Press).

Kristeva, J. (1991), *Strangers to Ourselves* (New York: Columbia University Press).

Kuehls, T. (2003), 'The Environment of Sovereignty', in Magnusson, W. and Shaw, K. (eds.) *A Political Space: Reading the Global through Clayoquot Sound* (Minnesota: University of Minnesota Press).

Laclau, E. and Mouffe, C. (2001), *Hegemony and Socialist Strategy: Towards A Radical Democratic Politics* (London: Verso).

Laird, S.A. (ed.) (2000), *Biodiversity and Traditional Knowledge: Equitable Partnerships in Practice* (UK: Earthscan).

Land Conservation Council (1982), 'Final Recommendations: South–Western Area District 2' (Melbourne: Land Conservation Council).

Land Conservation Council (1989), 'Mallee Area Review: Final Recommendations' (Melbourne: LCC).

Landry, D. and MacLean, G. (eds.) (1996), *The Spivak Reader: Selected works of Gayatri Chakravorty Spivak* (New York: Routledge).

Lane, M. and Corbett, T. (2005), 'The Tyranny of Localism: Indigenous Participation in Community–Based Environmental Management', *Journal of Environmental Policy and Planning* 7:2, 141–159.

Lane, M.B. and McDonald, G. (2005), 'Community–Based Environmental Planning: Operational Dilemmas, Planning Principles and Possible Remedies', *Journal of Environmental Planning and Management* 48:5, 709–731.

Lane, M.B. and Williams, L.J. (2008), 'Color Blind: Indigenous Peoples and Regional Environmental Management', *Journal of Planning Education and Research* 28:38–49.

Langton, M. (1993), 'Rum, Seduction and Death, Aboriginality and Alcohol', *Oceania* 63:3, 195–206.

Langton, M. (1996), 'What do we mean by Wilderness? Wilderness and Terra Nullius in Australian Art', *The Sydney Papers* 8:1, 11–31.

Langton, M. (1997), 'Estate Of Mind: The Growing Cooperation between Indigenous and Mainstream Managers of North Australia Landscapes and the Challenge for Educators and Researchers', <http://www.faira.org.au/niwg/estate.html> accessed 2 July 1997.

Langton, M. (1998), *Burning Questions: Emerging Environmental Issues for Indigenous Peoples in Northern Australia* (Darwin: Centre for Indigenous Natural and Cultural Resource Management).

Langton, M. (2002a), 'A New Deal? Indigenous development and the politics of recovery' Dr Charles Perkins Memorial Oration given at the University of Sydney, 4 October.

Langton, M. (2002b), 'Ancient Jurisdictions, Aboriginal Polities and Sovereignty', paper presented to the Indigenous Governance Conference, Canberra, 3–5 April.

Laslett, P. (ed.) (1988), *Locke: Two Treatises of Government* (Cambridge: Cambridge University Press).

Lawrence, D. (2002), *Kakadu: The Making of a National Park* (Carlton South: Melbourne University Press).

Latour, B. (1991), *We Have Never Been Modern* (Hemel Hempstead: Harvester Wheatsheaf).

Lattas, A. (1997), 'Aborigines and Contemporary Australian Nationalism: Primordiality and the Cultural Politics of Otherness', in Cowlishaw, G. and Morris, B. (eds.) *Race Matters: Indigenous Australians and 'Our' Society* (Canberra: Aboriginal Studies Press).

Lefebvre, H. (1991), *The Production of Space* (Oxford: Blackwell).

Lefebvre, H. (2003), 'Preface to the New Edition: The Production of Space', in Elden, S., Lebas, E. and Kofman, E. (eds.) *Henri Lefebvre: Key writings* (New York: Continuum).

Legg, S. (2007a), 'Beyond the European Province: Foucault and Postcolonialism', in Crampton, J.W. and Elden, S. (eds.) *Space, Knowledge and Power: Foucault and Geography* (Aldershot: Ashgate).

Legg, S. (2007b), *Spaces Of Colonialism: Delhi's Urban Governmentalities* (Malden: Blackwell).

Lewis, H. (1989), 'Ecological and Technological Knowledge of Fire: Aboriginal Versus Park Rangers in Northern Australia', *American Anthropologist* 91:4, 940–961.

Lewis, J.L. and Sheppard, S.R.J. (2005), 'Ancient Values, New Challenges: Indigenous Spiritual Perceptions of Landscapes and Forest Management', *Society and Natural Resources* 18:907–920.

Locke, J. (1988), 'Two Treatises of Government', in P. Laslett (ed.) *Locke: Two Treatises of Government* (Cambridge: Cambridge University Press).

Long, D.L. (2000), 'Cultural Heritage Management in Post–Colonial Polities: Not the Heritage of the Other', *International Journal of Heritage Studies* 6:4, 317–322.

Look Ear Pty Ltd (no date), 'Brambuk – the national park and cultural centres: Interpretation Plan', unpublished report.
Lucashenko, M. (2006) 'Not Quite White in the Head', in Stewart, F., Behrendt, L., Lopez, B. and Tredinnick, M. (eds.) *Where the Rivers Meet: New Writings from Australia* (Honolulu: University of Hawaii Press).
McCall, M.K. and Minang, P.A. (2005), 'Assessing Participatory GIS for Community–Based Natural Resource Management: Claiming Community Forests in Cameroon', *Geographical Journal* 171:340–356.
McGuirk, P. (2001), 'Situating Communicative Planning Theory: Context, Power, and Knowledge', *Environment and Planning A* 33:195–217.
McHoul, A. and Grace, W. (1993), *A Foucault Primer: Discourse, Power and the Subject* (London: University College London Press).
McKee, C. (2000), *Treaty Talks in British Columbia: Negotiating a Mutually Beneficial Future* (Vancouver: UBC Press).
Magnusson, W. (2003), 'Introduction: The Puzzle of the Political', in Magnusson, W. and Shaw, K. (eds.) *A Political Space: Reading the Global through Clayoquot Sound* (Minneapolis: University of Minnesota Press).
Mahar, C. (2005), 'Landscape, Empire and the Creation of Modern New Zealand', in Hooper, G. (ed.) *Landscape and Empire 1770–2000* (Aldershot: Ashgate).
Marsh, H. (2003). 'Yanner High Court Decision and Reconciliation', <http://www.austlii.edu.au/cgi-bin/disp.pl/au/other/IndigLRes/car/1999/8/wtpage14.htm?query=%7E%20yanner#disp2>, accessed 1 October 2003.
Merlan, F. (1991), 'The Limits of Cultural Constructionism: The Case of Coronation Hill', *Oceania* 61, 341–352.
Merlan, F. (1998), *Caging the Rainbow: Places, Politics, and Aborigines in a North Australian Town* (Honolulu: University of Hawai'i Press).
Mitchell, T.L. (1839), *Three Expeditions into the Interior of Eastern Australia: with Descriptions of the Recently Explored Region of Australia Felix and of the Present Colony of New South Wales* (London: T. and W. Boone).
Mouffe, C. (1999), 'Deliberative Democracy or Agonistic Pluralism?', *Social Research* 66:3, 745–758.
Muir, K. (1998), *'This Earth has an Aboriginal Culture Inside': Recognising the Cultural Value of Country* (Canberra: Australian Institute of Aboriginal and Torres Strait Islander Studies).
Myers, F. (1989), 'Burning the Truck and Holding the Country: Pintupi Forms of Property and Identity', in Wilmsen. E.N. (ed.) *We Are Here: Politics of Aboriginal Land Tenure* (Berkeley: University of California Press).
Nadasdy, P. (1999), 'The Politics of TEK: Power and the "Integration" of Knowledge', *Arctic Anthropology* 36:1, 1–18.
National Historic Preservation Act 1966 http://www.achp.gov/nhpa.html, accessed 4 September 2009.
Noxolo, P. (2009), '"My Paper, My Paper": Reflections on the Embodied Production of Postcolonial Geographical Responsibility in Academic Writing', *Geoforum* 40:55–65.

Nussbaum, M. (1990), *Love's Knowledge: Essays on Philosophy and Literature* (New York: Oxford University Press).
O'Faircheallaigh, C. (2008), 'Negotiating Cultural Heritage? Aboriginal–Mining Company Agreements in Australia', *Development and Change* 39:1, 25–51.
Ogden, S. (2007), 'Understanding, Respect, and Collaboration in Cultural Heritage Preservation: A Conservator's Developing Perspective', *Library Trends* 56:1, 275–287.
Palmer, L. (2001), 'Kakadu as an Aboriginal Place: Tourism and the Construction of Kakadu National Park', unpublished PhD thesis (Darwin: Northern Territory University, Aboriginal and Torres Strait Islander Studies).
Palmer, L. (2004), 'Bushwalking in Kakadu: A Study of Cultural Borderlands', *Social and Cultural Geography* 5:1, 109–119.
Palmer, L. (2006), '"Nature", Place and the Recognition of Indigenous Polities', *Australian Geographer* 37:1, 33–43.
Parks Victoria (1998), 'Grampians National Park Draft Management Plan' (Melbourne: DNRE).
Parks Victoria (2000), 'State of the Parks 2000, Volume 1 – The Parks System' (Melbourne: Parks Victoria).
Parks Victoria (2001), 'Parknotes: Grampians National Park Visitor Guide' (Melbourne: Parks Victoria).
Parks Victoria (2003), 'Grampians National Park Management Plan' (Melbourne: Parks Victoria).
Pearson, N. (1993), '204 Years of Invisible Title', in Stephenson, M.A. and Ratnapala, S. (eds.) *Mabo: A Judicial Revolution. The Aboriginal Land Rights Decision and its Impact on Australian Law* (St Lucia: University of Queensland Press).
Penney, J. (1979), 'The Death of Queen Aggie: Culture Contact in the Mid-Murray Region', unpublished Masters thesis (Melbourne: La Trobe University, Department of History).
Peterson, N. and Langton, M. (eds.) (1983), *Aborigines, Land and Land Rights* (Canberra: Australian Institute of Aboriginal Studies).
Pizzey, S. (1994), 'Ways of Seeing: Interpreting the Grampians National Park', unpublished brochure.
Pløger, J. (2004), 'Strife: Urban Planning and Agonism', *Planning Theory* 3:1, 71–92.
Porter, L. (2004), 'Planning's Colonial Culture: An Investigation of the Contested Process of Producing Place in (Post)colonial Victoria', unpublished PhD thesis, (Melbourne: University of Melbourne, Faculty of Architecture, Building and Planning).
Porter, L. (2006a), 'Planning in (Post)colonial Settings: Challenges for Theory and Practice', *Planning Theory and Practice* 7:4, 383–396.
Porter, L. (2006b), 'Rights or Containment? The Politics of Aboriginal Cultural Heritage in Victoria', *Australian Geographer* 37:3, 355–374.

Porter, L. (2006c), 'Unlearning One's Privilege: Reflections on Cross–Cultural Research with Indigenous Peoples in South–East Australia', *Planning Theory and Practice* 5:1, 104–109.

Porter, L. (2007), 'Producing Forests: A Colonial Genealogy of Environmental Planning in Victoria, Australia', *Journal of Planning Education and Research* 26:4, 466–477.

Porter, L. (2009), 'On Having Imperial Eyes', in Thomas, H. and Lo Piccolo, F. (eds.) *Ethics and Planning Research* (Aldershot: Ashgate).

Povinelli, E.A. (1993), *Labor's Lot: The Power, History, and Culture of Aboriginal Action* (Chicago: University of Chicago Press).

Powell, J.M. (1993), 'The Genesis of Environmentalism in Australia', in Garden, D. (ed.) *Created Landscapes: Historians and the Environment* (Carlton: The History Institute, Victoria Inc.).

Prakash, G. (1996), 'Who's Afraid of Postcoloniality?', *Social Text* 49:187–203.

Pratt, M.L. (1992), *Imperial Eyes: Travel Writing and Transculturation* (London: Routledge).

Rabinow, P. (ed.) (1984), *The Foucault Reader* (London: Penguin).

Rabinow, P. (1989), *French Modern: Norms and Forms of the Social Environment* (Cambridge Mass.: MIT Press).

Rangan, H. (1999), 'Bitter–Sweet Liaisons in a Contentious Democracy: Radical Planning Through State Agency in Postcolonial India', *Plurimondi* I:2, 47–66.

Reeves, D. (2005), *Planning for Diversity: Policy and Planning in a World of Difference* (London: Routledge).

Reps, J.W. (1965), *The Making of Urban America: A History of City Planning in The United States* (Princeton: Princeton University Press).

Reps, J.W. (1979), *Cities of the American West: A History of Frontier Urban Planning* (Princeton: Princeton University Press).

Reynolds, H. (1992), *The Law of the Land* (2nd ed) (Ringwood: Penguin).

Riley, M. (2002), *'Winning' Native Title: The Experience of the Nharnuwangga, Wajarri and Ngarla People* (Canberra: Australian Institute of Aboriginal and Torres Strait Islander Studies and the Native Title Research Unit).

Rowse, T. (1993), 'Rethinking Aboriginal "Resistance": The Community Development Employment Program (CDEP)', *Oceania* 63, 268–286.

Roy, A. (2006), 'Praxis in the Time of Empire', *Planning Theory* 5:1, 7–29.

Rudner, R. (1994), 'Sacred Geographies: Indian Country, Where Time, Land, Tradition, and Law are Joined – or Should Be', *Wilderness* 58:206, 10–28.

Ryan, S. (1996), *The Cartographic Eye: How Explorers Saw Australia* (Melbourne: Cambridge University Press).

Said, E.W. (1978), *Orientalism* (New York: Pantheon Books).

Said, E.W. (1983), *The World, the Text and the Critic* (Cambridge: Harvard University Press).

Said, E.W. (1993), *Culture and Imperialism* (New York: Alfred A Knopf).

Said, E.W. (1995), 'Afterword to the 1995 Printing', in *Orientalism* (London: Penguin).

Sandercock, L. (1976), *Cities For Sale: Property, Politics and Urban Planning in Australia* (Carlton: Melbourne University Press).
Sandercock, L. (ed.) (1998a), *Making the Invisible Visible: A Multicultural Planning History* (Berkeley: University of California Press).
Sandercock, L. (1998b), *Towards Cosmopolis: Planning for Multicultural Cities* (Chichester: John Wiley and Sons).
Sandercock, L. (2000), 'When Strangers Become Neighbours: Managing Cities of Difference', *Planning Theory and Practice* 1:1, 13–30.
Sandercock, L. (2003), *Cosmopolis II: Mongrel Cities in the 21st Century* (London: Continuum).
Sandercock, L. and Kliger, B. (1997), 'Multiculturalism and the Planning System' (Melbourne: Department of Landscape, Environment and Planning, RMIT).
Sanyal, B. (ed.) (2005), *Comparative Planning Cultures* (New York: Routledge).
Scholtz, C. (2006), *Negotiating Claims: The Emergence of Indigenous Land Claim Negotiation Policies in Australia, Canada, New Zealand, and the United States* (New York: Routledge).
Scott, J.C. (1998), *Seeing Like a State: How Certain Schemes to Improve the Human Condition Have Failed* (New Haven: Yale University Press).
Senese, G.B. (1991), *Self–Determination and the Social Education of Native Americans* (New York: Praeger).
Sharma, A. and Gupta, A. (2006), 'Introduction: Rethinking Theories of the State in an Age of Globalization', in Sharma, A. and Gupta, A. (eds.) *The Anthropology of the State: A Reader* (Malden: Blackwell).
Shaw, W.S. (2007), *Cities of Whiteness* (Malden: Blackwell).
Slemon, S. (1994), 'The Scramble for Post–Colonialism', in Tiffin, C. and Lawson, A. (eds.) *De–Scribing Empire: Post–Colonialism and Textuality* (London: Routledge).
Smith, L. (2001), 'Archaeology and the Governance of Material Culture: A Case Study from South–Eastern Australia', *Norwegian Archaeological Review* 34:2, 97–105.
Smith, L. (2004), *Archaeological Theory and the Politics of Cultural Heritage* (London: Routledge).
Smith, L.T. (1999), *Decolonizing Methodologies: Research and Indigenous Peoples* (Dunedin: University of Otago Press).
Smith, N. (1990), *Uneven Development: Nature, Capital and the Production of Space* (Oxford: Basil Blackwell).
Smyth, D. (2001), 'Joint Management of National Parks in Australia', in Baker, R., Davies, J. and Young, E. (eds.) *Working on Country: Contemporary Indigenous Management of Australia's Lands and Coastal Regions* (Oxford: Oxford University Press).
Soja, E.W. (2000), *Postmetropolis: Critical Studies of Cities and Regions* (Oxford: Blackwell).
Spence, M. (1999*), Dispossessing the Wilderness: Indian Removal and the Making of the National Parks* (New York: Oxford University Press).

Spivak, G.C. (1988), *In Other Worlds: Essays in Cultural Politics* (New York: Routledge).
Spivak, G.C. (1993), *Outside in the Teaching Machine* (London: Routledge).
Spivak, G.C. (1994), 'Can the Subaltern Speak?', in Williams, P. and Chrisman, L. (eds.) *Colonial Discourse and Postcolonial Theory: A Reader* (New York: Columbia University Press).
Stegner, W. (1969), *The Sound of Mountain Water* (New York: Doubleday).
Stephenson, M.A. and Ratnapala, S. (eds.) (1993), *Mabo: A Judicial Revolution: The Aboriginal Land Rights Decision and its Impact on Australian Law* (St Lucia: University of Queensland Press).
Stevens, S. (ed.) (1997), *Conservation through Cultural Survival: Indigenous Peoples and Protected Areas* (Washington DC: Island Press).
Stoler, A.L. (1989), 'Rethinking Colonial Categories: European Communities and the Boundaries of Rule', *Comparative Studies in Society and History* 31:134–161.
Stoler, A.L. (1995), *Race and the Education of Desire: Foucault's History of Sexuality and the Colonial Order of Things* (Durham: Duke University Press).
Stoler, A.L. (2004), 'Affective States', in Nugent, D. and Vincent, J. (eds.) *A Companion to the Anthropology of Politics* (Malden: Blackwell).
Strelein, L. (2003), *Members of the Yorta Yorta Aboriginal Community v Victoria [2002] HCA 58 (12 December 2002) – Comment* (Canberra: Australian Institute of Aboriginal and Torres Strait Islander Studies).
Swain, T. (1993), *A Place for Strangers: Towards a History of Australian Aboriginal Being* (Cambridge: Cambridge University Press).
Sutcliffe, A. (ed.) (1980), *The Rise of Modern Urban Planning 1800–1914* (London: Mansell).
Sutton, P. (1998), *Native Title and the Descent of Rights* (Perth: National Native Title Tribunal).
Te Runanga o Ngāi Tahu (2009), 'The claim history', http://www.ngaitahu.iwi.nz/About-Ngai-Tahu/Settlement/Claim-History.php, accessed 4 September 2009.
Tennant, P. (1990), *Aboriginal Peoples and Politics: The Indian Land Question in British Columbia, 1849–1989* (Vancouver: UBC Press).
Thomas, H. (2000), *Race and Planning: The UK Experience* (London: UCL Press).
Thomas, L. and Middleton, J. (2003), *Guidelines for Management Planning of Protected Areas* (Gland: IUCN).
Thomas, N. (1994), *Colonialism's Culture: Anthropology, Travel and Government* (Cambridge: Polity Press).
Tipa, G. and Nelson, K. (2008), 'Introducing Cultural Opportunities: A Framework for Incorporating Cultural Perspectives in Contemporary Resource Management', *Journal of Environmental Policy and Planning* 10:4, 313–337.
Torgovnick, M. (1997), *Primitive Passions: Men, Women, and the Quest for Ecstasy* (New York: Alfred A. Knopf).

Toyne, P. and Vachon, D. (1984), *Growing Up the Country: The Pitjantjajara Struggle for their Land* (Fitzroy: McPhee Gribble).

Tully, J. (1980), *A Discourse on Property: John Locke and his Adversaries* (Cambridge: Cambridge University Press).

Tully, J. (1995), *Strange Multiplicity: Constitutionalism in an Age of Diversity* (Cambridge: Cambridge University Press).

Tully, J. (2004), 'Recognition and Dialogue: The Emergence of a New Field', *Critical Review of International Social and Political Philosophy* 7:3, 84–106.

Umemoto, K. (2001), 'Walking in Another's Shoes: Epistemological Challenges in Participatory Planning', *Journal of Planning Education and Research* 21:17–31.

University of Ballarat (1997), 'Statement of Management Practices within the Floodplain State Forests of the Mildura Forest Management Area' (Melbourne: Government of Victoria).

Victorian Association of Forest Industries (no date), 'Forestry in Victoria: Key issues and facts.' Online source, http://www.vafi.org.au/documents/forestrykeyissuescomp.pdf, accessed 15 March 2009.

Vine Deloria, J. and Lytle, C. (eds.) (1984), *The Nations Within: The Past and future of American Indian Sovereignty* (New York: Pantheon Books).

Watson, A. and Huntington, O.H. (2008), 'They're Here – I Can Feel Them: The Epistemic Spaces of Indigenous and Western Knowledges', *Social and Cultural Geography* 9:3, 257–281.

Watson, V. (2006), 'Deep Difference: Diversity, Planning and Ethics', *Planning Theory* 5:1, 31–50.

Weaver, S. (1985), 'Political Representivity and Indigenous Minorities in Canada and Australia', in Dyck, N. (ed.) *Indigenous Peoples and the Nation–State: 'Fourth World' Politics in Canada, Australia and Norway* (Newfoundland: Institute of Social and Economic Research, University of Newfoundland).

Weiner, J.F. (2002), *Diaspora, Materialism, Tradition: Anthropological issues in the recent High Court appeal of the Yorta Yorta* (Canberra: Australian Institute of Aboriginal and Torres Strait Islander Studies).

Welch, J.R. and Ferguson, T.J. (2007), 'Putting Patria Back into Repatriation', *Journal of Social Archaeology* 7:2, 171–198.

Whatmore, S. (2002), *Hybrid Geographies: Natures, Cultures, Spaces* (London: SAGE).

White, A. (1634), *A relation of the successefull beginnings of the Lord Baltemore's plantation in Mary–land: Being an extracte of certaine letters written from thence, by some of the aduenturers, to their friends in England* (London: Anno. Dom.).

Willems–Braun, B. (1997), 'Buried Epistemologies: The Politics of Nature in (Post)Colonial British Columbia', *Annals of the Association of American Geographers* 87:1, 3–31.

Williams, R. (1965), *The Long Revolution* (Harmondsworth: Penguin).

Wilson, E. (1991), *The Sphinx in the City: Urban Life, the Control of Disorder, and Women* (London: Virago).

Wilson, M. and Yeatman, A. (eds.) (1995), *Justice and Identity: Antipodean Practices* (Wellington: Allen and Unwin).

Woenne–Green, S., et al. (1994), *Competing Interests: Aboriginal Participation in National Parks and Conservation Reserves in Australia: A Review* (Melbourne: Australian Conservation Foundation).

World Commission on Protected Areas (no date), 'Home page', website <http://www.iucn.org/about/union/commissions/wcpa/wcpa_overview/wcpa_about/index.cfm>, accessed 11 September 2008.

Wright, G. (1991), *The Politics of Design in French Colonial Urbanism* (Chicago: University of Chicago Press).

Yiftachel, O. (1996), 'The Internal Frontier: Territorial Control and Ethnic Relations in Israel', *Regional Studies* 30:5, 493–508.

Yiftachel, O. and Fenster, T. (1997), 'Introduction: Frontiers, Planning and Indigenous Peoples', in Fenster, T. and Yiftachel, O. (eds.) *Frontier Development and Indigenous Peoples* (UK: Pergamon).

Young, I.M. (1990), *Justice and the Politics of Difference* (New Jersey: Princeton University Press).

Young, I.M. (1995), 'Communication and the Other: Beyond Deliberative Democracy', in Wilson, M. and Yeatman, A. (eds.) *Justice and Identity: Antipodean Practices* (Wellington: Allen and Unwin).

Young, I.M. (2000), *Inclusion and Democracy* (Oxford: Oxford University Press).

Young, R.C. (1995), *Colonial Desire: Hybridity in Theory, Culture and Race* (London: Routledge).

Young, R.C. (2001), *Postcolonialism: An Historical Introduction* (Oxford: Blackwell).

Zahedieh, N. (2002), 'Economy', in Armitage, D. and Braddick, M. (eds.) *The British Atlantic World 1500–1800* (Hampshire: Palgrave Macmillan).

Zanetti, L.A. (1998), 'At the Nexus of State and Civil Society: The Transformative Practice of Public Administration', in King, C.S. and Stivers, C. (eds.) *Government is Us: Public Administration in an Anti–Government Era* (California: SAGE).

Index

Aoteoroa–New Zealand 3, 4, 7, 15, 22, 24, 30–31, 35, 37, 41, 49, 61, 64, 67–68, 79, 107, 109, 112, 125
    Aoraki/Mt Cook 79, 103–105
    Maori 22, 30–31, 67, 79, 103–104, 109
    New Zealand Company 65, 73
    Waikato 68
Assimilation 27, 29, 74
    Policy 28–31, 74
Australia 3, 4, 5, 7, 22, 23, 24, 35, 37, 38, 42, 49, 59, 91, 107, 112, 116, 132, 141
    Australian law and court cases 31–33, 67, 95, 109–110
    Brambuk Living Cultural Centre 10–11, 85, 88, 91–92, 126–138
    Coronation Hill 110–111
    Daly River 110
    'discovery' of 57–58
    Exploration of 59–65, 69–71
    Forestry in 96–97
    Gariwerd 5, 6, 7, 8, 10–11, 82–95, 126–139, 145, 146, 147, 148, 150
    Gunditjmara 10–11
    Jawoyn 111
    Kirrae Wurrung 10–11
    Land sales 73
    Nyah 5, 6, 7, 8–9, 19, 79, 96–100, 108, 113–126, 139–145, 146, 147, 148, 149
    Parramatta 123
    Swan Brewery 41, 107, 116
    Swan Hill 9, 99, 100, 142
    Tjapwurrung 10–11, 130, 131, 135
    Uluru 23, 88, 125
    Wadi Wadi 8–9, 100, 114–121, 139–145
    Wotjobaluk 10–11, 60, 93–94
    Yorta Yorta 32–33, 39

Canada 3, 4, 7, 22, 24, 27, 28–30, 31, 32, 37, 49, 73, 107, 109, 112
    Clayoquot Sound 100–102
    Geological survey of 58
    Kluane national park 125
    Nu–chah–nulth 58, 68, 79, 102
    Pacific North–West 1, 58, 68, 79
Carpet python 99–100
Citizenship 21, 24–25, 29, 34
Colonial
    British settler colonialism 3, 4, 31, 43, 44, 49, 58, 65, 66, 76
    Colonial office 7, 30, 47, 58, 67, 72, 73, 75
    encounter 5, 34, 35, 43, 45, 47, 61, 65, 68, 140
    space 15, 18, 21, 38, 43, 45, 46, 48, 49, 71, 74, 77, 147, 151
Colonisers 1, 4, 29, 31, 47, 48, 49, 51, 52, 56, 57, 59, 60, 63, 66, 67, 68, 72, 76, 78, 151
Cook, James 31, 58, 61
Cultural heritage 88, 105, 107, 108, 109, 111, 117, 121, 147, 153
    Archaeology 109, 114, 116, 122, 139
    Authenticity 90, 107, 111, 116
    Buffer zones 117–118
    Conservation 109, 113, 117, 123
    Indigenous 85, 86, 97, 108, 109, 122–123, 126, 132, 140, 142
    Management 19, 92, 107, 109, 110, 112, 113, 122, 123, 127, 128, 139, 140
    Officers 42, 114
    Partnership management 122, 123
    Register of 109, 110, 111, 112, 113, 115, 122, 123, 143
    Rock art sites 85, 86–89, 90, 132
    Site protection 97, 98, 109, 114
    Sites discourse 112, 115–117
    Struggle 115, 118–120

Culture
  Construction of 87–92, 101, 138
  Relativism 13, 14, 45
  Structure of meaning 2, 12, 15, 16, 26, 36, 43, 46, 49, 60, 63, 78, 108, 112, 141, 151

Deconstruction 17, 148, 156
  Unlearning 155–156, 158
Deliberative democracy 19, 125, 145, 146, 148
Difference
  Cultural 11–14, 17, 18, 24, 34, 40, 74, 122, 146, 147, 148
  Liberation 34, 37, 122, 148
  Oppression 35, 37, 149
  Politics of 17–18, 19, 25, 33–34, 41, 153, 154
  Scaling of bodies 36–37, 66
Discourse 17, 21, 26, 36–37, 39, 45, 47–48, 66, 79, 83, 87, 92, 93, 95, 112–115, 116–117, 119, 133, 137, 138, 140, 141, 154, 155
Dispossession 4, 6, 18, 21, 27, 28, 33–34, 37, 38–40, 45, 51, 76, 103, 126, 136, 151
  Cultural heritage 111, 116
  Exploration 60, 70–71
  Mission stations 74
  Reserves 28, 48
Doctrine of Discovery 27, 31, 66

Exploration 58, 60–61, 69–71

Forestry Victoria 9, 117, 144
Foucault, Michel 17, 36, 47, 48, 108–109, 155, 156
Fraser, Nancy 153–155

Genealogy 12, 13, 43–76
Governmentality 19, 43, 48, 107, 108–111, 113, 117, 123, 126, 140, 147

Hunting practices 93–95
Huxley, Margo 43, 48, 147, 149

Indigenous
  Identity 7, 26, 33, 34–38, 39, 122, 123, 126, 141, 147, 149

Inequality 12, 24
Land claims 7, 24, 26, 27, 29, 31–32, 74, 111, 122
Land rights 22, 25, 39, 77, 79, 101, 140
Resistance (see also struggle) 2, 18, 21–22, 26, 29, 30, 114, 115, 122, 123, 151, 153
Sacred 9, 23, 41, 100, 103, 107–124
Sovereignty 1, 21, 24–27, 31, 39, 41, 67–68, 74, 75, 101, 102, 110, 111, 122, 150
Struggle (see also resistance) 1, 18, 21–24, 2534, 38, 40
Unemployment 142, 145
IUCN 23, 80–84

Justice
  Equity 95, 153–155
  Land 1, 3, 5, 21–22, 146
  Procedural 146, 150
  Social 2, 18, 146, 150, 151, 158

Knowledge 3, 42, 146, 157
  Colonial 48, 69, 71, 76
  Local 51
  Planning 87, 44, 69, 82–84, 86–87, 95, 97
  Power 15, 17, 70, 76, 98, 108
  Production of 15, 35, 40, 79, 82, 152, 40
  Scientific 40, 41, 82, 84, 87, 95, 99, 110, 152, 111
  Traditional ecological or Indigenous 23, 38–39, 41, 82, 87, 102, 105, 107, 120, 141

Land
  Cultivation 4, 55 58, 60–67
  Improvement (see also Locke, John) 25–26, 56, 59–60, 61, 63–64, 68, 71, 74
  Waste 55–57, 63–64, 76
Latour, Bruno 13–14, 151
Lefebvre, Henri 14–15, 43, 45, 49, 52, 76, 77, 147, 152, 156
Locke, John 25–26, 44, 53–56, 57, 58, 63, 66–67, 77

Index

Logging (see also timber harvesting) 1, 6, 9, 22, 97, 99, 100, 101, 114–122, 134, 139–145
Love 157
   Hope 2, 157, 158
   Politics of 19, 153, 157–158

Mabo case 9, 22, 31, 32, 67
Marshall ruling 26–27, 75
Mitchell, Major Thomas 58, 60–61, 62, 68, 69, 70, 86, 90

Naming 10, 71, 76, 88, 90–93, 98
Native title 11, 31–33, 97, 126, 153
   Act 9, 32, 98, 140
   Claimants 7, 42, 91, 114, 119, 128, 139–140
   Holders 93
   Representative Body 139
   Rights 95
Natural resources
   Extraction 22, 113, 117
   Management of 24, 30, 80, 82, 86, 125
Nature, construction of 14, 36, 61, 77–105, 138, 151, 158

Planning
   Collaborative 11, 19, 78, 125–126, 139, 145–150, 154
   Community–based 125
   Cultural practice of 2–3, 11–17, 78, 147, 152–153, 156
   Epistemology 43–44, 147
   Environmental 1, 23, 79–88, 95, 105, 125, 145, 152
   Export of Britain 3, 50
   Law 50, 79, 95
   Ontology 13, 18, 43–44
   Origins / history 43, 49–50
   Spatial ordering 2–3, 12–13, 34, 39, 45, 76
   Technology 18, 43–45, 46–49, 52, 69–75, 108, 117, 151–153
Postcolonial 11, 34–35, 110, 154–155, 157
   Definition 12, 16
   Geographies 48
   Planning 18, 40–42, 105, 152

Politics 19, 22, 32, 77, 88, 90–93, 107, 113, 123, 145–149, 157–158
   Relations 17, 111, 119, 132
   States 35, 39, 113, 126, 139
   Studies 36–37, 48
Power
   Of the state 17, 108
   Relations 1, 11, 18, 27, 33, 39, 40, 79, 138
Primitivism 37–39, 42
   Traditionality 32, 33, 105, 111
Protected areas 62, 79–82
   Co–management 78, 103, 125, 147
   Estate 79, 80, 100
   Hierarchy 84, 85
   Joint management 23, 78, 105, 125, 129
   National parks 10, 79, 80, 82–95, 103–105
   Planning 18, 19, 77–78
   State forests 9–10, 84, 94, 96–100
   Tourism 83, 86, 88–90, 96, 114, 128–139
Public interest 11, 41, 54, 97

Racism /racial 5, 26, 35–36, 71, 126, 139, 146–147, 149, 151, 158
   Alcohol 140–141
Recognition of rights 25, 119, 131, 153–155
Research methodology
   Critical ethnography 5–6
   Methods 5–6, 15, 48–49
   Reflexivity 6–7
Romantic tradition 61–62

Space
   Abstract 52, 69, 76, 151, 152
   Cartesian 45–46, 62, 75, 152
   Colonial 15, 21, 38, 43, 48–49, 71, 74, 77, 147, 151
   Hierarchisation of 18, 76, 77, 87, 152
   Perceived, conceived, lived 14–15, 45
   Production of 14–16, 45–46, 76
   Values in 56–68
Spatial
   Culture 17–19, 67, 83, 86, 97, 152–153, 155–156
   Ontology 18, 43–44
   Practice 15, 36, 51, 81, 83, 152

Spivak, Gayatri 17, 33, 35, 122, 155–156
Squatters/squatting 9, 47, 60–63, 67, 69, 71
Stereotype 37, 42, 140–141, 148
Survey 47, 52, 58–60, 69–76, 86, 114–115, 127, 139

Terra nullius 31, 52, 67, 71
Timber harvesting 84, 96–100, 114–120, 139, 142, 144
Town building 63, 65, 76
Treaty 22–23, 27, 28–30, 75, 153
   James Bay Cree 22
   Nuu–chah–nulth 102
   Waitangi 22, 30, 41, 67–68, 79, 103
Tully, James 55–56, 123, 153–154

United Nations
   Convention on Biological Diversity 23
   Declaration of Rights of Indigenous People 23
   UNESCO Man and Biosphere 23, 100–102
   World Heritage Convention 23

United States 7, 24, 26–28, 36, 37, 65, 75, 109, 122
   Cherokee 65
   Chinook Nation 121–122
   Navajo 113
   Papkolea 148
   Pennsylvania 72
   Virginia 50, 59, 71
   Yellowstone 62
Unsettle 2, 14, 16, 41, 81, 98, 101, 123, 150, 154, 158
Utilitarian 59, 62–63, 76, 77, 84

Violence 16, 24, 26, 35, 57, 65, 74–75, 147, 151, 153, 157
   Epistemic 156, 158

Wakefield, Edward Gibbon 72–73
Wilderness 61–62, 64, 67, 77–79, 80–81, 87, 102

Young, Iris Marion 34–37, 44, 68, 148, 153